THE REPUBLIC IN CRISIS, 1848–1861

The Republic in Crisis, 1848–1861, analyses the political climate in the years leading up to the Civil War, offering for students and general readers a clear, chronological account of the sectional conflict and the beginning of the Civil War. Emerging from the tumultuous political events of the 1840s and 1850s, the Civil War was caused by the maturing of the separate, distinctive forms of social organisation in the North and South and their resulting ideologies. John Ashworth emphasises factors often overlooked in explanations of the war, including the resistance of slaves in the South and the growth of wage labour in the North. Ashworth acquaints readers with modern writings on the period, providing a new interpretation of the American Civil War's causes.

John Ashworth is Professor of American History at the University of Nottingham in England. He is the author of numerous books, including *Slavery, Capitalism and Politics in the Antebellum Republic* (Cambridge 1995, 2007), the second volume of which won the James A. Rawley award given by the Southern Historical Association.

D0514185

THE REPUBLIC IN CRISIS, 1848–1861

JOHN ASHWORTH

University of Nottingham

CAMBRIDGE
UNIVERSITY PRESS

CAMBRIDGE UNIVERSITY PRESS
Cambridge, New York, Melbourne, Madrid, Cape Town,
Singapore, São Paulo, Delhi, Mexico City

Cambridge University Press
32 Avenue of the Americas, New York, NY 10013-2473, USA

www.cambridge.org
Information on this title: www.cambridge.org/9781107639232

First published 2012

Printed in the United States of America

A catalog record for this publication is available from the British Library.

Library of Congress Cataloging in Publication data
Ashworth, John, 1950–
The republic in crisis, 1848–1861 / John Ashworth.
p.   cm.
Includes bibliographical references and index.
ISBN 978-1-107-02408-3 (hardback) – ISBN 978-1-107-63923-2 (paperback)
1. United States – Politics and government – 1845–1861.   2. United States – History –
Civil War, 1861–1865 – Causes.   I. Title.
E415.7.A75   2012
973.7'11–dc23   2011047817

ISBN 978-1-107-02408-3 Hardback
ISBN 978-1-107-63923-2 Paperback

CONTENTS

LIST OF MAPS AND CARTOONS

CHRONOLOGY OF EVENTS

1619	Arrival of the first African slaves in Virginia.
1776	The American Revolution results in the founding of the United States of America.
1787	Slavery is made illegal in the North West Territory.
1787	The U.S. Constitution states that Congress may not ban the slave trade until 1808. The Constitution also gives some protections to slaveholders, though without mentioning slaves or slavery by name.
1793	Eli Whitney's invention of a cotton "gin" increases the demand for slave labour.
1800	Gabriel Prosser, an enslaved blacksmith, organises a slave revolt.
1800	Thomas Jefferson, a Republican, defeats John Adams, a Federalist, and wins the presidency.
1808	Congress bans the importation of slaves from Africa.
1800–1820	Gradual disintegration of the Federalist party and thus of the first party system.
1820	The Missouri Compromise bans slavery north of 36° 30'.
1822	Denmark Vesey's slave revolt in South Carolina.
1828	Election of Andrew Jackson at the head of the party that will become known as the Democratic party.
1831	Nat Turner's slave revolt in Virginia.
1831	William Lloyd Garrison founds the *Liberator*, advocating the immediate abolition of slavery.
1833–1834	Formation of the Whig party, which creates the second party system (of Democrats against Whigs).

1846	The Wilmot Proviso attempts to ban slavery in territory gained from Mexico.
1846–1848	War with Mexico.
1850	The Compromise of 1850 admits California into the Union as a free state, decrees that the status of slavery in Utah and New Mexico territories is to be decided by popular sovereignty, outlaws the slave trade in Washington DC, and creates a much more stringent Fugitive Slave law.
1852	Harriet Beecher Stowe's novel, *Uncle Tom's Cabin*, appears.
1854	Congress passes the Kansas–Nebraska Act, establishing the territories of Kansas and Nebraska and repealing the Missouri Compromise of 1820.
1854	The Know Nothing (or American) party, displaying hostility to immigrants, enters politics and achieves some notable successes.
1854–1856	Collapse of the Whig party.
1856	The newly formed Republican party contests its first presidential election.
1857	The *Dred Scott* ruling from the Supreme Court decrees that Congress does not have the right to ban slavery in the territories and that African Americans are not citizens.
1859	John Brown attempts to launch a slave revolt at Harpers Ferry, Virginia.
1860	The Democratic party splits and nominates two candidates for president: Stephen A. Douglas and John C. Breckinridge.
1860	Election of Abraham Lincoln, a Republican, to the White House.
1860–1861	Between December and February seven states of the Deep South secede to form the Confederate States of America.
April 1861	President Lincoln re-provisions Fort Sumter, prompting the outbreak of the Civil War.

April 1861	In a presidential proclamation Lincoln calls for 75,000 troops to put down the rebellion of the southern states.
1861	In April and May, four more states join the Confederacy.
1863	President Lincoln issues the Emancipation Proclamation.
1865	The Civil War ends, Lincoln is assassinated, and the Thirteenth Amendment abolishes slavery.

INTRODUCTION

The American Civil War occupies a privileged position in history. It was the greatest event in the life of the most powerful country the world has ever seen. Not surprisingly, therefore, it has attracted considerable scholarly interest, mainly from historians within the United States but also from many outside. This book is not intended to be merely another account of the years leading up to that seismic conflict, although the extraordinarily dramatic story is indeed told here. Instead it reinterprets the conflict, arguing that it was the almost inevitable product not of chance or "contingency", but of the profound differences between North and South.[1]

In the first century or so after the outbreak of the war, historians sought to explain what had gone wrong in 1861. They offered many interpretations, interpretations which are still sometimes endorsed today. At that time, however, many scholars made an assumption about the slaves of the South that no reputable historian would now endorse. The assumption was that the slaves were suited to slavery; African-American slaves, it was said, were naturally inclined to accept their enslavement.[2]

At that time, prior to the 1950s and 1960s, little effort had been made to study the social history of the slaves, and racist stereotyping still prevailed. Since the 1960s, however, both these deficiencies have been

---

[1] This interpretation is at odds with some recent writing. See Edward Ayers, *In the Presence of Mine Enemies: War in the Heart of America, 1859–1863* (New York, 2003); Nelson Lankford, *Cry Havoc: The Crooked Road to Civil War* (New York, 2007); Russell McClintock, *Lincoln and the Decision for War: The Northern Response to Secession* (Chapel Hill, NC, 2008).

[2] Thus Ulrich B. Phillips, for example, in *American Slavery, Negro Slavery* (Baton Rouge, 1918), p. 291, referred to the slaves' "courteous acceptance of subordination" and their "readiness for loyalty of a feudal sort".

rectified. We now know that the slaves in their hundreds of thousands yearned for freedom and, accordingly, resisted slavery, occasionally violently, more often in a far quieter, less dramatic but still vitally important manner. What the general public and even many specialists in the period have not yet grasped are the processes by which this resistance played itself out politically. In fact, as we shall see, slave resistance was a fundamental, perhaps the most fundamental, cause of the Civil War. There have been many valuable histories of the 1850s and of the sectional conflict. But in failing to incorporate this factor into their causal schemas, these works are severely defective.[3] Moreover their failure to explain the Civil War adequately entails a failure to assess the role of the slaves not only in creating the conflict but also in bringing about the abolition of slavery and thus their own liberation. We are dealing, then, with a major distortion of the historical process at what is a vital moment in the history of a great nation.

Slave resistance was not, of course, the only cause of the sectional conflict. Nor is it the only one that standard histories have overlooked. In the North the years of intensifying sectional antagonism were also years in which wage labour was becoming increasingly widespread. This was no coincidence. Although almost entirely ignored by Civil War historians, the spread of wage labour, as we shall see, in fact underwrote both the economic and the moral critiques of slavery. And these were the critiques that allowed the North to mobilise opposition to slavery in the South and ultimately, on the battle field, to bring about its destruction. This book will argue that the growth of wage labour must therefore take its rightful place as another principal, though almost entirely unrecognised, cause of the Civil War.

One problem that confronts historians is to integrate these causal processes with a narrative of the events of the 1850s. In the political arena slave resistance was not immediately apparent in the events of the late 1840s and 1850s. Slaves were not, after all, participants in the political process. They did not vote, had no representatives in

---

[3] Two works to which this generalisation applies are David Potter, *The Impending Crisis, 1848–1861* (New York, 1976) and James M. McPherson, *Battle Cry of Freedom* (New York, 1988). These are two of the most widely used – and widely admired – single volumes on the politics of the 1850s. But it is interesting to note that a recent volume on the origins of the Civil War also completely ignores the question of slave resistance – as did almost all of its academic reviewers. See Marc Egnal, *The Clash of Extremes: The Economic Origins of the Civil War* (New York, 2009).

Congress and were not consulted when white Americans made the key decisions. Although wage workers were, in general, able to vote and had representatives in Congress, they too were not directly involved in the key decisions. Those decisions were made by members of the white elite, northern and southern. None of this means, however, that these apparently rather powerless groups can be ignored in an account of the coming of the Civil War, and the pages that follow, without losing their focus on the role of the elites who did make the decisions, will seek to illustrate in all their complexity the processes by which the influence of these other groups was felt.

The discerning reader will quickly see that this interpretation of the sectional conflict places great emphasis not only upon these relatively disadvantaged groups but also (and relatedly) upon the economic changes that were taking places in these years. This is not a new emphasis, though it will be seen that my understanding of the impact of these economic changes differs from that of most scholars.

Another characteristic of this account is that it also places heavy emphasis upon *ideology*, which I treat essentially as world view.[4] Ideology is a set of ideas, attitudes and beliefs which together make up a view of society, of government and of human nature – in short a view of the world. We can expect an ideology to be comprised of ideas which are relatively consistent with one another. But we should also recognise that there may be tensions, sometimes even outright contradictions within these belief systems. Even more important we should recognise that ideologies sometimes illuminate reality but sometimes serve to obscure it. For example, as we shall see, in the decades before the Civil War, the ideology of the Democratic party illuminated some of the inequalities that existed within American society, and simultaneously obscured others. As a result it offered protection to the elite group (the slaveholders of the South) whose privileges it covertly furthered.

It will also become apparent to the reader that, again and again, when I identify what seem to be the errors of what some historians have termed a "blundering generation" of Americans,[5] I seek to explain how

---

[4] Some scholars employ the German term "Weltanschauung" as a synonym for world view.

[5] Here I am referring, as students of the period will know, to the Civil War "revisionist" historians who argued that the war was brought about by blunders on the part of statesmen who simply lacked the abilities necessary to lead the nation in challenging times. Implicit

those errors flowed directly from more basic perceptions, perceptions that were integral to the ideology or world view of the group in question. I then often seek to identify the economic interests served, whether consciously or not, by these ideologies. This is an approach, going from "blunders" (though in fact denying that they should be seen as blunders) to ideology to economic interest, that will be unfamiliar to many readers and students, and it results in there being some passages of the book that non-specialists may find difficult.[6] I have of course tried to be as clear and lucid as possible in the exposition of these ideas; this is the minimum that the reader can expect of any author.

Finally I should like to offer thanks to some friends, relations, colleagues and editors, who have, in one way or another, facilitated the completion of this volume. My father, Eric Ashworth, read the entire manuscript and offered many valuable suggestions, as did my good friend (and former teacher) Michael Heale. Heather Forland also read the book and gave me an enormous amount of help and encouragement to complete it. Eric Foner and James Oakes were among those who initially suggested that I should write the volume and it has benefited greatly from the comments of Frank Towers and Bruce Levine. I have learnt a great deal from each of these scholars. Frank Smith of Cambridge University Press gave me every encouragement to embark upon the project; at CUP responsibility for the volume subsequently fell to Emily Spangler, Abigail Zorbaugh and Eric Crahan to each of whom I am very much indebted. A special thanks must go to Luane Hutchinson for her superb and highly efficient copy editing. Although I would dearly like to blame all these people for the errors that remain in the book, unfortunately I cannot quite bring myself to do so.

John Ashworth
November 2011

(or even explicit) in this view was the claim that better statesmen would have avoided war. This volume rejects this claim entirely.

[6] It is probably the case that the discussion of the relationship of the Democratic party to slavery in Chapter 2 is the most difficult section of the book.

I

THE UNITED STATES
IN 1848

A Nation Imperilled

I

Eighteen forty eight was the year of revolutions in Europe. In the United States it seemed like business as usual, at least insofar as the stability of the nation was concerned. There was no revolution expected here. And none came. Nevertheless within little more than a dozen years, there would indeed be a revolution, a cataclysm which would set in train some devastating social, political and economic changes and, at the same time, claim the lives of far more men and women than had been casualties in Europe in its year of revolutions. Few Americans glimpsed this possibility in 1848.

Many instead, and understandably, congratulated themselves on not merely the stability but also the overall success of their nation. Contrary to the expectations of some European observers at the time and subsequently, the "experiment" that had been the American Republic in 1776 had been a triumphant success. This success had been political, economic and military.[1]

Its political manifestation was obvious. The United States, as of March 1848 following the recent war and peace treaty with Mexico, comprised a huge nation covering not 890,000 square miles, as in 1776, but instead almost three million. There were now not thirteen but, by mid-1848, thirty states. Equally important the nation's political institutions had advanced at what seemed an equally breathtaking pace. The Federal Constitution, drawn up and put into operation in the late 1780s, had survived not only unscathed but as an object of veneration

---

[1] The success was also, it could be argued, cultural. This question is beyond the scope of the present volume.

to all but a small minority of Americans, or at least of white Americans. Presidents had come and gone, Congresses had been elected and then turned out as the Constitution stipulated, and a federal judiciary had operated sometimes controversially but never so as to bring large numbers of Americans to question the viability of their Republic. It was all much as the more optimistic of the nation's founding fathers might have hoped.

As far as the economy was concerned, it was a similar success story. Since 1800 gross national product had increased approximately sevenfold, with a doubling of per capita income. The population was growing by approximately a third every decade. Internal trade, extremely difficult in the eighteenth century, had been transformed by the digging of canals and the building of turnpikes, steamboats and now railroads. Meanwhile the value of goods exported had soared from a little over twenty million dollars in 1790 to more than 138 million in 1848. Similarly the value of the nation's manufactured goods had in the forty years before 1850 increased almost sixfold. This expansionary process had not been uninterrupted; indeed the most recent significant interruption had come recently, in the late 1830s and early 1840s, but from the mid-to-late 1840s growth had resumed, and at an accelerating pace. There seemed little reason to doubt that it would continue for the foreseeable future. This seemed further reason for celebration. Time would show that it was not.[2]

Were Americans united? A superficial glance would suggest that they were. While many of Europe's ethnic minorities were questioning their allegiances to the nations of which they were a part, and others were challenging established hierarchies and seeking to replace them with more liberal or radical alternatives, in the United States a shared loyalty to the nation encompassed all but a small minority, or at any rate a small minority of the white Anglo-Saxon males who wielded all the power. The most exploited groups of all, the slaves of the South and the Native Americans, comprised only a small part of the total population and, for the most part, lacked all political rights or the strength to

---

[2] Douglass C. North, *The Economic Growth of the United States 1790–1860* (New York, 1966), pp. 221, 233; Susan Lee and Peter Passell, *A New Economic View of American History* (New York, 1979), pp. 52–62; John Ashworth, *Slavery, Capitalism and Politics in the Antebellum Republic* vol 1, *Commerce and Compromise, 1820–1850* (Cambridge, 1995), p. 91.

obtain them by force. Women also lacked the vote but only a handful of men or women believed this to be wrong; they would in 1848 form the first women's rights convention the world had seen, to the derision of most commentators. An observer might thus have concluded that, in contradistinction to Europe, the United States of 1848 was indeed a united nation.

II

Appearances were deceptive. Beneath this unity lay the seeds of the revolution that would burst forth in 1861. It was scarcely surprising that a nation spread over so large an area as the United States now occupied should exhibit marked regional diversity. A sharp and obvious contrast existed between the comparatively long-established states of the East and those of the West (what would now be the Midwest), some of which had been settled only a few years. As all observers noted and expected, the processes of economic development were more advanced in the older states of the East. Contrast, however, did not necessitate conflict, and if the only sectional difference had been between East and West there would in 1848 have been little cause for concern. Far more ominous, even in 1848, were the differences between North and South, with the institution of slavery at their heart.

Slavery had existed throughout the Union in 1776, but in part because of the idealism of 1776, enshrined in the American Revolution's rhetoric of liberty and equality, it had been very gradually abolished in the North, a process not completed until the 1820s. The disruption to the northern economy had been very limited. In 1776 many southerners had assumed that in their region too slavery would disappear. But its role here was too great. In the eighteenth century its strongholds were the tobacco-growing areas of Virginia and Maryland and the parts of South Carolina and Georgia where rice and indigo could be cultivated. In the 1790s a technological breakthrough occurred with the invention by Eli Whitney of a new cotton engine, or "gin", which removed the seeds from cotton, previously a highly labour-intensive process, and thus made its cultivation profitable across much of the Lower South (and even a few areas in the Upper South). The acquisition of new land in the South West, together with the often forcible expulsion of the Native Americans from it, now combined with an almost insatiable demand from Europe for raw cotton. The result was the spectacular growth of the cotton kingdom. In 1791 the United States exported fewer than two hundred thousand pounds of cotton; by 1815 the figure was in excess of eighty million. The process continued. By 1850 the value of cotton exported would be four times the 1815 figure.[3]

American slavery was by now explicitly racial; its victims were African Americans, though a few had skins so white that they could not be distinguished from Caucasians. As of 1848 there were fifteen slave states, forming in effect three tiers. These were the states of the Border South (Delaware, Maryland, Missouri and Kentucky), the Middle South (Virginia, North Carolina, Arkansas and Tennessee), and the Deep South (South Carolina, Georgia, Florida, Alabama, Mississippi, Louisiana and Texas). Although Virginia had more slaves than any other state, the proportion of slaves in the total population was greater in the Lower than in the Middle South, and lowest in the Border South. South Carolina and Mississippi were exceptional in having a majority of their populations enslaved. In Delaware meanwhile the slave population was less than three per cent of the total, while in Missouri, a state destined to play a key role in the politics of the 1850s, the figure (as of 1850) was approximately thirteen per cent. It is a striking though not perhaps surprising fact that, across the South as a whole, proslavery sentiment (among the whites) was directly proportional to the percentage of the population enslaved. South Carolina was in the vanguard of the movement for southern rights and for southern independence; Delaware scarcely counted as a southern state at all.[4]

The growth in the total slave population had itself been startling. In 1808 the African slave trade had been closed and many contemporaries had expected the institution to wither away as a result. But alone among new world slave regimes, the slaveholders of the South had seen their human chattels increase in number decade on decade through natural reproduction combined with, as some masters saw it, the paternal regard lavished upon them. We need not accept these claims to recognise

---

[3] Arthur Zilversmit, *The First Emancipation: The Abolition of Slavery in the North* (Chicago, 1969); North, *Economic Growth*, pp. 231, 233. For a different view of the technological impact of the cotton gin, see Angela Lakwete, *Inventing the Cotton Gin: Machine and Myth in Antebellum America* (Baltimore, 2003).

[4] Useful data on slaveholding can be found at http://www.sonofthesouth.net/slavery/slave-maps/slave-census.htm.

that slavery in the United States by the mid-nineteenth century was less savage than it had been in previous times and somewhat less malign than in most other slaveholding countries. By 1850 there were approximately three million slaves in the South; at the time of the Revolution there had been half a million.

These slaves were owned by a comparatively small number of southerners. Only one in three families possessed slaves, though once again the proportion was highest in the Deep South, lowest in the border areas. The loyalty of the non-slaveholders to their states and thus to slavery was real, but not uniform and certainly not unlimited, especially in the most lightly enslaved areas.[5] This potential for conflict would play a key role in the politics of the 1850s and in precipitating a Civil War in 1861. It was not, however, as important as the attitude of the slaves themselves to their own enslavement.[6]

III

Although the experiences of the millions of black Americans who lived in slavery in the United States were extraordinarily varied, one generalisation can be offered. In their millions they bitterly resented being slaves. With few exceptions, they wanted to be free. Slavery is an exploitative system, but the exploitation on which it rests is naked and highly visible to its victims. The slave works, the master appropriates the fruits of this labour and without the consent of the slave. Whatever is returned to the slave in the form of food, clothing or "luxuries" is at the discretion of the master. One does not need to be educated or literate or well-informed to perceive the exploitative nature of this relationship. As we shall see, this is one of the key weaknesses of the system.

Abundant evidence exists to show that slaves of all ages, of both sexes, from all parts of the Old South perceived it and yearned for freedom. As one of them put it, "my heart ached within me to feel the life of liberty". Another later and poignantly recalled that he "used to wonder why it was that our people were kept in slavery". He "would look

[5] A recent work that emphasises the opposition of the non-slaveholders to the slaveholders' rule is David Williams, *Bitterly Divided: The South's Inner Civil War* (New York, 2008).
[6] Lawrence Shore, *Southern Capitalists: The Ideological Leadership of an Elite* (Chapel Hill, NC, 1986); Ashworth, *Slavery, Capitalism and Politics in the Antebellum Republic* vol 2, *The Coming of the Civil War 1850–1861* (Cambridge, 2007), pp. 82–96.

at the birds as they flew over my head or sung their free songs upon the trees, and think it strange, that, of all God's creatures, the poor negro only was held in bondage". He insisted that "no slaves think they were made to be slaves".[7] Even if this were an exaggeration, and some slaves were instead content with their situation, the slaveholders had to respond to the dangers posed by those who were not. As a result slave resistance, taken in conjunction with the southern response to that resistance, would be a fundamental, perhaps the most fundamental, cause of sectional conflict and thus of civil war. Until recently it has been entirely ignored by historians.[8]

Slave resistance took many forms. First and most dramatic was the deliberately undertaken act of violence. This might be directed against an individual slaveholder and take the form of arson, poisoning or an act of physical aggression. In the most extreme cases of all, there were attempted insurrections. In the United States these were few and far between, reflecting the slaves' extremely limited prospect of success. In 1831 Nat Turner had led the most famous slave revolt in American history, which had resulted in the deaths of more than seventy whites and caused widespread panic, together with ferocious reprisals, in Southampton County, Virginia and throughout the South. There would be no comparable uprisings in later years. But this must not be taken

---

[7] John Blassingame, *Slave Testimony* (Baton Rouge, LA, 1977), pp. 688, 135.

[8] No historian did more than Kenneth M. Stampp to alert scholars to slave resistance – in his writings on slavery. In his writings on the origins of the Civil War, he ignored the subject entirely. See Stampp, *The Peculiar Institution: Slavery in the Ante-Bellum South* (New York, 1956), pp. 9, 92, 140. As historian John W. Blassingame put it, "there is overwhelming evidence in the primary sources, of the Negro's resistance to his bondage and of his undying love for freedom"; "the slave's constant prayer, his all-consuming hope, was for liberty"; *The Slave Community: Plantation Life in the Antebellum South* (rev. ed., New York, 1979), pp. 192, 193. For examples of works stressing black resistance, see Raymond A. Bauer and Alice H. Bauer, "Day to Day Resistance to Slavery", *Journal of Negro History* XXVII (1942), 388–419; Gabor Boritt and Scott Hancock, eds. *Slavery, Resistance, Freedom* (New York, 2007); Steven Hahn, *A Nation Under Our Feet: Black Political Struggles in the Rural South from Slavery to the Great Migration* (Cambridge, MA, 2003), *The Political Worlds of Slavery and Freedom* (Boston, 2009); James Oakes, *Slavery and Freedom: An Interpretation of the Old South* (New York, 1990); Leslie Howard Owens, *This Species of Property: Slave Life and Culture in the Old South* (New York, 1976); Walter Johnson, *Soul by Soul: Life Inside the Antebellum Slave Market* (Cambridge, MA, 1999); Deborah Gray White, *Arn't I A Woman: Female Slaves in the Plantation* (New York, 1985); William A. Link, *Roots of Secession: Slavery and Politics in Antebellum Virginia* (Chapel Hill, NC, 2003). This is also a main theme of both volumes of my *Slavery, Capitalism and Politics*. For a balanced assessment of the extent of slave resistance, see Peter Kolchin, *American Slavery, 1619–1861* (New York, 2003).

to mean that slave rebellion was irrelevant to the growing sectional conflict. As we shall see, southerners had to respond again and again to the *potential* for violence from their slaves and in so doing took actions that threatened white liberties and in the process deeply antagonised the North. In this way slave violence, or the potential for it, indirectly promoted the antislavery cause and aggravated the sectional conflict.[9]

Only slightly less dramatic as a form of resistance were the attempts made by slaves to run away, in the most extreme cases to the North. Once again it did not matter that only a small number of slaves attempted this in any one year. Once again the potential for resistance was all important, in this case because it resulted in southerners pressing for legislation to facilitate the recapture of these slaves. Once again the actions taken to combat slave resistance produced resentment and a significant intensification of antislavery sentiment in the North.

There were other, apparently far more mundane, forms of resistance. On a day-to-day basis slaves could, and did, disrupt the work routine, damage crops and machinery, or feign illness. These actions, about which slaveholders complained again and again in their letters, journals and diaries, impaired the performance of the southern economy. One should not press this point too far, since the South, like the North, was experiencing rapid economic growth in the late 1840s, a process that would continue and indeed accelerate into the 1850s. It did, however, serve to convince northerners of the economic inferiority of slave labour, which seemed simply to lack the incentives that motivated free labour.

More important was the process of economic development which slavery imposed upon the South, or perhaps it would be better to say the lack of economic development. In 1850 ninety per cent (by value) of the nation's manufactured goods came from the North. Urbanisation was, of course, far more advanced in the eastern than in the western states, but in the same year while the proportion of the population in the North East living in urban areas was in excess of twenty-five per cent, in the South East it was below ten per cent. Although some slaves were used in manufacturing industry and were also to be found in cities, it is striking

[9] Eugene D. Genovese, *From Rebellion to Revolution: Afro-American Slave Revolts in the Making of the New World* (New York, 1979); Herbert Aptheker, *American Negro Slave Revolts* (New York, 1943). See also Edward B. Rugemer, *The Problem of Emancipation: The Caribbean Roots of the American Civil War* (Baton Rouge, LA, 2008).

that no slave regime in the history of the world has managed to industrialise or urbanise. Up to and including the time of its final gasp in 1865, the Old South would prove no exception.[10]

Why was this? It was not because slaves could not be employed profitably in industry. On the contrary, the most important study of the subject finds that profits were even higher there than in agriculture.[11] Nor were opportunities lacking in urban environments, where slaves could be employed in myriad ways or hired out to others, or even left to hire themselves out to others (with the master having to do little other than to pocket the payment obtained from the hirer). Profitability was not the problem. Instead there were two major constraints. One of them was the phenomenon we have already encountered: slave resistance. Slaves had a reputation for misusing tools, and this gave a careful master an incentive to keep them in agriculture where the value of capital equipment employed and thus the potential for damage was far lower. Moreover white workers were employed both in industry and in cities in the South, and whenever they faced competition from slaves, complaints were frequently voiced. The slaveholders were fully aware that their very existence depended upon the acquiescence in the regime of the non-slaveholding whites, a clear majority, we should remember, of the white population of the South. Furthermore, in cities there were "undesirable" groups with whom slaves might all too easily consort. These comprised not only poor whites but also free blacks, a most undesirable class, from the slaveholder's perspective, whose very existence challenged the claim that blacks needed to be enslaved for their own benefit. Southerners frequently commented on the dangers posed by urbanisation and industrialisation. According to James Henry Hammond, one of South Carolina's most prominent statesmen, "whenever a slave is made a mechanic, he is more than half freed". "The field", another southerner concluded, "is the proper sphere of the negro".[12]

---

[10] Ashworth, *Slavery Capitalism and Politics*, I, pp. 90–108. For a different view of the South, see (amongst other recent works) John Majewski, *Modernizing a Slave Economy: The Economic Vision of the Confederate Nation* (Chapel Hill, NC, 2009); L. Diane Barnes, Brian Schoen and Frank Towers, eds. *The Old South's Modern Worlds: Slavery, Region, and Nation in the Age of Progress* (New York, 2011). See also Towers, *The Urban South and the Coming of the Civil War* (Charlottesville, VA, 2004).

[11] Fred Bateman and Thomas Weiss, *A Deplorable Scarcity: The Failure of Industrialization in the Slave Economy* (Chapel Hill, NC, 1981), pp. 106, 113.

[12] *De Bow's Review*, XXIV (1858), p. 581, VIII (1850), pp. 25–26.

The second constraint had to do not so much with slave resistance as with the very nature of slavery as a form of investment. The demand for slaves' labour in agriculture was highly seasonal: it was greatest by far at harvest time. But it was not possible for masters to shed their slaves at other points in the cycle in the way that employers could shed wage workers when their labour was not needed. So it made economic sense for the slaves at those times to be employed on other tasks. Consequently plantations attempted to be self-sufficient; other than in their export crop, their involvement in trade was extremely limited. And when the slaves were growing their own food, the masters had no incentive to introduce labour-saving technology, since the slaves had nothing else to do. The absence of specialisation in food production, together with the lack of demand from the plantations, implied the underdevelopment of towns wherever slavery was prevalent, in sharp contrast with the situation in the North. And the failure to introduce labour-saving technology implied that in the South, unlike in the North, labour would not be expelled from agriculture into industry. Little wonder then that the South lagged so far behind in the processes of both urbanisation and industrialisation.[13]

Most, though not all, southerners congratulated themselves on their overwhelmingly agricultural economy and rural society. Moreover they were fully aware of another of the effects of slave resistance, this time on the relationship between the slaveholders and the non-slaveholding whites in the South. As we have already noted, the slaveholders understood the importance of the non-slaveholders' support, or at least acquiescence. If the slaves had been machines, with no capacity for resistance, the relationship between slaveholders and non-slaveholding whites would scarcely have been a concern. As it was these less affluent (as they almost always were) whites were needed. They were needed to come to the aid of the slaveholders should there be any slave unrest. They were needed to man the patrols that maintained discipline and "order" in the black-belt areas of the South, the localities where the slaves were most numerous. At all costs they must not make common cause with the slaves and unite with them in an attack upon the

---

[13] Robin Blackburn, *The Making of New World Slavery: From the Baroque to the Modern, 1492–1800* (London, 1997); Charles Post, The *American Road to Capitalism* (Boston, 2011).

slaveholding elite. They must not even form a separate power base in the South, one over which the masters had no control, and one which might create the alarming prospect of a prosperous and thriving but slaveless South. In theory, the South could have attempted to industrialise on the basis of white labour. Some southerners advocated this. But others saw the danger clearly. As Christopher Memminger of South Carolina warned, if white labourers became an important political force in the South, they would soon "raise hue and cry against the Negro and be hot Abolitionists". In the words of another prominent southerner, "every city" of the South "is destined to be the seat of free soilism".[14]

As a result the South, and especially the Deep South, bestowed its highest accolades not upon those who engaged in commerce or manufacturing but instead upon the plantation owner, whose livelihood depended upon slave labour. In the North these constraints on economic development were absent, and the northern economy progressed accordingly. But when northerners looked at the South, they were struck by the contrast between the two regional economies and did not doubt that theirs was superior. The effect once again was to deepen their hostility to slavery. In this indirect way, as in so many others, slave resistance again intensified antislavery sentiment. How important was this? Within less than two decades, the forces of northern antislavery would, at gun point, destroy slavery south of the Mason–Dixon line.

IV

The slaveholders lived cheek by jowl with their allegedly inferior, childlike slaves and believed they understood them. Here they were profoundly and fatally mistaken. A curious irony resulted. Although the slaves longed for freedom, they took care not to let the masters know it. One slave later recalled that when white men were present, "no slave would dare...to say that he wished for freedom". Another remembered that in front of white men, they would "go so far as to say they would not leave their masters for the world". The slaveholders were duped.[15]

---

[14] Christopher Memminger quoted in Robert Starobin, *Industrial Slavery in the Old South* (New York, 1970), pp. 209–210; *Southern Quarterly Review* XXVI (1854), pp. 431–457.

[15] Blassingame, *Slave Testimony*, pp. 135, 690.

If they were dupes, however, they were not hypocrites. Although the modern world finds slavery repellent, it would be a mistake to believe that all humans at all times have instinctively recoiled from it. Southerners occasionally expressed guilt about slavery, but such admissions were few and far between. Instead, in their hundreds of thousands, they sincerely believed in it. The claims made for slavery had grown with its growing economic success. In the early years of the Republic, it had usually been defended as a "necessary evil": any direct attempt to remove it would create chaos and upheaval. The South might have been better off without slavery but was saddled with it.[16]

From the 1830s, however, southerners had been faced with a more militant antislavery movement in the North and the "necessary evil" argument would no longer suffice. But it would be quite wrong to assume that the changing attitude towards slavery in the South was mere opportunism. Instead the ever-deeper dependence of the southern economy upon slave labour, together with attacks from the North, made intelligent southerners re-examine the institution. Would God allow them to prosper on the basis of a labour system that He condemned? Had the slaves not been given the inestimable benefits of Christianity? Were blacks in America not more prosperous than elsewhere? Did they not need, for their own good, to be enslaved? More and more southerners gave new answers to these questions, answers that together confirmed that slavery should now be viewed as a "positive good".[17]

By mid-century a body of proslavery thought was forming. It held that blacks were inherently inferior and would remain so for the foreseeable future. They therefore needed the protection of their masters, who gave them food, clothing and shelter, together with Christian teaching. Unlike the wage labourers of the North, who were vulnerable to unemployment and starvation when economic conditions worsened, the slave was protected by a wise and caring master. Slavery was, according

[16] Many scholars have argued for widespread slaveholder guilt. It is a claim for which there is little evidence, is essentially a projection of the values of our own age, and signals a failure to respect the distinctiveness of the past.

[17] On the proslavery argument, see Drew G. Faust, "A Southern Stewardship: The Intellectual and the Proslavery Argument", *American Quarterly*, XXXI (1979), 63–80; Faust, *A Sacred Circle: The Dilemma of the Intellectual in the Old South, 1840–1860* (Baltimore, 1977); Eugene D. Genovese, *The World the Slaveholders Made: Two Essays in Interpretation* (rev. ed., New York, 1988); William S. Jenkins, *The Proslavery Argument in the Old South* (Chapel Hill, NC, 1935); Shore, *Southern Capitalists*; Larry E. Tise, *Proslavery: A History of the Defense of Slavery in America, 1701–1840* (Athens, GA, 1987).

to the more extreme defenders of the institution, not merely acceptable, but actually superior to the free-labour system of the North.

Moreover, proslavery theorists insisted, slavery was highly beneficial to the non-slaveholding whites as well. Slaves, it was claimed, did the menial jobs that society required and this in turn allowed all white southerners to enjoy much greater esteem than would otherwise be possible or than was even now possible in the North, where menial labour had to be performed by whites. An extension of this argument came when proslavery writers held that slavery fostered not merely greater equality of esteem (among whites) but also greater equality of wealth and income (once again among whites). Finally it was claimed, even more paradoxically, that slavery actually promoted a love of liberty from which, once again, all whites would benefit. Southerners pointed with pride to the disproportionate influence they had exerted in the nation's history. George Washington, Thomas Jefferson, James Madison, Andrew Jackson – all were key figures in the success story that was the American Republic. All had furthered the cause of American liberty. All had been slaveholders. Thanks in part to their experience of slavery, all had been blessed with, and had inculcated in their fellow countrymen, a keen awareness of the benefits of freedom.[18]

It is important to note that this entire intellectual edifice was built on the premise that slavery served slaves well. Here we encounter a final paradox. Although, as we have seen, southerners responded to the resistance, or the potential for resistance, of their slaves, they simultaneously and quite sincerely denied its existence. How could this be? In fact the slaveholders' logic was impeccable, however distorted their vision. According to southerners, slaves were in themselves quite content under slavery unless and until they were "tampered with", incited, or provoked by pernicious influences, sometimes within the South, more often outside it. What were these influences? Southerners did not hesitate to identify the culprits. They might be abolitionists and other anti-slavery agitators, white or black, mainly though not exclusively in the North. They might also be free blacks in the South. They might be visitors to the region, either from the North or from abroad. They might be

---

[18] These arguments were not without problems, in that southerners often got themselves into logical difficulties with them. See my *Slavery, Capitalism and Politics*, I, pp. 192–285.

the despicable minority of southern whites who fraternised with slaves and thus challenged the racial barriers upon which the entire social system depended. These were the groups scapegoated.

So southerners utterly misunderstood the nature of the threats surrounding them. The threat from the North came precisely because there were groups in the South, slaves and non-slaveholding whites, whose loyalty to the regime might be suspect. The threat from the non-slaveholding whites was in turn so great because of the potential resistance of the slaves. The ultimate source of the difficulty was thus the slaves themselves, the very group about whose inherent loyalty the masters were most confident.

V

By 1848 southerners were faced with intensifying antislavery sentiment in the North. Just as the South's increasing dependence on slave labour had encouraged southerners to revise their opinion of the peculiar institution, so the same process led to a revision of attitudes in the North. The revolutionary generation had been content in the cosy assumption that slavery was moribund; one could oppose it, but one need take no action, since it was clearly doomed. As late as 1810 this assumption was perhaps still tenable. At that time slavery was clearly on its way out in the North, and the recent closure of the African slave trade held out the possibility that the same might be true of the South. In 1816 the American Colonization Society (ACS) was founded. It sought to colonise or repatriate either free blacks or slaves (whose masters might free them precisely because repatriation would then follow). Although some slaveholders did take up this option, their numbers were pitifully small, nowhere near enough to dent the institution itself. By 1830, indeed before 1830, it was obvious to all clear-sighted observers that slavery was flourishing in the South and that it was, in organisational terms, effectively unopposed throughout the nation.[19]

Partly in response to this development, and partly in response to changing conditions in the North itself (which we shall examine shortly), the 1830s saw the birth of a new era in the history of antislavery in

---

[19] Eric Burin, *Slavery and the Peculiar Solution: A History of the American Colonization Society* (Gainesville, FL, 2005).

the United States. On 1 January 1831 William Lloyd Garrison began to publish in Boston the *Liberator*. In its very first issue, he avowed his purpose: "I do not wish to think, or speak, or write, with moderation…I am in earnest – I will not equivocate – I will not excuse – I will not retreat a single inch – AND I WILL BE HEARD".[20]

Garrison and other antislavery radicals, both black and white, made a number of assertions, from which they assuredly did not retreat. First, slavery was a sin. Second, the conscience, which was the voice of God, or the nearest possible approximation to it, confirmed that it was indeed a sin. Third, compromise with slavery was compromise with sin and was therefore sinful itself. To tolerate slavery was to disobey the voice of conscience and was to encourage others to sin. These would be the key principles of the abolitionists, as they were known, from 1831 to the emancipation of the slaves during the Civil War.[21]

In the early 1830s this logic drove Garrison first to reject the ACS on the grounds that it embraced compromise and thus perpetuated slavery. Next it drove him to denounce the nation's churches, when most of them failed to join the crusade against slavery. Third, it led him to believe that all the nation's political parties were, in varying degrees, corrupt. They functioned on the basis of compromise, once again stultifying the voice of conscience within. Finally it led him to denounce the Federal Constitution and the Union itself, on the grounds that both tolerated slavery.

These were extremely radical and alarming conclusions. Most southerners believed that if Garrison had been inspired by any supernatural force, it must surely be the Devil rather than the Christian God whom

---

[20] William Lloyd Garrison, "To the Public", *Liberator*, Jan. 1, 1831.

[21] The best analysis of abolitionist thought is Ronald G. Walters, *The Antislavery Appeal: American Abolitionism After 1830* (Baltimore, 1976). Other valuable works include Gilbert Hobbs Barnes, *The Antislavery Impulse, 1830–1844* (2nd ed., New York, 1964); Louis Filler, *The Crusade Against Slavery, 1830–1860* (New York, 1960); Lawrence J. Friedman, *Gregarious Saints: Self and Community in American Abolitionism, 1830–1870* (Cambridge, 1982); Paul Goodman, *Of One Blood: Abolitionism and the Origins of Racial Equality* (Berkeley, 1998); Aileen S. Kraditor, *Means and Ends in American Abolition: Garrison and His Critics on Strategy and Tactics, 1834–1850* (New York, 1970); Timothy P. McCarthy and John Stauffer, eds. *Prophets of Protest: Reconsidering the History of American Abolitionism* (New York, 2006); Lewis Perry, *Radical Abolitionism: Anarchy and the Government of God in Antislavery Thought* (Ithaca, NY, 1973); Lewis Perry and Michael Fellman, eds. *Antislavery Reconsidered: New Perspectives on the Abolitionists* (Baton Rouge, LA, 1979); Peter F. Walker, *Moral Choices: Memory, Desire and Imagination in Nineteenth-Century American Abolition* (Baton Rouge, LA, 1978).

they worshipped. But the great majority of northerners too found Garrison's principles repugnant. Even those who disliked slavery found his views far too extreme. Nevertheless the abolitionist movement grew. It attracted blacks and whites. Within a decade there were probably more than a thousand local abolition societies with a total of well over a hundred thousand members. These groups did not necessarily agree with one another. Some, unlike Garrison, were prepared to enter politics and they formed the Liberty party. Some, unlike Garrison, did not accept that the Constitution condoned slavery and, as a result, did not denounce the Union. Some, unlike Garrison, did not advocate the rights of women. Some contained African Americans, others did not. But all were viewed with great alarm in the South.[22]

The first decade of the movement saw the first examples of a process that would recur again and again before reaching the finale that was the outbreak of armed hostilities in 1861. The abolitionists (and later other, more moderate antislavery groups like the Republicans) would put pressure on, there would be a reaction in the South, and as a result more northerners, some of whom had not shared the original antislavery objectives, would in turn react against the South. Thus in the mid-1830s the abolitionists sent petitions to Congress seeking, among other goals, the abolition of slavery in the nation's capital. Southerners, fearing that mere discussion of this issue in the halls of Congress would legitimate the demand (and also serve to incite any slaves within earshot), responded by demanding a gag rule, by which the petitions would be tabled without discussion. The result was to identify antislavery with the right of freedom of speech. In much the same way, and at the same time, when abolitionists sought to flood the South with antislavery pamphlets, southerners, again fearful of the effect upon slaves and non-slaveholding whites, reacted by censoring the mails and preventing delivery of the pamphlets. Again many northerners resented this curtailment of white civil liberties. Finally in 1837 came the murder of Elijah Lovejoy in Alton, Illinois. Lovejoy became abolitionism's first martyr: he met his death at the hands of an anti-abolition mob. Many northerners were outraged. In each case abolitionist activity deepened

---

[22] Dwight L. Dumond, *Antislavery: The Crusade for Freedom in America* (New York, 1961), pp. 245–258. See also Bruce Laurie, *Beyond Garrison: Antislavery and Social Reform* (New York, 2005); Reinhard O. Johnson, *The Liberty Party, 1840–1848: Antislavery Third Party Politics in the United States* (Baton Rouge, LA, 2009).

the division within the nation over slavery. Abolitionism and proslavery sentiment grew together, each reinforced by the growth of the other.[23]

On the other hand it would be an error to conclude that the anti-slavery movement did not at the same time reflect changing conditions within northern society. Its most obvious affinity was perhaps with the religious revivals that had swept the nation repeatedly since colonial times. Evangelical Protestants taught that the son of God had been sent to atone for mankind's guilt and could bring salvation and regeneration by the Holy Ghost. The righteous would be blessed. Moreover salvation was open to all. In huge numbers, evangelicals believed that the growth of religious piety and benevolence would herald the "millennium", a golden age or era of Christian prosperity and dominance, after which there would be Christ's second coming. Slavery had long been regarded as a symbol of man's sinful nature with the slave, or perhaps the entire social system, or perhaps human nature itself, rather than the slave-holder, held to blame. But if, as the evangelicals insisted, sins were erad-icable, it surely followed that slavery could be eradicated too.[24]

Nevertheless the vast majority of evangelicals did not become aboli-tionists, nor were all abolitionists evangelicals. And the desire to purge the world of sin, or at least to battle against it, had not in the past been taken to imply criticism of slavery, which had rarely been challenged before the final quarter of the eighteenth century. Clearly other factors were present.

VI

The United States in 1848 was experimenting with a new social system, one which was essentially untried. This was not, however, the slave-labour system, an example of which was to be found in the South, and which had a long and undistinguished pedigree going back thousands of years. Instead it was the wage-labour system of the North. Although individuals and small groups had been employed for wages for many centuries, the idea that men (and women) in their hundreds of thou-sands could be dependent on wages for their livelihood was quite novel.

---

[23] See Russel B. Nye, *Fettered Freedom: Civil Liberties and the Slavery Controversy 1830–1860* (Urbana, IL, 1972).

[24] One of many good books on American religion in these years is Richard Carwardine, *Evangelicals and Politics in Antebellum America* (New Haven, CT, 1993).

And the idea that these men (though not the women) might at the same time enjoy political rights was unprecedented and would, for almost all of human history, have seemed fanciful or absurd.

The status of the wage labourer has traditionally been an extremely humble one. Americans were heirs to a long and venerable tradition, going back to Ancient Greece, of hostility to wage labour. In early modern England and colonial America, wage labourers were held to be inferior to those who possessed even the minutest fragment of land to farm for themselves. What most struck commentators about wage workers was their dependence or servility. Others feared that they lacked any stake in society and were thus a dangerous and disturbing element in the body politic. By contrast the farmer, and especially the yeoman farmer who owned his own land, seemed a model of manly independence, fit to enjoy the rights of republican citizenship. This was very much the attitude of Thomas Jefferson, as expressed in his celebrated *Notes on Virginia* in the 1780s. As we shall see, it was also the attitude of Andrew Jackson and the Democratic party of the 1830s and 1840s.[25]

In the following decades these attitudes began to change dramatically. It would be a pardonable exaggeration to claim that in the nineteenth century, the United States went from a belief that democracy was incompatible with wage labour (on a large scale) to an assumption that a successful free society and democratic government depend on wage labour and are scarcely possible without it. From the 1830s onwards the abolitionists were in the vanguard of this movement. The adjustment to the arrival of wage labour on a large scale would bring with it a new hostility to slavery.

The process was a complex one. If, as must be the case (assuming the entire social system were not doomed), the wage labourer were indeed a fit citizen for a Republic, what were the qualities that he possessed? What was it that rooted him in society, that kept him loyal to the social order? Abolitionists (and some other Americans too) gave several answers; for anyone who acted upon those conclusions rigorously and wholeheartedly, as abolitionists assuredly did, each mandated an uncompromising opposition to, and hatred of, slavery.

[25] Christopher Hill, "Pottage for Freeborn Englishmen: Attitudes to Wage Labor", in Hill, *Change and Continuity in Seventeenth-Century England* (London, 1974), pp. 219–238. See also John Ashworth, *"Agrarians" and "Aristocrats": Party Political Ideology in the United States* (London, 1983).

First, the wage worker had the opportunity to rise in society. Thus he might cease to be a wage labourer and might even become an employer of wage labourers in his turn. According to *The Emancipator*, another abolitionist newspaper, "the truth" was "that the *great body* of the young men of New England, and a large portion of the young women, work for wages, acquire the means of becoming either employers or operatives in their own shops or on their own farms". It followed that "to assume the existence of a distinction between employers and paid workmen, as a permanent state, is either to dream or to deceive". In the United States, the writer continued, "the wheels of fortune revolve too rapidly, and the rich and poor change places too frequently, to allow a foundation for such an agitation as this".[26] The driving force of the entire system was, of course, self-interest: the prospect of upward mobility gave the worker a huge incentive to labour. At this point the antislavery implications became apparent. The slave simply lacked these incentives. In the vast majority of cases he could never cease to be a slave.[27] Moreover because his labour was given under duress, it could not, abolitionists were confident, energise an economy and foster its development. Nor was it properly respected. As a result "indolence" and "dissipation" ruled in the South. According to abolitionist Charles Beecher, "slavery degrades labor, discourages education, science, art; enfeebles commerce, blights agriculture, and continually works society towards barbarism". As northerners re-examined the basis of their labour system and stressed the incentives available to wage workers (as to other northerners), in increasing numbers they found it difficult to ignore the antislavery implications.[28]

This was not the only way in which the features that legitimated the northern wage-labour system simultaneously deepened opposition to southern slavery. Even if he did not rise in society, the free worker had the priceless benefits afforded by home and family. From the second quarter of the nineteenth century, in the more economically advanced regions of the North, a gap was opening between work and home. In an

[26] *The Emancipator*, Dec. 31, 1840.
[27] In theory the slave might have been offered the enormous incentive of his freedom. But manumissions (the freeing of slaves by their owners) became increasingly infrequent not least because of the slaveholders' fears of free blacks. They were, moreover, committed to the notion that slavery was beneficial for the slave.
[28] Rev. Charles Beecher, "The God of the Bible Against Slavery", *Antislavery Tracts* no 17 (n.p., n.d.), 3.

agricultural society the two are one: work is done on the farm; the farm is the home. But the spread of new commercial opportunities and the inability of fathers to pass on a viable farm (especially in New England) pushed more and more young men towards work outside the home. A simultaneous decline in the number of apprentices working within the household paved the way for a new ideology of domesticity, especially since men could now less easily combine moral, religious and domestic responsibilities with work outside the home. It now seemed to many northerners as though there were a God-given division of labour between the sexes, with virtue centred upon home and family. The family began to be seen as a refuge from the outside world, in extreme cases a "haven in a heartless world".[29] This was the abolitionist's view of home and family. According to Boston abolitionist Theodore Parker, home could be "likened to a little conservatory or glass house, so formed as to keep in the sun and to keep out the cold, and create a milder atmosphere, where delicate plants may grow into hardihood, till they can bear the bleak exposure of the common field". Home was "the place wherein we must cultivate all the narrow virtues which cannot bear the cold atmosphere of the outside world". But where did all this leave slavery, an institution which denied its victims these benefits? The slave had no legalised marriage; children could be taken from their parents at the master's whim. The home too was at the mercy of the master. To the abolitionist this was little short of diabolical. "The worst abuse of the system of slavery", wrote Harriet Beecher Stowe, author of *Uncle Tom's Cabin*, greatest of all works of antislavery propaganda, "is its outrage upon the family".[30]

For the abolitionist the home was an indispensable source of stability and social harmony. Alongside it he placed the individual conscience. Here was a third benefit, of incalculable value, available to all northerners in their free-labour economy. If the wage worker lacked

[29] Stephanie Coontz, *The Social Origins of Private Life: A History of American Families, 1600–1900* (London, 1988); Nancy Cott, *The Bonds of Womanhood: 'Women's Sphere' in New England, 1780–1835* (New Haven, CT, 1977); Amy Dru Stanley, "Home Life and the Morality of the Market", in Melvyn Stokes and Stephen Conway, eds. *The Market Revolution in America: Social, Political and Religious Expressions, 1800–1860* (Charlottesville, VA, 1996), pp. 74–96.

[30] Theodore Parker, *Sins and Safeguards of Society* (Boston, n.d.), pp. 209, 212, *Lessons from the World of Matter and the World of Man* (Boston, 1865), pp. 200–202; Harriet Beecher Stowe, *The Key to Uncle Tom's Cabin* (London, n.d.), p. 257.

the productive, and especially landed, property that Thomas Jefferson, for example, had extolled as the best foundation for individual virtue, he could instead consult and obey his conscience. How much reliance could he place upon it? According to Theodore Parker, "it is the function of conscience to discover to men the moral law of God". The conscience offered the closest approximation possible to the word of God. Abolitionists were convinced that the conscience mandated opposition to slavery; only by silencing its voice within could the slaveholder continue with his merciless exploitation of his fellow man. Moreover the very essence of slavery was its denial to the slave of the right to consult and obey his conscience. Slavery was thus a violation of this, perhaps the most fundamental of all human rights.[31]

Two further points should be made here. First, the blessings of northern society that mandated antislavery were available to all, or almost all, northerners. It was not only the wage worker who had the opportunity to prosper, to consult the voice of conscience within, or to experience the joys of the family circle. But the wage worker assuredly did possess them, and their common possession helped erase the distinction between wage work and other forms of economic activity. The wage worker was thus assimilated into the mainstream of northern society.

Second, if there were indeed a correlation between the growth of wage labour and the growth of antislavery sentiment, the implications for the United States in 1848 were profoundly alarming. Just ahead, in the 1850s, lay the fastest growth in the numbers of wage labourers yet seen in any decade.[32] So just as economic growth south of the Mason–Dixon line had allowed, and continued to allow, slavery to tighten its grip upon the South, so the same growth process in the North was accelerating northern development, deepening the contrast with the southern economy, and above all, generating values that made slavery seem increasingly unacceptable. In other words the very process of economic expansion, upon which Americans understandably were congratulating themselves in 1848, had within it the seeds of conflict, of crisis, and of catastrophe.

---

[31] Theodore Parker, *The Slave Power* (reprint: New York, 1969), p. 292.
[32] Stanley Lebergott estimates that by 1860, forty per cent of Americans were employed as wage workers, the vast majority, of course, in the North. See Lebergott, "The Pattern of Employment Since 1800", in Seymour Harris, ed. *American Economic History* (New York, 1961), pp. 281–310, esp. pp. 290–291.

VII

Just as Americans took pride in the progress of their economy, they were also able to congratulate themselves on their country's physical expansion. In 1803 Thomas Jefferson had doubled the size of the nation when he had purchased Louisiana, a huge territory comprising all or part of what are now fourteen states of the Union. Other territorial acquisitions followed until, by the start of 1848, there were twenty-nine states, with a thirtieth, Wisconsin, entering the Union later that year.

What of slavery in these territories? In 1820 a crisis had arisen over precisely this question, as applied specifically to the territory of Missouri. Missouri had slaves within it and applied to join the Union as a slaveholding state. Many northerners were shocked; the application compelled them to question their comforting assumption that slavery was in steady retreat. Some northerners accordingly moved to ban slavery from Missouri. A fierce conflict between North and South was now sparked, though the only violence was verbal and consisted of fears voiced and threats issued about a civil war. The crisis was resolved by means of a compromise. To appease Missourians and southerners generally, Missouri was admitted into the Union as a slave state. At the same time, and purely as a counterweight, the new state of Maine was created, thus preserving the balance of free and slave states (then twelve each). Even more important, a line was drawn across the remainder of the Louisiana Purchase territory at 36° 30′. Below the line, slavery was to be allowed; above it (except in the state of Missouri itself), it was prohibited.[33]

The importance of the Missouri Compromise cannot be overestimated. It confirmed the principle that Congress could exclude or permit slavery in the nation's territories, a principle that would not be effectively challenged for a third of a century. It also highlighted the importance of the political equilibrium between North and South. The Constitution, almost all commentators and statesmen believed, gave no authorisation to Congress to abolish slavery in the states where it existed. But what if the Constitution itself were amended? A three-fourths majority of the states would be able to do just that. Southerners were increasingly

---

[33] On the Missouri crisis, see especially Glover Moore, *The Missouri Controversy, 1819–1821* (Lexington, KY, 1966) and Robert Pierce Forbes, *The Missouri Compromise and Its Aftermath: Slavery and the Meaning of America* (Chapel Hill, NC, 2007).

The Missouri Compromise

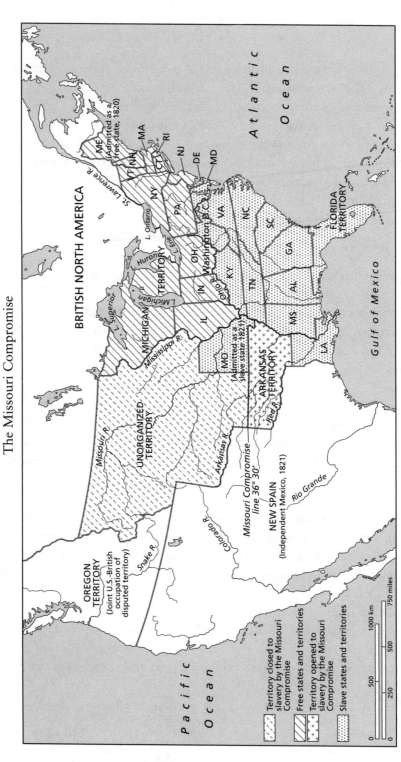

conscious of this possibility with each passing decade, and with the growth of antislavery sentiment in the North.

In the 1820s and the 1830s the question of slavery in the territories went into abeyance. New states were admitted into the Union in pairs, one slave and one free. But in the 1840s the issue resurfaced in the most dramatic way. Once again slave resistance or the potential for it was at the heart of the controversy. This time Texas provided the flashpoint. Texas had originally been part of Mexico, and slavery had been abolished there. But Americans from the South continued to emigrate there, taking their slaves. In 1836 Texas secured her independence from Mexico and sought admission into the Union. For a variety of reasons the request was declined. But in the early 1840s it became apparent to some southerners that, under the influence of Britain, now militantly hostile to slavery, Texas might actually free all the slaves within her boundaries. The leading campaigner for the annexation of Texas was John C. Calhoun of South Carolina. Partly out of fears for slavery, Calhoun had in the 1830s led his state's attempt to nullify federal tariff laws, claiming that the Constitution allowed each and every state in effect to prevent, within its own boundaries, the operation of any federal law of which it disapproved. Clearly this would have given the South a form of insurance against any future actions taken at Washington against slavery. But President Andrew Jackson had faced South Carolina down, and Calhoun had had to abandon nullification. Now he sounded the alarm about the dangers to slavery not only in Texas but also throughout the South. According to Calhoun, Texas was "an exposed frontier", which could not in its present form be defended against "the aggressions of the abolitionists". He did not of course acknowledge or understand that abolition itself was feasible only because the slaves did not wish to remain slaves. Instead he urged the annexation of Texas partly on the familiar grounds that slavery was clearly in the interests of the black population.[34]

The presidential election of 1844 had turned on the question of the immediate annexation of Texas, and the victory of James K. Polk

[34] Calhoun to William R. King, Dec. 13, 1844, in Franklin Jameson, ed. "The Correspondence of John C. Calhoun", 2 vols *Annual Report of the American Historical Association for 1899* (Washington DC, 1900), II, p. 632. On Texas, see especially William W. Freehling, *The Road to Disunion: Secessionists at Bay* (New York, 1990) and Joel H. Silbey, *Storm Over Texas: The Annexation Controversy and the Road to Civil War* (New York, 2005).

confirmed that annexation would follow. Texas accordingly took its place in the Union in 1845. But in response Mexico broke off diplomatic relations with the United States. There were now boundary disputes to be resolved between the two nations. President Polk ordered General Zachary Taylor to take his troops into the disputed area and subsequently to the Rio Grande. The President also attempted to purchase a large amount of territory from Mexico, but the Mexican government refused. In April 1846, Mexican troops crossed the Rio Grande onto disputed territory and a skirmish took place. Polk was now able to claim that Mexico had invaded U.S. territory and accordingly obtained a declaration of war from Congress in May 1846. The war would be concluded only in 1848.[35]

Polk himself was an enthusiastic exponent of the doctrine of "Manifest Destiny", which held it to be "manifest" that the United States' "destiny" was to occupy the whole of the North American continent. In the 1840s Americans had their eye upon Oregon (and even, in some cases, the whole of Canada), as well as large chunks of Mexico (and even, in some cases, the whole of Latin America). The problem with this expansionist programme was that it reopened the question of slavery in the territories.

Many northerners had objected strongly to the annexation of Texas. Even more objected, on moral grounds, to the war that was being waged with Mexico. A still larger number were bitterly opposed to the prospect of acquiring land from Mexico and then planting slavery upon it. Accordingly in June 1846, David Wilmot, a congressman from Pennsylvania, moved a resolution in the House of Representatives, which was forever linked with his name. The Wilmot Proviso stipulated that slavery should never be allowed in any territory that might be acquired from the Mexican war. The Proviso failed to become law, but it sounded an alarm and announced that the question of slavery in the territories was about to rise to the very top of the political agenda. The issue of "free soil", the exclusion of slavery from new territories still to be settled, was highly explosive. No contemporary issue was more controversial; none possessed so much potential to destroy the Union.[36]

---

[35] Robert W. Johannsen, *To the Halls of the Montezumas: The Mexican War in the American Imagination* (New York, 1986).

[36] For contrasting views on the sectional crisis, see Michael F. Holt, *The Fate of Their Country: Politicians, Slavery Extension, and the Coming of the Civil War* (New York, 2004) and

VIII

As of 1848 the successes upon which Americans could congratulate themselves were many and real. The economic growth, either of recent years or of the entire period since independence, was spectacular, the political achievements, involving the maintenance of a republican government over a nation that was large in 1776 and was now more than twice that size, equally so. Militarily the nation had not only maintained itself but was in the process of defeating a neighbouring country and could anticipate another huge accession of territory as a result. Surely there was much here to be proud of.

But although few Americans realised it, the sectional controversy, with slavery at its heart, threatened to negate all these achievements. Economic growth was confirming the attachment of the South to its forced labour system even as it created an ever-growing antislavery constituency in the North. The system of representative government, of which Americans were equally proud, could not itself quell the controversy over slavery. Indeed the attempt to spread that system across the entire continent might be the nation's "manifest destiny", but would it not merely aggravate that controversy as North and South competed for control of the newly acquired territory? Underlying and animating the clash over slavery was both the resistance of the slaves themselves in the South and the process by which the wage labourer was being integrated into society in the North. Neither the resistance nor the process could be checked by either economic growth or territorial expansion. Meanwhile the military triumphs that were being reported in the war with Mexico were in reality still less a cause for congratulation. They would reopen the question of slavery in the territories and, within little more than a dozen years, Americans would employ their ever-growing military expertise against one another – and with deadly effect.

Elizabeth R. Varon, *Disunion! The Coming of the American Civil War, 1789–1859* (Chapel Hill, NC, 2008). See also Bruce Levine, *Half Slave and Half Free: The Roots of Civil War* (New York, 2005).

2

———

CRISIS AT MID-CENTURY, 1848–1851

I

Eighteen forty eight was a presidential election year. Despite the controversy over slavery, recently reignited by the Wilmot Proviso, the two major political parties, Democrats and Whigs, were not, or at least did not wish to be, primarily concerned with the issue in any of its forms. At the start of 1848 each party was able to recruit and win elections in all sections of the Union, with neither of them officially committed either for or against slavery. Each maintained a kind of neutrality on the issue. But this neutrality was highly precarious.

The Democrats had come into formal existence in the 1820s as the party which placed Andrew Jackson in the White House. Nevertheless they could legitimately trace their origins back to the 1790s when Thomas Jefferson, whom they almost universally revered as their patron saint, had battled the Federalists. Jefferson's party had been known as Republican, but its creed was very similar to that with which Democrats were identified from the 1820s and 1830s. Equally there were clear continuities (as well as discontinuities) between the policies adopted and the attitudes taken by their opponents, the Federalists, in the 1790s and the Whigs in the 1830s, 1840s and 1850s. In short the first party system (as scholars term it) of the 1790s was, in some important respects, a rehearsal for the second, which came into existence with the creation of the Whig party in 1833–1834 and which would last into the mid-1850s. Historians have debated the political functions of the second party system and many have noted the degree to which national party organisations served to mediate sectional tensions and keep the country together.[1]

What did the Democrats believe? The party took its cue from Jefferson, some of whose core principles were expressed in his *Notes on Virginia*.[2] Jefferson extolled the yeoman farmer who owned his own land, arguing that such a farmer was independent, free and, accordingly, virtuous. Jefferson had also insisted that an inactive government, and especially an inactive federal government, was essential to the maintenance of liberty. Jefferson, and later the Democrats under Andrew Jackson and his successors, strove to keep government out of the economy. They championed both the principle of "state's rights", the advocacy of which would curtail the role of the federal government, and the strategy of laissez-faire, adherence to which would curtail the role of all governments. Democrats believed with Jefferson that men in office, in government, would be all too likely to use the powers of government either to enhance their own wealth and privileges or to favour certain interest groups in the community, at the expense of the people as a whole.

It is imperative to understand (as some historians have failed to do) that, from a modern perspective, the Democratic commitment to laissez-faire is highly paradoxical. In the modern world, laissez-faire, the rolling back of government intervention in the economy, is widely favoured by industrial, commercial and financial interests on the grounds that it is best to allow the capitalist market, the free-enterprise system, the freedom to regulate itself. The laws of supply and demand should be allowed free play. Laissez-faire is thus quite compatible with, is indeed often defended in the name of, an economy in which large blocks of industrial or financial capital are present.

In the era of Thomas Jefferson and Andrew Jackson, however, the United States was different. As late as 1837, when Jackson left office, agriculture employed more than eighty per cent of the nation's

---

[1] On Democratic and Whig ideology see John Ashworth, *"Agrarians" and "Aristocrats": Party Political Ideology in the United States, 1837–1846* (London, 1983); Thomas Brown, *Politics and Statesmanship: Essays on the American Whig Party* (New York, 1985); Frederick Kohl, *The Politics of Individualism: Parties and the American Character in the Jacksonian Era* (New York, 1989); Daniel Walker Howe, *The Political Culture of the American Whigs* (Chicago, 1979); Rush Welter, *The Mind of America, 1820–1860* (New York, 1975).
[2] Thomas Jefferson, *Notes on the State of Virginia* (new ed., New York, 1964).

workforce and accounted for almost seventy per cent of commodity output. This was a nation of small farmers. They inhabited, moreover, a world in which there was a chronic shortage of capital. Lacking capital, many of these small farmers favoured a "safety-first" approach, by which they would limit their involvement in the market and meet as many of their own wants as possible. They would then exchange what has been described as a "marketable surplus" of their own goods for the essential items they could not themselves produce. Involvement in the market was risky, since dependence on market vicissitudes could result in the ultimate calamity: loss of land and farm.[3]

Where then was the capital needed for economic growth to come from, if not from these risk-averse farmers? The answer some Americans gave was: from government. Government would charter banks and construct, perhaps with help from private individuals and companies, internal improvements (roads, canals and later railroads). The federal government would also levy a tariff on imported manufactured goods in order to raise their price and thereby allow American manufacturing to take root and flourish. These were the policies generally favoured by the Whigs. But the key point is that they were opposed by Democrats on the grounds that they were unjust. If banks were encouraged by special privileges such as limited liability, reducing the danger that the stockholders and directors would lose all their property, who would bear this risk or take the loss? If tariffs raised the price of imported manufactured goods, who would pay for this subsidy to the nation's manufacturers? According to Democrats it would be the rest of the community, and especially the farmers. Democrats therefore tended to oppose (though by no means invariably or with entire uniformity) such measures. In advocating laissez-faire and the withdrawal of government from these activities, they were, they believed, maintaining the agrarian republic so beloved of Thomas Jefferson and Andrew Jackson. In the ideological universe of the Jacksonian era, therefore, laissez-faire was a doctrine espoused by those who were hostile to capitalist development on the grounds that it was inegalitarian, unjust and destructive of the

[3] Douglass C. North, *Growth and Welfare in the American Past* (Englewood Cliffs, NJ, 1966), pp. 19–22; Christopher Clark, *The Roots of Rural Capitalism: Western Massachusetts, 1780–1860* (Ithaca, NY, 1990); Gavin Wright, *The Political Economy of the Cotton South: Households, Markets, and Wealth in the Nineteenth Century* (New York, 1978), pp. 62–63.

agrarian society. Meanwhile, their political rivals, the Whigs, looked to government intervention as a spur to the development and diversification of the American economy. This was one of the primary sources of party conflict during the era of the second party system. Only by freeing himself from the assumptions of the present can the historian grasp this fact.

In the same way Democrats insisted that individual liberty should not be compromised by a government that imposed a particular moral code upon the citizen. They demanded laissez-faire not merely in the economic arena but in the moral sphere too. The individual must be left free to make his own moral choices. As we shall see, the 1840s and 1850s would witness the emergence of a powerful temperance or Prohibition movement. Orthodox Democrats might well endorse the goals of the movement, the elimination of alcohol, but, if government coercion were involved, they would reject the means. An interventionist government once again was a threat to both freedom and equality.

At the same time there was a still more basic difference between the two major parties in the realm of what might be termed political theory.[4] Although the Whigs had more confidence in those who wielded the powers of government (and were prepared to trust them to legislate in matters pertaining either to the economy or to individual morality), the Democrats on the whole placed more faith in the people (though as we shall see, "the people" had to be white as well as male). It is important to recognise not only that capitalism was really in its infancy in the United States (with the paradoxical effects on the parties' attitude towards government we have already noted) but also that democracy (once again for adult white males) was still not, at the time of Andrew Jackson's election, a consensual issue in the nation. The Democrats were wont to enthuse about the nation's political system, precisely because it gave an unprecedented degree of power to the people. Thus in the words of one Democrat, American democracy had "done more, in fifty years, to elevate the moral and political condition of man, than has been achieved by any other civil institutions since the Christian era". Here was "perhaps the greatest achievement of modern times".[5]

---

[4] There has been a tendency among historians to overlook this fact, a residue perhaps of the once widespread assumption that "consensus" over democracy and capitalism characterise the American past.

[5] Samuel McRoberts, *To the Members of the General Assembly of Illinois* (n.p., n.d.), p. 7.

It would be an error to dismiss these utterances (which were made with great regularity) as a cynical attempt to court popularity. The overwhelming majority of Whigs did not speak in this way. Instead they feared that such attitudes would breed a dangerous overconfidence in American democracy, a disregard for the lessons and the accumulated wisdom of the past. Moreover they viewed the standard Democratic eulogy of the people as blatant demagoguery, a dangerous and subversive appeal to popular passion that would threaten stable government and the rule of law. We should remember that in the second quarter of the nineteenth century there were few if any examples of democratic governments anywhere in the world that had not collapsed into either anarchy or tyranny. Some Whigs, especially the more conservative among them, openly referred to this possibility and consequently shrank from emulating Democratic populism.

The Democratic party, when it came into existence in the 1820s, was not clearly identified with the values with which it would subsequently be associated. But the pressure of events had clarified the party's outlook. In the early 1830s President Jackson had confronted the state of South Carolina over nullification, the attempt on that state's part to prevent the operation of a federal law within its boundaries. Jackson had made it clear that, although he championed the rights of the states, and was indeed suspicious of federal power, he would not tolerate nullification, which would have virtually destroyed federal power entirely. Moreover Jackson had, prior to the presidential election of 1832, vetoed the bill for the recharter of the Bank of the United States, by far the largest financial institution in the entire nation. He had then removed the federal government's deposits from the Bank. Why did he take these actions? Once again the reasons have often been misunderstood by historians but it is clear that the key factor was his dislike of banks on the grounds that they were engines of inequality, benefiting some groups at the expense of the remainder of the community. Banks, like tariffs, threatened to undermine republican America by creating an "aristocracy", a group of wealthy individuals who might not enjoy the titles of a European aristocracy but who nevertheless were similarly privileged.[6]

---

[6] John Ashworth, *Slavery, Capitalism and Politics in the Antebellum Republic* vol 1, *Commerce and Compromise, 1820–1850* (Cambridge, 1995), pp. 369–414.

In 1837 the nation experienced a financial Panic, followed by an economic recession from which recovery did not come until the mid-1840s. These years of economic gloom marked the high tide of Democratic radicalism. With the national bank destroyed, the Democrats in almost every state of the Union now turned against the state banks. In some cases they aimed to reform the banks, perhaps by requiring them to hold a larger amount of reserves in specie (gold and silver), perhaps by preventing them from issuing small banknotes. (At this time every bank was able to issue paper money.) In other cases the Democrats sought to destroy the banks entirely. Their success varied from one state to another, depending on the strength of the Whig opposition and also on the extent to which they could dominate the minority, as it usually was, within their own party who did not share these anti-bank sentiments. Moreover the bank war within the states varied also in the pace at which it was waged. In most cases its most intense phase occurred when economic despondency was deepest, but this was not invariably so.[7]

The history of the Whig party was different. It had come into existence in 1833–1834 essentially in opposition to Andrew Jackson's veto of the Bank of the United States and his removal of the government's deposits from the bank. Many Whigs were, from the start, committed to Henry Clay's American System, which called for a national bank, a protective tariff and a carefully planned, federally constructed network of internal improvements (roads, canals and later railroads). But not all. As yet party members could agree on little more than the need to criticise and condemn "King" Andrew Jackson for the expansion in presidential power over which he had presided. But once again the pressure of events clarified a party's outlook. By the early 1840s the Whig party was committed to attempting to re-create a national bank, and to raising the level of tariff duties in the United States, as always in the belief that this would promote manufacturing within the country and lessen its dependence on imported European goods.[8]

Who supported the Democrats and who the Whigs? Not surprisingly those who were successful within the market economy, or who

[7] James R. Sharp, *The Jacksonians versus the Banks: Politics in the States after the Panic of 1837* (New York, 1970).
[8] Michael F. Holt, *The Rise and Fall of the American Whig Party: Jacksonian Politics and the Onset of the Civil War* (New York, 1999).

were persuaded that they had the capacity for such success, tended to vote Whig. This might mean white-collar or skilled workers, or perhaps farmers and slaveholders who lived in areas more integrated into the market economy. By contrast the typical Democratic voter was more likely to be an unskilled worker or a farmer living farther away from the main arteries of commerce. Immigrants, and especially Irish Catholic immigrants, also gave the Democrats disproportionate support, for reasons that had to do with both economics and ethnicity. But these generalisations are subject to many qualifications and each party recruited from all points on the social as well as the geographical compass.[9]

In 1840 the Whigs had won their first presidential election. At this point they pressed ahead with their legislative programme. But the death of President William Henry Harrison within a short time of taking office had placed Vice-President John Tyler in the White House. Tyler had not shared Harrison's views, or those of the vast majority of his fellow Whigs. Had he remained Vice President, this would scarcely have mattered. As it was, a breach opened up between the President and the remainder of the party, and the country was treated to the spectacle of a president being formally expelled from the party of which in a formal sense he appeared to be the head. President Tyler then, with help from Democrats like John C. Calhoun of South Carolina, set about annexing Texas to the Union. The election of 1844 had been, in part, a referendum on the annexation of Texas, and the victory of Democratic candidate James K. Polk was a confirmation that Texas would be accepted, indeed welcomed, into the Union.

Polk's presidency was, at least by reference to the aims which he had set himself, extremely successful. Not only was Texas annexed but the protective tariff (on imported manufactured goods) was lowered, in accordance with classic Democratic theory. The idea of a national bank was buried as Polk instead reintroduced the Independent Treasury system, first passed under Jackson's successor in the White House, Martin Van Buren. The Independent Treasury allowed the government to keep

[9] See, for example, Donald B. Cole, *Jacksonian Democracy in New Hampshire, 1800–1851* (Cambridge, MA, 1970); Sharp, *Jacksonians versus Banks*; J. Mills Thornton III, *Politics and Power in a Slave Society: Alabama, 1800–1860* (Baton Rouge, LA, 1978); Harry L. Watson, *Jacksonian Politics and Community Conflict: The Emergence of the Second Party System in Cumberland County, North Carolina* (Baton Rouge, LA, 1981).

its funds entirely separate from the nation's banking system and thus accorded well with Democratic hostility to banking. Polk's other goal was, as we have already noted, to acquire more territory and to this effect he stirred up conflict and war with Mexico.

In 1848 then, the nation's politics had reached a crossroads. Economic recovery had, in all but a small minority of states, blunted Democratic radicalism. The bank failures of the late 1830s and early 1840s were now a thing of the past. Meanwhile the tariff had also ceased to be so divisive an issue. The reduction in rates produced by the Democrats' Walker tariff of 1846 had been denounced by the Whigs as spelling doom for the nation's manufacturers but for a variety of reasons these predictions proved inaccurate. There was now far less to divide the parties than earlier in the decade. Moreover Whig suspicions about Democratic populism, Whig fears of demagoguery and of political radicalism had largely (though not entirely) abated. They too were casualties of the new prosperity. So a new consensus was emerging on the issues which had traditionally separated Democrat and Whig. At the same time, however, conflict between the sections was deepening and this would subject the party system to a series of severe, ultimately fatal, stresses.

II

What of the major parties and slavery? Within each of them there was a spectrum of opinion. But this is not to say that the two spectrums were identical. In the South after 1837, or perhaps 1841, there were far fewer overtly proslavery Whigs than Democrats; in the North there were more overtly antislavery Whigs than Democrats.

Whig attitudes are easier to understand. The two most prominent Whigs, until their deaths in 1852, were Henry Clay of Kentucky, himself a slaveholder, and Daniel Webster of Massachusetts. Each could be termed antislavery, though in a highly qualified and, a critic might say, ineffectual way. Each disliked the institution of slavery, partly on moral grounds (slavery was unjust to the slave) but also on grounds of political economy (slavery retarded the South). But each recognised that a huge amount of property was tied up in the institution. Moreover each acknowledged that there was no easy way of dispensing with it, given the racial prejudice that existed throughout the nation. Finally, each feared that anything other than the mildest antislavery would jeopardise the future of the Union. The two luminaries concluded, therefore, that the task of the prudent statesman was to balance the injustice of slavery against the inexpediency and indeed the impossibility, in anything but the very long term, of eliminating it. In practice this meant moderation, a strict refusal to indulge in either proslavery polemics or antislavery diatribes.[10]

Both men were, however, as early as 1848, coming under pressure even within their own sections. There were some southern Whigs who were more antislavery than Clay (such as his kinsman Cassius Clay, also of Kentucky) but they were an almost negligible force in all but one or two states. More important was the larger contingent of southern Whigs who were critical of Clay for the opposite reason: he was too hostile to slavery. Georgia was the strongest Whig state in the Deep South and by the late 1840s Whig leaders there like Alexander H. Stephens and Robert Toombs were distancing themselves from any public criticism of slavery. Other Whigs in the Deep South occasionally insisted that slavery was a "positive good", though usually they hedged their claim with reservations about climatic or other conditions. What was the dominant Whig view in the South as a whole? Given that the Upper South was, in electoral terms, the southern Whig heartland, it had probably been, in the 1840s, the extremely moderate view of Henry Clay.

In the North the situation was reversed. Very few northern Whigs believed that Daniel Webster by the late 1840s was too militantly antislavery. Instead he was widely condemned for the opposite reason: betraying the antislavery cause. In the eyes of the abolitionists he was one of those who undermined their entire crusade by refusing to acknowledge the primacy of the moral argument. They thus denounced him for the very quality on which he based his claim to statesmanlike pre-eminence: the ability to balance principle and expediency. Moreover many northern Whigs were also highly critical. William Seward of New York, for example, although not an abolitionist in the Garrison mould, believed that the Whig party should strive to "improve" American society and that removing slavery should be an essential part of that improvement. In some northern states those who thought like Seward

---

[10] Ashworth, *Slavery Capitalism and Politics*, I, pp. 350–355.

were as prominent and powerful within the Whig party as those who took their cue from Daniel Webster.[11]

Whig policies, it should be noted, had an appeal to both North and South, regardless of the presence or the absence of slavery. The commercially minded agriculturalists, whether northern farmers or southern slaveholding planters, had reason to welcome the banks and the internal improvement projects championed by the Whig party. Likewise with the tariff which had an obvious appeal not merely to northern manufacturers but also to those who wished to see the South diversify into manufacturing itself as well as southern growers of hemp and sugar, which also received protection from the tariff. Moreover Whigs north and south could embrace the party's political conservatism in equal measure. The fear of Democratic populism and Democratic radicalism was present within the party both north and south of the Mason–Dixon line.

The problem for the Whig party nationally, however, was that with the passage of time, and under the impact of the sectional controversies emerging in the late 1840s, in the North the more liberal, antislavery wing of northern Whiggery was growing – at the expense of the Webster wing. Meanwhile in the South the recovery of cotton prices in the mid- and late 1840s meant that the Whig dream of a more diversified southern agriculture was slowly fading. In short, time was not on the side of Whig unity. Even as early as 1848 it was clear that the sectional controversy would place great, perhaps ultimately intolerable, strains upon that unity. Even in that year it was apparent even to a casual observer that while northern Whigs were overwhelmingly in favour of the Wilmot Proviso, southern Whigs, though not as vehemently opposed to it as southern Democrats, took a radically different view. The same casual observer might well have doubted whether this situation could persist.

III

The relationship of the Democratic party to slavery in these years was more complex and cannot be understood without reference to the party's origins in the Jeffersonian era. The case of Thomas Jefferson himself

---

[11] Glyndon G. Van Deusen, *William Henry Seward* (New York, 1967), p. 119.

is highly instructive. In his *Notes on Virginia*, the Sage of Monticello had written: "Those who labor in the earth are the chosen people of God". What did he mean? It is easier to say what he did not mean. He did not mean that those who labour in the earth are the chosen people of God. We know this because of all groups in Virginia those who spent the greatest proportion of their collective time labouring in the earth were – the slaves, owned in large numbers by many southerners, including one Thomas Jefferson of Virginia. So Jefferson did not mean the slaves. If he had, this would have been a demand for the abolition of slavery: one could scarcely enslave "the chosen people of God". But no one who read Jefferson believed he meant the slaves. And when Andrew Jackson and other Democrats offered similar encomia on agriculture and the landed interest, they were not referring to slaves either. In the same way, when Democrats (and Jeffersonians before them) pronounced eulogies on the people it was white, not African-American, people, they were alluding to.[12]

In Jefferson's rhetoric there was no explicit disclaimer to the effect that certain racial groups were now being excluded from consideration. Thus the Declaration of Independence, written by Jefferson, seemed to proclaim the freedom and equality of "all men" although in any normal sense of the term it clearly did not. Once again this practice would continue into the Jacksonian era and beyond. When heaping praise upon agriculture, upon the people and upon American democracy, the Democrat simply ignored the existence of slavery throughout the American South.

Moreover when Jefferson spoke of the agricultural interest, he did not mean merely farmers. He also included slaveholding planters. To the modern reader it might seem surprising that among the "chosen people of God" were not the slaves but instead the masters who owned and exploited them, Jefferson himself of course being one. Once again there was no explicit reference made but this is the only possible construction of Jefferson's remarks. And once again this practice would continue into the Jacksonian era. In "Jeffersonian Democracy" and in "Jacksonian Democracy", the slave had disappeared from view, and meanwhile the slaveholding planter had been assimilated to the farmer as a worthy and virtuous member of the community.

[12] Jefferson, *Notes on Virginia*, p. 157.

Thus the Democratic tradition, though highly attuned to inequalities in the commercial, financial or industrial sectors, was largely oblivious to the inequalities within agriculture. Yeoman farmers and slaveholding planters (and farmers) were to be celebrated in equal measure. Until the advent of the territorial question in the mid-1840s, the ownership of slaves was not widely believed to pose a major threat to the equality upon which American democracy depended. In these years Democrats were highly sensitive to inequalities produced by banks, tariffs or other legally conferred special privileges, but the great majority of them were equally insensitive to the blatant inequality between slaveholders and non-slaveholding whites, to say nothing of the still more blatant inequality between slaveholders and slaves. Almost all Democratic pronouncements about liberty, equality, democracy and the people must be seen in this light.[13]

Even this, however, does not dispose of all the complexities in the relationship between Democratic ideology, as enunciated by those in the mainstream of the party, and slavery. One must ask how it was that members of the slaveholding elite of the South, men like Jefferson, John Taylor of Caroline and later Andrew Jackson and James K. Polk, were able to embrace democracy (for adult white males) in the way they did. Jefferson himself lived through the French Revolution, from which most elites around the world, including the northern elite for which Federalists like John Adams and Alexander Hamilton had been spokesmen, recoiled in horror. But Jefferson and the party he led in the 1790s hailed it as marking a great advance for liberty and equality. How was this possible?

Once again slavery is at the heart of the issue. Jefferson and those who followed him were able to enthuse about equality, democracy and liberty because equality, democracy and liberty were to be for whites only. They were not to apply at all to the most exploited group in the community: the slaves. To put it somewhat differently, northern

---

[13] For different views of the relationship between the Democratic party and slavery see Jonathan H. Earle, *Jacksonian Antislavery and the Politics of Free Soil, 1824–1854* (Chapel Hill, NC, 2004); Daniel Feller, "A Brother in Arms: Benjamin Tappan and the Antislavery Democracy", *Journal of American History* 88 (June 2001), 48–74; Sean Wilentz, "Slavery, Antislavery, and Jacksonian Democracy", in Melvyn Stokes and Stephen Conway, (eds), *The Market Revolution in America: Social, Political, and Religious Expressions, 1800–1880* (Charlottesville, VA, 1996), pp. 202–223; Wilentz, *The Rise of American Democracy: Jefferson to Lincoln* (New York, 2005).

Federalists and Jeffersonian Republicans were alike adamantly opposed to conferring political rights on the most exploited (or even simply the poorest) members of their respective communities. But the result was a bitter conflict over the question of democracy for white men, since the poorest and most exploited groups in Virginia for example were, of course, black men and women. To this extent, therefore, the slaves substituted in republican thought for the poorer whites of the North.[14] In effect slavery produced a different alignment of classes in the South. It allowed Jefferson to embrace highly egalitarian ideals – but only because those ideals excluded slaves. It allowed him to reach out for the support of the poorer white citizens of Virginia (and other states) – but only because the dominant class in the South, the class of which he was himself a prominent member, exploited black slaves rather than white farmers.[15]

The result was a creed which not only had been embraced in good part because of slavery but which, as a result, continued to afford protection to the slaveholding interest. The relationship between Democratic thought and slavery is thus a complex and subtle one. One or two disclaimers are in order. It is important to note that the principles which Democrats espoused did not themselves depend for their appeal upon slavery. The twin ideals of state's rights and limited government, the insistence on popular control over government, the attachment to the agrarian interest, the resentment of financial inequalities, the resistance to laws that diminished individual choice on what were essentially moral issues – all these were deeply rooted in the European past. Indeed many Democratic ideas bear a remarkable similarity to those advanced by groups like the Levellers during the English Revolution, an era in which chattel slavery did not even exist. Similarly, many northerners, who had no contact with slavery, rallied to the principles of Jefferson, Jackson and Polk. Nor was it the case that all slaveholders everywhere, or even in the southern part of the United States inevitably embraced them. Slavery and the principles with which the Democrats were identified could, and did, exist independently of one another.

---

[14] This is not to say, of course, that the role of slaves in the South was in other ways like that of the poor in the North; on the contrary it is imperative to recognise that the difference between the labour systems in the two sections was of enormous significance.

[15] Many scholars find it unpalatable to believe that that American democracy was promoted by American slavery.

Nevertheless these doctrines gave special protection to slavery in the South, and this was no random effect. They comprised a creed that was at once democratic (for adult white males) and functionally proslavery. It is important to note that they were not explicitly proslavery: Jefferson, Taylor, Jackson and those in the party's mainstream did not engage in the proslavery theorising to which John C. Calhoun of South Carolina and some other southern leaders were now so strongly committed. We shall look at their explicit views on slavery later. But each of their key doctrines afforded shelter to slavery and to slaveholders. Thus limited government and state's rights, if strictly adhered to, removed the threat to slavery from Washington and as a consequence from any potentially hostile northern majority that might be formed. The insistence upon individual autonomy in the moral sphere allowed Democrats to demand that individual white males be allowed to decide whether or not they should own black slaves without any legal coercion from government. The Democratic doctrine that all should be left undisturbed by government in the enjoyment of the fruits of their labour was invaluable to slaveholders, since, as we have seen, it ignored the existence of the slave and simultaneously removed from view the inequalities generated by slaveholding.

The result was that the Jeffersonian tradition operated not directly or explicitly to promote slavery but rather to disable antislavery. Slavery was an *unrecognised* or *invisible* underpinning, an unacknowledged condition of Jeffersonian and Democratic thought. In consequence, the northerner who had no interest in slavery but who accepted this creed was likely to end by defending southerners' rights to hold their slaves, unmolested by the federal government and unchallenged by abolitionism. Such at any rate was the situation until the advent of the territorial question in the 1840s.

There were several consequences, each of them enormously important. First was the affinity between the Democratic party, or perhaps we should say the Jeffersonian tradition since it had been apparent since Jefferson's era, and the South. To see this clearly it is necessary to look not at the late 1840s or at any single decade but instead at the entire period from 1790 to 1861. In the 1790s opposition to the Federalists began and was always strongest in the South. In the presidential election of 1796, John Adams, the Federalist candidate, ran strongly in the North. In the South, however (and also in the West), the results were reversed. Here Adams obtained a mere two electoral votes, while Jefferson amassed fifty. This pattern was present also in 1800, though not so starkly revealed. In the 1820s it reappeared. In 1828 Adams's son swept New England, while his opponent, Andrew Jackson, carried every state south and west of Maryland. Thus Jacksonian like Jeffersonian Democracy derived its initial impetus from the South. And as we shall see, thirty years later, in the final decade of the antebellum republic, the identification of the Democratic party with the South would be still more apparent, as the presidential elections of 1856 and 1860 would demonstrate. In the intervening years and especially for the decade or so after the Panic of 1837, the political parties enjoyed good support in every section of the Union. With each passing decade the issues might well change and change dramatically. Slavery, the crucial issue in 1856 and 1860, had no real salience in 1796 and was of limited significance in 1828. However, if we treat the years from the 1790s to the Civil War as a single unit, and characterise the antebellum republic as a single regime, then a clear pattern is apparent. Although the political fortunes of the major parties might vary from one year to another, nonetheless in that regime the Democratic party was dominant. And the South was dominant within the Democratic party. And the slaveholders were dominant within the South.

In the 1850s major changes would take place within the Democratic party. But it would retain many of the principles with which it had traditionally been associated. As we shall see, these proved highly advantageous to the slaveholders. If we do not recognise the link between slavery and the Democratic party, we shall have to conclude that this was a mere coincidence. But if instead we recognise that Jeffersonianism, without its leaders ever being aware of it,[16] always bore the imprint of the class interest of the planters, it comes as no surprise that it should be of benefit to that class when a crisis developed. As we shall also see, the price would be that the hitherto concealed class interest became increasingly visible so that by the 1850s the Democracy was seen by all and sundry as the party of the southern slaveholder, the party, in the then-current parlance, of the Slave Power.

---

[16] It is important to note that men and women are not fully conscious of all the forces which operate upon them. To say that Jeffersonianism was functionally proslavery is not, therefore, to say that either Jefferson or those who followed his lead were necessarily aware of the fact.

Even at that time, and to a far greater extent in earlier decades, northern Democrats had been the main supporters of the South. Throughout the North Federalists and Whigs were much more likely to display hostility to the South and her peculiar institution. In the 1830s and early 1840s southerners had pressed for a "gag" law, which would prevent congressional discussion of antislavery petitions. In these years the question of slavery in the District of Columbia was also discussed by the nation's lawmakers and voted on as were issues like the colonisation of free blacks, the recognition of Haiti, the imprisonment of northern black sailors in South Carolina, the capture of fugitive slaves, and the repeal of the three-fifths compromise in the Federal Constitution.[17] In each case the pro-southern position won more votes from northern Democrats than from northern Whigs. This pattern had been present in the 1820s when Jefferson's party had faced the Federalists and would be still more apparent in the 1850s when the Democrats were opposed by the Republicans.[18]

In the South meanwhile, the Democrats were more militant defenders of slavery than the Whigs, at least from the late 1830s onwards.[19] It was not that the Whigs were necessarily willing to allow northerners to attack the institution; it was rather that they were more willing to accept that the great majority of northerners were trustworthy and that slavery was accordingly safe within the Union. Southern Democrats as a result typically denounced southern Whigs for being disloyal to the South and her peculiar institution.

Thus the Democratic party was, in a profound sense, oriented towards the South, however many votes it might amass in the North. But the party was not monolithic, and especially not in its attitude towards slavery. Instead there were three positions taken, two of them very much confined to minorities within the party. The first was an

[17] The recognition of Haiti raised important issues about race and the dangers posed, at least symbolically, to slavery in the South. The three-fifths clause, which counted each slave, for purposes of representation, as three-fifths of a person, raised equally important issues about the protection that should be extended to slavery and slaveholders.

[18] See Thomas B. Alexander, *Sectional Stress and Party Strength: A Study of Roll-Call Voting in the United States House of Representatives, 1836–1860* (Nashville, TN, 1967), p. 73 and *passim*.

[19] In the late 1830s John C. Calhoun, who had been acting with the Whigs, but without sharing their basic outlook, returned to the Democrats. Of all groups in Congress he and his small band were slavery's most fervent defenders.

explicit proslavery which would trumpet forth the virtues of slavery at any and every opportunity. This was the approach of John C. Calhoun who had been Jackson's running mate in 1828, but who had broken with the administration over nullification and then rejoined the party in 1837. Calhoun commanded great respect and even admiration within the South but it is important to note that his views were never Democratic orthodoxy during his lifetime. Indeed Calhoun himself was never entirely sure whether the Democratic party was even trustworthy. From the early 1830s he strove to make the Union safe for slavery and the South. Sometimes he concluded that the party was, or could be made, safe, especially if John C. Calhoun were to be placed at the head of it. This was his strategy when he had sought, rather unrealistically it should be said, the Democratic nomination for the presidential election of 1844. At other times he concluded that the party was irremediably corrupt and that southerners should unite in defence of slavery regardless of party lines. This was his strategy when a little later in that same presidential campaign he concluded, much more realistically, that the Democrats did not after all want him as their standard bearer. As a result of this disappointment Calhoun had then urged the immediate annexation of Texas to the Union on explicitly proslavery grounds. Not surprisingly these oscillations aroused the deepest suspicion in other Democrats, who accused him of a "rule or ruin" approach. But this overt proslavery was very much a minority position within the Democratic party nationally and even, in the 1840s, within the ranks of southern Democrats.[20]

At the other extreme within the party, there was another small minority of antislavery Democrats. Needless to say, they were confined to the North or the Border South. They tended to come from the more radical wing of the Democratic party. Thus in New York, for example, they were from the radical "Barnburner" element, the group most enthusiastic about Democratic economic policy, rather than the conservative "Hunker" contingent, which displayed many Whiggish attitudes. This was no coincidence. With a deeper commitment to equality than their more conservative colleagues, these Democrats were opposed both to bankers and to slaveholders, in each case because those groups threatened the equality upon which democracy depended. Typical of

[20] Thornton, *Politics and Power in a Slave Society*, p. 132.

antislavery Democrats was David Wilmot of Pennsylvania, author of the famous Proviso.[21]

Wilmot's antislavery was real but it differed sharply from that of William Lloyd Garrison, for example. Wilmot acknowledged that he had little interest in pronouncing upon the morality of slavery and even less interest in benefiting its black victims. Instead he objected to the political and economic damage slaveholders wrought upon the white population. Wilmot and his fellow radical Democrats accepted that slavery within the states was a subject over which they had no control. But they objected strenuously to the attempt to spread it into the western territories, including, of course, the territory that might now be obtained as a result of the war with Mexico. Wilmot believed that, like bankers and manufacturers, the slaveholders were attempting to seize control of the federal government and use it for their benefit, and to the detriment of the remainder of the community. How common was this view within the Democratic party? It was widespread in New York, for example, and Missouri. But its proponents were in a decided minority in the North as a whole, to say nothing of the entire nation.[22]

This brings us to the third and, by a wide margin, predominant view. It was the view we have already examined, well represented by, among others, Andrew Jackson himself, "Old Hickory", and by James K. Polk, "Young Hickory". These Tennesseans, along with many other Democrats from all regions of the country, believed that, in the words of Jackson's favourite newspaper editor, Francis P. Blair, as far as slavery was concerned, "there is no debatable ground left upon the subject". Since the Constitution had made specific and explicit provision for slavery, there was now nothing left to discuss. All men of good faith could see this. Hence it followed that those who attempted to agitate the slavery question, whether abolitionists or secessionists, Free Soilers or nullifiers, must be traitors. Jackson and his followers denounced each group of extremists with equal vehemence. Accordingly it was said to have been one of Old Hickory's greatest regrets that during the nullification crisis he had lost an opportunity to march into South Carolina in order to hang John C. Calhoun, the man recently elected as his vice-president![23]

[21] Herbert D. A. Donovan, *The Barnburners* (New York, 1925).
[22] Chaplain Morrison, *Democratic Politics and Sectionalism* (Chapel Hill, NC, 1967); *Congressional Globe*, 31st Congress, 1st Session, Appendix, pp. 941–942.
[23] Washington *Globe*, May 1, July 10, 1833.

This was also the attitude adopted by James K. Polk when the question of territorial expansion arose. Polk won the Democratic nomination in 1844 because he combined orthodox Democratic views on traditional party issues like banking and the tariff with a willingness to endorse the immediate annexation of Texas, together with the "reoccupation" of much of the Oregon territory. Unlike Martin Van Buren, who had been the favourite to win the nomination, Polk had no qualms about seeing another large slave state immediately added to the Union. But unlike Calhoun Polk did not call for the annexation of Texas on the grounds that slavery must be protected. Instead Texas, like Oregon, must join the Union because it was America's "Manifest Destiny" to spread across the continent and acquire territory on the Pacific.[24]

The entire episode illustrated in microcosm the complex relationship between slavery and the Democratic party. Polk did not explicitly or consciously act in defence of slavery. The mainstream Democrats did not in any way privilege slavery over free labour or single slavery out for special treatment within the federal government. But once again the effect was to promote the slaveholding interest. The defence of agrarian values, the refusal to take the welfare of the slave into account, indeed the failure even to notice the slave in this context, the total indifference to the moral issues involved in slaveholding, the assimilation of the planter to the farmer – all these features of Democratic ideology converged as they had many times in the past, and would again in the future, to promote the slaveholding interest.

The problem for the South, however, and for the Democratic party, was that the war with Mexico could only aggravate the slavery question. Democrats could acquiesce in the existence of slavery in the South. Like Thomas Jefferson himself they could even dismiss northern antislavery as a desperate and hypocritical attempt on the part of anti-Democratic reactionaries to win elections by unscrupulous means. But the spread of slavery into the West and the creation of new slave states was, for some northern Democrats, another matter. In the late 1840s and the 1850s increasing numbers of them refused to accept it.

---

[24] Frederick Merk, *Manifest Destiny and Mission in American History: A Reinterpretation* (New York, 1963); Albert K. Weinberg, *Manifest Destiny, A Study of Nationalist Expansionism in American History* (Baltimore, 1935); Charles G. Sellers Jr., *James K. Polk: Continentalist* (Princeton, NJ, 1966).

Moreover the party was faced with an even greater threat, though one which would not be fully realised until the mid-1850s and beyond. Until the advent of the territorial question Democratic ideology meant that the party had a potent disabling effect on the antislavery cause. But if antislavery grew in strength in the North, as a result of changes within northern society, was there not a danger that this effect would be reversed? If the Democrats remained hostile to the antislavery movement, was there not a possibility that in the North, and thus in the nation as a whole, the antislavery cause might instead have a potent disabling effect on the Democratic party itself? Few glimpsed this danger in 1848. We now know, however, that it was all too real.

IV

As far as the stated objectives of the conflict were concerned, the Mexican War was enormously successful – for the United States. Military and naval victories came one after another over the sixteen months of war, some of them against numerically superior Mexican forces. When Mexico surrendered, the United States received an enormous accession of territory. By the terms of the Treaty of Guadalupe Hidalgo, the Mexican cession, as it was termed, increased the size of the United States by almost a third. It added to the Union an enormous tract of land, which corresponded to what President Polk had originally desired (though the President had subsequently had his sights on even more), and which comprised present-day California, New Mexico, Arizona, Nevada and Utah. Now, however, came the thorny question of slavery in these territories.

There were four possible solutions. One was to enact the Wilmot Proviso, by which slavery would be excluded from the Mexican cession. This policy was admirable in its clarity and popular in the North, especially with the Whigs, as always more likely to be hostile to slavery than northern Democrats. But southerners were able to block it in the Senate, and President Polk was utterly opposed to it. Moreover some southerners agreed with John C. Calhoun that its passage would, and should, mean the break up of the Union. Calhoun himself had a different solution. This was to affirm the right of all Americans to move into any and all territories with their property, slaves included. According to Calhoun the Constitution conferred no power upon Congress or anyone else to prevent southerners from taking their slaves into the western territories. Only states, he insisted, could bar slavery. This approach was every bit as unambiguous as the diametrically opposed one taken by David Wilmot, thus every bit as controversial, and accordingly, as far as national unity was concerned, every bit as ruinous.

This left two possible, compromise solutions. One, the simpler, was to extend the Missouri Compromise line at 36° 30' across to the Pacific. Many southerners and some northerners, such as James Buchanan of Pennsylvania and, for a time, Stephen A. Douglas of Illinois, endorsed this policy. The fourth solution was a new one, an idea first put forward by Daniel Dickinson of New York and later taken up by Lewis Cass of Michigan and subsequently becoming most closely identified with Stephen A. Douglas. This was the notion of popular sovereignty. Popular sovereignty meant authorising not Congress but instead the settlers who migrated into the territory concerned to determine whether they would, or would not, have slavery in their midst. There was a certain ambiguity in the policy, since its proponents did not agree on the point at which the decision should be taken. Should it be taken as soon as the territorial legislature was established? Or should it be taken what might be years later at the moment when the territory became a state? Clearly this was an important distinction, since a ban on slavery in the territorial phase would obviously doom its prospects at the time of statehood. But popular sovereignty had its adherents, not least because it meant different things to different people.

The territorial question was not the only divisive sectional issue in 1848. Another arose over fugitive slaves. Without actually mentioning slavery, the Constitution required a fugitive to "be delivered up on Claim of the Party to whom such Service or Labor may be due". But the first Fugitive Slave Act of 1793 was being, especially in the 1840s, circumvented by north-eastern states, some of which now forbade their officials from arresting free blacks or accepting jurisdiction in fugitive slave cases. Some cases, such as *Prigg v. Pennsylvania* (1842), had achieved national prominence and although the U.S. Supreme Court in effect found for the slaveholder, the outcome was of little practical value to southerners. In the Van Zandt case (1847), a group of Kentuckians seeking to recapture some alleged fugitives were forced to leave Michigan under threat of violence and were even fined for trespass. By the late 1840s pressure accordingly mounted for a new

Fugitive Slave Act. Northerners had at first responded to the question of fugitive slaves on a piecemeal basis or simply to safeguard the rights of their free black population. But by the 1840s resistance to the law was becoming, as it would remain after 1850, part of a planned antislavery strategy. Antislavery polemicists claimed that violations of northern rights were inherent in legislation for the return of fugitive slaves and indeed inherent in slavery itself. On the northern side therefore the fugitive slave question both reflected and created antislavery sentiment. Here was another fruitful source of sectional discord.[25]

With the territorial question acquiring additional urgency, and the fugitive slave issue flaring up anew, the political parties approached the presidential election of 1848. Whilst sectional issues were increasingly prominent, the old party issues, like the tariff and the banking question had, as we have noted, lost much of their salience. Given that the parties could relatively easily maintain national unity on these financial questions, but not on the sectional ones, it was clear that the approaching election would differ from any which Whig and Democrat had previously contested.

V

President Polk declined to stand for re-election. His Secretary of State, James Buchanan, was a frontrunner for the Democratic nomination. On the territorial question Buchanan favoured an extension of the Missouri Compromise line at 36° 30′, the policy the Polk cabinet had endorsed. But Lewis Cass of Michigan was also in the field and Cass instead endorsed popular sovereignty, with its inherent ambiguity carefully left intact. Cass had been an object of hatred to some northerners, especially the radical Democrats who blamed him for Martin Van Buren's failure to win the presidential nomination in 1844. It is an indication of the declining importance of the old Jacksonian issues that Cass, largely on the basis of his position on popular sovereignty, won the nomination.

The Whig nomination confirmed the increasing irrelevance of the old issues. Most northern Whigs had actually condemned the Mexican

---

[25] Don E. Fehrenbacher, *The Slaveholding Republic: An Account of the United States Government's Relations to Slavery* (New York, 2001).

war as immoral, but ironically the military victories secured in Mexico were achieved by Whig Generals Zachary Taylor and Winfield Scott. Of the two, Taylor had much the weaker links to the Whig party; indeed he had never even voted. This proved decisive, though not in the way that might be expected. He won. His lack of political experience meant that he also lacked any political liabilities inherited from the past. This was crucial.

While the Democratic platform (unlike the candidate) did not endorse any specific policy for the territories (though it condemned the Wilmot Proviso), the Whigs went further and did not have a platform at all. In addition to being a General, Taylor was a Louisiana planter who owned more than a hundred slaves. Thus to southerners he appeared eminently safe, another enormous political asset. The Whigs had in any case long believed that Congress, rather than the executive, should be the focus of government in Washington so it was possible for them to argue that Taylor's inexperience did not matter unduly.

Taylor and Cass were not the only candidates in the field. As both parties manoeuvred to avoid any explicit commitments for or against slavery, dissidents in each section took, or attempted to take, more decisive action. At the Democratic convention in Baltimore in May 1848, the Alabama delegation, inspired by William Lowndes Yancey, attempted to make the Democratic platform more explicit. The "Alabama Platform" as it was known declared that neither Congress nor a territorial legislature had the power to exclude slavery from a territory. This, of course, was the Calhoun position. It was overwhelmingly rejected. Yancey then walked out of the convention, but he was able to take virtually no one with him. A Democratic split was thus averted; Democratic ambiguity had triumphed over the proslavery forces.

The antislavery forces in the North, however, were another matter. Some northern Democrats were by now deeply disillusioned with their party. They were stung by the fact that Polk's expansionist plans had been fully implemented, as far as territory to the south was concerned. But the President had compromised with Great Britain over Oregon. Moreover the New York radical Democrats, the Barnburners, bitterly resented the more conservative wing of their own party, the Hunkers, and each faction sent a delegation to the Democratic convention, with each claiming to be the true representatives of the state. When the Convention sought to divide New York's votes between the two factions, the Barnburners walked out and then in their own convention nominated Martin Van Buren for the presidency on a platform that called for "Free Soil", the exclusion of slavery from the territories.

This was now a signal not only for other like-minded northern Democrats but also two other groups to rally in support. First came a phalanx of antislavery or "Conscience" Whigs. Just as southern Whigs were pleased with the nomination of a slaveholder, so some (though not all) northern antislavery Whigs were disgusted. Men like Charles Francis Adams (son of the former president), Joshua Giddings of Ohio and George Julian of Indiana were of this persuasion. They had long been locked in an intra-party battle with the "Cotton Whigs", who had traditionally looked with favour upon, and had had lucrative economic ties with, southern planters. Charles Sumner of Massachusetts expressed their contempt for the Whig nominee in memorable language when he attributed Taylor's success to "an unhallowed union, conspiracy rather let it be called, between the politicians of the Southwest and the politicians of the Northeast, between the cotton-planters and fleshmongers of Louisiana and Mississippi, and the cotton-spinners and traffickers of New England; between the Lords of the Lash and the Lords of the Loom".[26]

Although these Whigs had no liking for Martin Van Buren, they were willing to swallow their prejudices in order to further the antislavery cause. So with the third group that made up the Free Soil party of 1848. Although some out-and-out abolitionists like William Lloyd Garrison continued to shun politics entirely, on the grounds that political involvement would inevitably mean compromise and a dilution of the antislavery cause, others had never endorsed this view. They had formed the Liberty party, which had contested the presidency in 1840 and 1844 though with derisory results. In 1848, however, many party members concluded that the possibility of an outright victory under Van Buren would allow them to consent to a dilution, though certainly not a total abandonment, of their antislavery principles. The Free Soil party then drew up a platform that played down the moral evils of slavery and instead stressed the need to keep the territories free for the benefit of white labour. This was antislavery, of a moderate kind in comparison with the stance of a William Lloyd Garrison, but of a radical kind in comparison with the position of Henry Clay or Daniel Webster.

[26] *The Works of Charles Sumner* 15 vols (Boston, 1870–1893), II, p. 81.

The presidential election of 1848 pits Zachary Taylor (Whig) against Lewis Cass (Democrat) as the two main candidates. Here Taylor, recently nominated at the Whig national convention in Philadelphia, is represented by a cannon ball (note the portrait of Taylor on it) about to knock Cass into a large hat.

KNOCK'D INTO A COCK'D HAT.

The election campaign confirmed the difficulty each of the major parties was now experiencing with the slavery question. In order to blunt the appeal of the Free Soilers, northern Whigs claimed that Taylor would leave the key issues to Congress. Thus, it was claimed, if Congress passed the Wilmot Proviso, Taylor, despite being a slaveholder himself, would not veto it. In the South meanwhile one of Taylor's strongest supporters was Alexander H. Stephens, who was on record as saying that the passage of the Proviso would constitute grounds for secession. In short the Whigs made contradictory claims about Taylor and the Proviso. The General himself did nothing to remove the uncertainty. The Democrats experienced similar problems. In the North they claimed that popular sovereignty would create free states galore; in the South the potential for new slave states and the party's rejection of the Wilmot Proviso were stressed. The old financial issues of the Jacksonian era received little attention.

Taylor was the victor. He and Cass each won fifteen of the thirty states, but since Taylor's states had more electoral voters he was duly elected. Van Buren ran well in some states, especially New York (though without capturing it), and attracted in total just fewer than 300,000 votes. This was a huge increase on the Liberty vote polled four years earlier. Even though the Free Soilers espoused a much milder form of antislavery this outcome, together with the nine congressmen the party elected, was an indication of the extent to which sectional issues had climbed up the political agenda. Beyond that, however, it was far from clear what the victory meant, either to the parties or to the sections.[27]

VI

With controversy simmering over the fugitive slave issue and sometimes boiling over when the territorial question was being considered, there was a clear need for action. This need became still more urgent when gold was discovered in California. The actual discovery came in early 1848 but the following months and especially the following year saw a large influx of Americans (and other nationalities) into the area. The gold rush and the "forty-niners" immediately created an urgent

[27] Joel H. Silbey. *Party Over Section: The Rough and Ready Presidential Election of 1848* (Lawrence, KS, 2009).

problem in that California was literally lawless, virtually without any effective administration.

Many Americans in all regions of the country were eager to see it formally organised first as a territory then as a state, the standard process by which new states entered the Union. But northerners and southerners once again clashed over the desirability of allowing slavery to expand. Northerners, rehearsing all their arguments about the blighting effect of the institution, made much of the fact that it did not exist in California, Mexico having abolished slavery throughout her provinces. Many southerners, on the other hand, insisted that slavery could nevertheless be viable in the area, demanded that whatever its viability their constitutional right to take their property into the territories should be fully respected, and claimed that the debt peonage that did exist in California was in any case akin to slavery.[28] California thus became yet another source of sectional conflict, and a pressing one at that.[29]

Under the impact of the rising tide of antislavery sentiment and especially the threat he discerned in the Wilmot Proviso, John C. Calhoun now finally decided that the future of the South depended upon the break-up of the party system. He wrote a lengthy document entitled the *Southern Address* in which he urged southerners to unite in defence of their interests. Southern rights in the territories must be maintained, not, he pointed out, because southerners necessarily insisted on extending slavery, but because a denial of these rights would immediately reduce southerners "from being equals, into a subordinate and dependent condition".[30] Unfortunately for Calhoun, however, only 48 southerners in Congress (out of 121) signed the Address, even after it had been softened to appease more moderate opinion. The principal reason was that southern Whigs remained aloof, partly because they

---

[28] Debt peonage was a form of bonded labour in which a person was forced to pay off a loan with direct labour often over an extended period of time.

[29] Standard surveys on the politics of these years include Holman Hamilton, *Prologue to Conflict: The Crisis and Compromise of 1850* (New York, 1964) and Allan Nevins, *Ordeal of the Union: Fruits of Manifest Destiny* (New York, 1947). See also Mark J. Stegmaier, *Texas, New Mexico and the Compromise of 1850* (Kent, OH, 1996), though in my opinion this work exaggerates the role of the Texas boundary disputes.

[30] See "Address of the Southern Delegates in Congress to their Constituents", in Richard K. Crallé, ed. *The Works of John C. Calhoun* 6 vols (Columbia, SC, 1851-1855), VI, pp. 285-313.

were always more moderate on sectional questions and partly because they were confident that the newly elected President Taylor would protect their interests.

This confidence soon evaporated, however. It gradually became apparent that Taylor was prepared to admit California and even New Mexico into the Union as free states, bypassing the territorial stage entirely, and in accordance with the stated wishes of the citizens there. Many southerners objected strenuously but at least they preferred this to the Wilmot Proviso, which placed slavery in the territories under a federal ban. Then it emerged that Taylor would not even veto the Wilmot Proviso, should it be passed. The ultimate shock came when the president warned that he would oppose any attempt at secession with military force.

By now emotions were running high. The House of Representatives, where there was no clear majority for either party, could scarcely organise itself, even the election of a Speaker proving enormously controversial and difficult. There were fistfights in Congress, duels were threatened, secession and civil war openly discussed. Though antislavery northerners were convinced (as they would be for another decade) that threats of secession were mere bluffs, they were mistaken; most southerners who spoke that way were in deadly earnest. Most Americans believed that their nation was in crisis.

Some nevertheless were confident that there was still scope for compromise. Henry Clay of Kentucky took the lead and announced a package of proposals, some meant to benefit the North, some the South and some seeking to mediate between the two. Congress debated them for months but in the end they were rejected, probably because they were voted on as a single package, in the form of an "omnibus" bill. Leadership of the pro-compromise forces now passed to Stephen A. Douglas of Illinois. He was aided by the unexpected death of President Taylor in July 1850, which placed in the White House Millard Fillmore, a conservative Whig and a friend of the Compromise measures. As a result, and after some of the most memorable debates in the whole of U.S. history, the Compromise measures were passed, one by one.

What had the Compromise of 1850 achieved? There were five provisions. First, California was to enter the Union as a free state, bypassing the territorial stage (as Taylor and others had proposed). Second, the slave trade, though not slavery itself, was prohibited in the District of Columbia. These measures pleased most northerners, infuriated many southerners. Third, a new and far more stringent fugitive slave act was passed. This time, most southerners were pleased, many northerners infuriated. Fourth, a border dispute between New Mexico and Texas was settled by means of a $10 million payment to Texas. Finally, the status of slavery in New Mexico and Utah was to be determined on the basis of popular sovereignty, though with the ambiguities in the doctrine (concerning the timing of the decision) to be settled, it was hoped, at some future date by judicial ruling. The last two measures were more neutral in effect than the first three, though southerners were able to claim that the Wilmot Proviso had been decisively, and they hoped, finally rejected.

On 7 September 1850 when the last of the measures went through, there were extraordinary scenes in the nation's capital. A hundred-gun salute was fired, skyrockets were launched and bands began to play "The Star-Spangled Banner" and "Yankee Doodle". Bonfires, processions and serenades followed, and word went round that it was the duty of every patriot to get drunk. Most Americans rejoiced; their country had been saved.

VII

It is not only with hindsight that one may doubt whether the individuals primarily responsible for the settlement of 1850 were really the saviours of their country. But first they must be identified. The credit for the compromise belonged primarily to the moderates on the sectional issues, northern Democrats and southern Whigs. There was nothing new in this alignment. As we have observed, northern Democrats had long been more sympathetic to the South, more immune to antislavery than northern Whigs. As we have also seen, southern Whigs were, in general, far less likely to advance explicitly proslavery arguments and far more likely to respect northern economic progress and trust northern opinion, including future northern opinion, than southern Democrats. There were of course exceptions. Thus Daniel Webster delivered one of the most celebrated speeches of his entire career in March 1850 in favour of the Compromise, expressing sentiments for which he was excoriated by the antislavery crusaders of Massachusetts. Equally important was President Fillmore's unwavering support for the Compromise which contrasted sharply with the attitude of his predecessor in the White House, Zachary Taylor. Both Fillmore and Webster argued, in classic conservative fashion, that it was incumbent upon the

The Compromise of 1850

Pacific
Ocean

BRITISH CANADA

Atlantic
Ocean

St. Lawrence R.

ME

VT NH MA
RI
NY CT NJ
PA DE
MD
Mason-Dixon line
OH VA
L. Ontario
L. Erie NC
SC
L. Huron
L. Superior MI
L. Michigan
WI IN KY TN GA
IL
IA AL
Mississippi R. MO
Missouri R. AR Ohio R. FL
MINNESOTA Red R. MI
TERRITORY Arkansas R. LA
Missouri Compromise line 36°30'
UNORGANIZED
TERRITORY TX
Snake R. Colorado R.
OREGON UTAH Rio Grande
COUNTRY TERRITORY
NEW MEXICO
TERRITORY Gulf of Mexico
CA MEXICO

Unorganized territory

Free states and territories

Slave territories

Open to slavery by
popular sovereignty
(Compromise of 1850)

0   500   1000 km

0   250   500   750 miles

wise statesman to set aside his personal sentiments either for or against slavery in the interest of the common good and in the name of national unity. Nevertheless it was appropriate that the most prominent of all the pro-Compromise figures were Henry Clay and Stephen A. Douglas, respectively a southern Whig and a northern Democrat.

The alignment of 1850 had pitted the moderates against the extremists. Northern Whigs and southern Democrats tended to oppose the Compromise, though for opposite reasons. Thus William Seward of New York, an antislavery Whig, made a celebrated speech in which he prophesied the doom of slavery and, even more controversially, insisted not only that the Constitution conferred the power on Congress to exclude slavery from the territories but also that a "higher law" than the Constitution, by which he meant of course the law of God, mandated the same policy. These were doctrines which would have pleased even William Lloyd Garrison but to conservatives throughout the country they smacked of anarchy – for who was to determine God's law? – and demagoguery.

For Seward and those who thought like him, the failure to exclude slavery from New Mexico and Utah, together with the new Fugitive Slave Act, meant that the Compromise was fatally flawed. Meanwhile many southerners, and especially southern Democrats, also inveighed against it but for opposite reasons. In March John C. Calhoun had delivered or, to be more accurate, had had delivered his final speech to the United States Senate. The South Carolinian had been too weak to address the Senate himself. By the end of the month he would be dead, but not before he had confirmed his opposition to the Compromise. In June 1850 a convention of militant southerners had met in Nashville, also with the aim of stiffening southern resistance. Many delegates argued strongly that the exclusion of slavery from California would destroy the equilibrium in the Senate between free and slave states, and that the abolition of the slave trade in the nation's capital would furnish a deadly precedent for a series of antislavery measures emanating from the federal government and culminating in abolition and the emancipation of all the slaves in the South. As for the Fugitive Slave Act, these southerners claimed that it would prove impossible to enforce, such was the extent to which northern public opinion had already been "corrupted".

Two problems now confronted the pro-Compromise forces. The immediate one was to "sell" the measures to their own constituents;

the second was to make them stick in the longer term, to ensure that the Compromise of 1850 became a final resolution of the sectional conflict rather than a mere stage in its evolution. The first was difficult but by no means impossible. The second would prove to be of an entirely different magnitude.

VIII

In the immediate aftermath of the passage of the Compromise measures, statesmen who were facing re-election, and even some who were not, were compelled to confront their constituents. In some states of the Union important debates were now conducted which revolved not merely around the Compromise itself but also around the causes of the sectional conflict as a whole. This was particularly so in the South and the debates and struggles that took place offer a valuable glimpse into the state of public opinion there.

In South Carolina, a unique confrontation took place. It pitted not the advocates of the Compromise against its enemies, which was the alignment in some other states, but rather advocates of immediate secession by South Carolina alone against those who found the idea of a dissolution of the Union not unappealing but who insisted that South Carolina should act only in concert with other southern states. The result was a crushing defeat for the separate-state secessionists. It is important to note that South Carolina was the one state in which the second party system (which had pitted Democrat against Whig) had never really taken root, largely because sectional animosities in effect precluded significant support for the national Whig party.[31] The three other states of the South where proslavery sentiment was strongest were Georgia, Alabama and Mississippi. In all three the mainly Democratic opponents of the Compromise, now calling themselves a Southern Rights party, were confronted by a coalition of Whigs and pro-Compromise Democrats, now styling themselves a Union party. And in each state the pro-Compromise Union forces triumphed. In Georgia for example, Howell Cobb easily defeated Charles McDonald,

[31] As the Charleston *Mercury* observed a decade later, South Carolina had for ten years favoured a dissolution of the Union, the difference of opinion in 1851 being over the means rather than the ends – *Charleston Mercury*, 10 March 1860.

the Southern Rights candidate, in the gubernatorial election of 1851. The Union party also won almost all Georgia's seats in Congress and in addition sent Robert Toombs to the United States Senate. The outcome was similar in Mississippi with Jefferson Davis defeated in the gubernatorial election of 1851 by Henry Foote, and in Alabama where the Union candidates were victorious in the legislative elections of the same year.[32]

This seemed like a victory for the sectional moderates, and in a sense it was. The anti-Compromise forces indeed had stopped far short of demanding secession, so their defeat testified to the depth of unionist sentiment in each of the three states (though not in South Carolina). However, a closer look at the situation testifies also to the fragility of unionist sentiment in each of them. The Southern Rights parties in reality lost because their appeal was undercut by the Unionist parties, who themselves laid down stringent conditions for their state's continued commitment to the Union. These conditions were most clearly spelt out in the so-called Georgia Platform. This platform was drawn up by a convention of Georgia unionists that assembled in December 1850 specifically to consider the Compromise. The delegates agreed that whilst the state of Georgia could not "wholly approve" of the Compromise, she would nevertheless "abide by it as a permanent adjustment of the sectional controversy". They then put forward a series of resolutions, of which the following was by far the most important:

> *Resolved,* That the State of Georgia, in the judgment of this Convention, will and ought to resist, even (as a last resort) to the disruption of every tie which binds her to the Union, any future act of Congress abolishing slavery in the District of Columbia, without the consent and petition of the slaveholders thereof; or any act abolishing slavery in places within the slaveholding States, purchased by the United States for the erection of forts, magazines, arsenals, dock-yards, navy-yards, and other like purposes; or any act suppressing the slave trade between slaveholding States; or any refusal to admit as a State any Territory applying, because of the existence of slavery therein; or any act prohibiting the introduction of slaves into the territories of Utah and New Mexico, or any act repealing or materially modifying the laws now in force for the recovery of fugitive slaves.

[32] Michael F. Holt, *The Political Crisis of the 1850s* (New York, 1978), p. 92.

This resolution was a warning to the North. Time would show that the most important condition was the one that related to the introduction of new slave states. Georgia would secede if Congress, under northern control, refused to admit a state into the Union because of the existence of slavery within it.[33]

Thus although Unionism triumphed in these three key states of the Deep South, it was a highly conditional Unionism. Moreover the mid-century struggle over the Compromise marked a first step in the collapse of the second party system. Not for the first time, Whigs in the Deep South were trapped. They were pressured on one side by southern Democrats, who constantly accused them of infidelity to the South and her interests, and on the other by their own northern wing, whose clear antislavery proclivities made co-existence within the same political organisation extremely difficult. In each of these three states the Whig party never recovered. Indeed by the time of the presidential election of 1852 the party's managers had written off the entire Deep South.[34]

It was only with hindsight that this first stage in the disintegration of the second party system, which had pitted Democrat against Whig since the mid-1830s, became apparent. Elsewhere the party system held up much better. In the Upper South, the southern Whig heartland, the Compromise was generally quite popular. Southern Whigs from these states had been among its firmest supporters in Congress and election results together with opinion expressed within the states confirmed that public opinion had not been misrepresented. In Virginia such opposition as there was came overwhelmingly from the Democrats, with both the Old Dominion's Senators opposed, but the major Democratic newspaper in the state (and perhaps in the entire South), the Richmond *Enquirer*, like its neighbour and rival the Richmond *Whig* endorsed it. Although the Compromise did not require ratification by the states, there is no doubt that it would have been formally approved in the Upper South.[35]

So too in the Lower North. Here it was the Democrats who were the stronger pro-Compromise group, reflecting once again the functionally

[33] The Georgia Platform may be conveniently located at http://georgiainfo.galileo.usg.edu/gaplatfo.htm
[34] Holt, *Whig Party*, p. 733.
[35] Nevins, *Fruits of Manifest Destiny*, p. 367.

proslavery orientation of Democratic ideology. In the Upper North, however, where antislavery sentiment was strongest, the Compromise continued to have its enemies. The real sticking point was the Fugitive Slave law which many northerners simply refused to comply with. The most ardent enemies of slavery, viewing not only slavery but also compromise with slavery as sin, categorically refused to come to the aid of the slave catcher. Here was a major problem. Some southerners were arguing that their loyalty to the Union was conditional upon a faithful execution of the law in the North but as early as 1851 it was becoming evident that compliance with it would never be total.

In the Upper North especially antislavery groups, including antislavery Whigs, believed that the Compromise threatened to block all progress on slavery. They were therefore extremely unhappy with it and especially repudiated the idea that it was a final settlement of the sectional conflict. These problems would surface again and again in the future.

Nonetheless, northern opinion as a whole, as far as it can be gauged in an era before opinion polls were taken, rallied to the Compromise. A collective sigh of relief was breathed once it became clear that no southern state planned to leave the Union. In late 1851 Democrats pledged to the Compromise achieved conspicuous victories in both Pennsylvania and New York, along with Massachusetts probably the most important states in the entire North. Undoubtedly the advocates of compromise were helped by the extensive northern commercial and manufacturing interests that depended on trade with the South. [36]

By the end of 1851 therefore, the nation had survived the greatest challenge to its continued existence it had yet faced. The Compromise had been "sold" to the nation and the Union, for the present at any rate, appeared safe. Whether this safety was real, however, and how long it would last, were questions upon which a discerning observer might have found much to ponder.

---

[36] Nevins, *Fruits of Manifest Destiny*, pp. 399–400.

3

IMMIGRANTS, ALCOHOLICS AND THEIR ENEMIES

Ethnocultural Issues, 1851–1854

I

By the early 1850s, at the time the slavery question was causing alternating waves of consternation and complacency, politics in the nation were also heavily influenced by two other issues, which historians often describe as "ethnocultural". For some years temperance reformers had been active in some states of the Union, seeking to reform not merely the alcoholic but also, in part in order to ensure that he did not become an alcoholic in his turn, the occasional tippler. In other words Prohibition of alcohol became the stated goal of these enthusiasts. A little later an even more important movement developed when opposition to the political power of immigrants crystallised into what was universally referred to as the Know Nothing party. Prohibition had a significant impact on politics in some states; the Know Nothing, or, as it was formally known, the American party had, if only for a brief period, a still larger one in most states and at the federal capital too.

II

By 1852 the temperance movement was entering upon its era of greatest success, at least before its famous triumph in the twentieth century. Originating in the early nineteenth century in an attempt to prevent, at local level and by the use of moral suasion only, the intemperate use of alcohol, it changed in the 1830s as reformers began to demand total abstinence, enforced by laws that would be state-wide in their operation.

Their first conspicuous triumph came in 1846 in Maine when a prohibitory law was passed. This was tightened up in 1851 in a law which was dubbed the "Maine Law" throughout the nation. By 1855 no fewer than thirteen states or territories had passed Maine Laws. New England together with the "little" New Englands (the areas in the North West where enclaves of Yankees were to be found) was and remained the heartland of the temperance movement. It is difficult to know for certain but it is likely that the combined membership of the organisations campaigning for Prohibition, groups like the Sons of Temperance and the American Temperance Union, totalled more than a million.[1]

These reformers did not doubt that they were doing God's will and were convinced too that the removal of alcohol would be a means to an end; it would do no less than clear the way, many believed, for a millennialist triumph in the young nation. Temperance was thus closely linked to the Protestant evangelical revivals that periodically swept the United States in the antebellum years.[2] Just as the religious revival invited the sinner to repent, so the temperance reformer invited the drinker to renounce his wicked ways, sign a pledge committing himself to total abstinence and thus enjoy his new found spiritual, and spirituous-liquor free, purity.[3]

Despite this concern with ethereal matters, the temperance advocate was convinced that the renunciation of alcohol would bring, in addition, an array of earthly benefits. Often mistaking causes for consequences, reformers believed that alcohol brought in its wake poverty, crime and destitution. Neal Dow, the leading temperance reformer of the antebellum era, when delivering his inaugural message as Mayor of Portland in 1851, announced that "the traffic in intoxicating drinks

---

[1] The best book on the temperance movement is Ian R. Tyrrell, *Sobering Up: From Temperance to Prohibition in Antebellum America, 1800–1860* (Westport, CT, 1979). See also Alice Felt Tyler, *Freedom's Ferment: Phases of American Social History From the Colonial Period to the Outbreak of the Civil War* (Minneapolis, MN, 1944), pp. 308–350; John A. Krout, *The Origins of Prohibition* (New York, 1925); Joseph R. Gusfield, *Symbolic Crusade: Status Politics and the American Temperance Movement* (Urbana, IL, 1963); Jed Dannenbaum, *Drink and Disorder: Temperance Reform in Cincinnati from the Washingtonian Revival to the WCTU* (Urbana, IL, 1984).

[2] Richard Carwardine, *Evangelicals and Politics in Antebellum America* (New Haven, CT, 1993), pp. 61–102; Whitney R. Cross, *The Burned-Over District: The Social and Intellectual History of Enthusiastic Religion in Western New York, 1800–1850* (New York, 1950), p. 211.

[3] Tyrrell, *Sobering Up*, p. 67; Gusfield, *Symbolic Crusade*, p. 168. Temperance enthusiasts actually claimed that religious enthusiasm could, and should, make up for the loss of intemperate drinking via "enchanting visions". See J. G. Adams and E. H. Chapin, eds. *The Fountain: A Temperance Gift* (Boston, 1847), p. 239.

tends more to the degradation and impoverishment of the people than all other causes of evil combined". "There is", the Mayor affirmed, "no fact better established than this".[4]

Prohibition would thus bring not merely spiritual but also economic regeneration. Its promoters were mindful of the problems encountered by the wage worker and laid heavy emphasis on the benefits he could expect from total abstinence from alcohol. He would work more effectively and so would be less vulnerable to unemployment. No longer frittering away his wages on alcoholic beverages, he would be able to save more. The employer too would benefit, since productivity would assuredly rise. And as far as the community as a whole was concerned, Prohibition would bring with it a reduction in taxation, since the numbers of the destitute in need of assistance would fall dramatically. It was arguments like these which carried the day with large numbers of voters in the early 1850s.

Temperance was also a response to changing patterns of work especially in the North, as larger units of production, more expensive machinery and stricter market discipline became the norm. This placed a large premium on regular and predictable output achieved by sober and disciplined workers during the working day. Accompanying this process was an increasing separation between employer and employee. The booming towns of the North experienced greater residential segregation as employees ceased to live with employers. In a parallel development, leisure time became separated from work to a greater extent than previously. As a result a cultural and spatial gap opened up between employer and worker and the rowdiness of the working class neighbourhoods in which the taverns and grog shops were usually located seemed to the temperance reformer not merely an affront to decency but also an impediment to moral and material progress, in short to everything that he or she held dear. In this sense temperance was, in part, an attempt made by employers and their allies to re-establish their former influence over the lives and pastimes of their workers. It was thus in good part a response to the problems brought by the spread of wage labour.[5]

[4] Neil Dow, *The Reminiscences of Neil Dow* (Portland, ME, 1898), p. 331.
[5] Tyrrell, *Sobering Up*, pp. 275–276; Paul Johnson, *A Shopkeeper's Millennium* (New York, 1978), pp. 55–61.

Itinerant workers aggravated these problems. Those who dug the canals and built the railroads (the Irish were disproportionately represented here) necessarily made up a transient population that was largely immune to traditional appeals for temperance on the basis of moral suasion. Such workers were difficult to integrate into local communities and the demand for a statutory, state-wide ban on alcohol owed much to their presence.

However shocked they might be by current levels of poverty, crime and sin, temperance reformers believed that American society was, or could relatively easily become, fundamentally sound. It offered to the virtuous extraordinary opportunities, both moral and material. The poor need not in the United States (and especially in the North) remain poor; they merely needed to resist the blandishments of the tavern, or the bottle, and avail themselves of the economic opportunities showered upon them. Material and moral progress would thus go hand in hand.

III

It is scarcely surprising that the temperance movement should have been centred upon the North East. The economic processes which had spawned the movement were far more advanced there than elsewhere. And they were least in evidence in the South. As a result, of the thirteen states or territories that enacted prohibitory laws between 1851 and 1855, no fewer than eight were in the East. Only one was a slaveholding state and that one, Delaware, scarcely counted as part of the South.

Temperance advocates did not form a distinct party. Instead they sought pledges of support from existing parties. This, of course, gave each of those parties at least a potential dilemma, since Prohibition was as unpopular with some groups as it was popular with others. The parties responded, however, in different ways.

Most sympathetic were the small (in the early 1850s) antislavery groups that might call themselves "Independent Democrats", "Free Soilers", "Abolitionists" or members of the Liberty party. These groups shared many of the attitudes of the temperance advocates. Both movements believed (in general) in using the power of government to bring about moral reform. Moreover both posed similar questions. Was the drunkard not the "slave" of alcohol? Did alcohol not prevent its victim from following the voice of conscience within, exactly like slavery? Did both evils not wreak havoc upon the family, that most sacred of institutions? "The one group in the state on which the Prohibitionists could count", Neal Dow recalled in his autobiography, "was the anti-slavery element", and historians have confirmed that this pattern existed across much of the North in the early 1850s, when the Prohibition movement was at its peak.[6]

By contrast the Democrats were the party most hostile to the temperance movement, at least in their official, theoretical pronouncements. Although many Democrats favoured temperance themselves, the tradition of Jefferson and Jackson condemned the attempt to impose it by legislative statute. As we have seen, classic Democratic theory led party members to denounce the presumptuousness of a select few attempting to establish a dictatorial control over the remainder of the community. According to one party member, it was simply "not part of the duty of the state to coerce the individual man except so far as his conduct may affect others, not remotely and consequentially, but by violating rights which legislation can recognise and undertake to protect". The contrary approach, he continued, "leaves no room for individual reason and conscience, trusts nothing to self-culture, and substitutes the wisdom of the Senate and Assembly for the plan of moral government ordained by Providence". Temperance laws thus, in theory, violated Democratic notions of liberty and equality as well as the Democratic commitment to laissez-faire and limited government. Accordingly New York Governor Horatio Seymour acquired a reputation as one of the nation's leading "wets" when he vetoed a prohibitory law on the grounds that "we have but one petition to our law-makers – it is to be let alone".[7]

In practice, however, Democrats could not remain immune to the groundswell of opinion that was forming in some areas in support of temperance. Some of them sought a middle position on the issue, expressing a willingness to support "moderate" laws against drunkenness but

---

[6] Dow, *Reminiscences*, p. 289; Krout, *Origins of Prohibition*, pp. 176–177; Tyrrell, *Sobering Up*, p. 264.

[7] John Bigelow, ed. *The Writings and Speeches of Samuel J. Tilden* 2 vols (New York, 1885), I, p. 282; Thomas M. Cook and Thomas W. Knox, eds. *Public Record: Including Speeches, Messages, Proclamations, Official Correspondence, and Other Public Utterances of Horatio Seymour* (New York, 1868), pp. 5, 10–11.

opposing all "ultra" measures. As a result some of the states which embraced Prohibition did so when under Democratic control.

If Democrats found it difficult to maintain their ranks under the pressures imposed by temperance enthusiasts, the Whigs were subjected to still greater stresses. There were many affinities between Whigs and temperance reformers. Both warmly welcomed the economic changes underway in the United States and especially the North East. Both believed that the United States offered boundless opportunities to the poor but industrious worker. Both looked to government to preside over the "improvement", both moral and material, of the people. Both found congenial the notion that an elite should direct the affairs of the community. Finally both groups believed they represented respectability; a middle-class aura surrounded Whig and temperance advocate alike.

For these reasons Whigs were, in general, more receptive to temperance than Democrats. On the other hand there were, as some party members did not hesitate to point out, some powerful reasons for the party to distance itself from the temperance cause. The more conservative, elite Whigs enjoyed their fine wines and saw no reason to give them up; why should the moderate, self-controlled drinker be denied his pleasure? Religious conservatives, meanwhile, questioned the scriptural authority of the temperance movement; did it not rather strain credulity to depict Jesus Christ as a confirmed teetotaller? Moreover some of the advocates of temperance seemed themselves almost intoxicated with the ardour of their cause and some Whigs were as suspicious of the enthusiasm that accompanied the temperance movement as they were of the abolitionist's passionate advocacy of the slave's freedom.

Even this did not exhaust the fears of some in the party. Immigrants were a frequent target of temperance propaganda. The Irish and Germans, in particular, were often singled out for criticism. Although many Whigs had themselves endorsed such sentiments, and the party had frequently flirted with nativism in the past,[8] many party regulars noted the rapid increase in the levels of immigration and wondered if they could afford to alienate such a large constituency. Finally although Whigs and temperance reformers alike wished to establish or

---

[8] Historians often refer to those espousing anti-immigrant sentiment as "nativists" and the sentiment itself as "nativism".

re-establish order in their communities, many Whigs wondered whether the injection of so hugely controversial a subject into politics would not generate additional political bickering and social conflict. As we shall see, these concerns were in good part borne out and the result was to hasten the demise of the temperance movement. It was not surprising therefore that many Whigs were strongly opposed to a formal endorsement of Prohibition. Whenever temperance has been agitated, one Whig warned, "the Whig party has always lost ground".[9]

As a result the Whigs, like the Democrats, were unable to maintain party discipline on the temperance question. Each party was divided and its stance varied from state to state and sometimes from year to year. As we shall see, the effect was to blur the political landscape and increase the political chaos of the early 1850s.

IV

Temperance reformers were not the only group to draw attention to the increasing levels of immigration in these years. The Know Nothing party sprang into existence in direct response to the huge numbers of immigrants now arriving from Europe and for a time enjoyed an extraordinary degree of success. Once again the effect was to create political instability and to undermine the existing political parties.

Between 1845 and 1855 ten times the number of immigrants entered as had arrived in the previous thirty years. In the peak year, 1854, more than 400,000 came. The largest ethnic groups were the Irish and the Germans. Some were attracted by the greater political and religious freedom on offer in the United States, but far more were driven out of their homelands as their agricultural smallholdings became increasingly unviable, partly owing to overpopulation on the land as well as natural disasters like the potato famine in Ireland. These immigrants were drawn by the real prospect of economic betterment in the United States.[10]

---

[9] Robert Morris to Hamilton Fish, 10 February 1852, quoted in William Gienapp, *The Origins of the Republican Party, 1852-1856* (New York, 1987), p. 47.

[10] There is a large literature on immigration. See, for example, Marcus Lee Hansen, *The Atlantic Migration, 1607-1860* (Cambridge, MA, 1940); Kerby A. Miller, *Emigrants and Exiles: Ireland and the Irish Exodus to North America* (New York, 1985); Oscar Handlin, *Boston's Immigrants: A Study in Acculturation* (New York, 1959); Mack Walker, *Germany and the Emigration, 1816-1865* (Cambridge, MA, 1964).

When they reached the United States, they did not spread out evenly throughout the nation. The vast majority went to the North. With the important exceptions of New Orleans and some of the larger cities of the Upper South, the slave states proved unattractive to them. This was partly because many important and powerful southerners made it clear that they did not want immigrants. The fear was that at best they would swell the population of the cities of the South, an unwelcome prospect as we have seen, given the difficulties of controlling slaves in an urban environment. Worse still the immigrant might actually agitate against slavery.

As a result immigrants went disproportionately to the free-labour North, where demand for their services was greatest. Many German and Scandinavian immigrants settled in the rural North; the Irish, however, were concentrated in the nation's largest cities. As a consequence by the 1850s, immigrants outnumbered the native born in a host of Midwestern cities (Chicago, Detroit, Milwaukee) and were close to that mark in many in the East (New York, Brooklyn, Buffalo). It was thus not surprising that they encountered hostility from some of the native born.

This nativist hostility was primarily to their religious faith, their political activities and the links between them. The majority of the newly arrived Irish, and a significant proportion of the Germans, were Roman Catholics. It was the Irish who attracted most hostility. Most of the recent arrivals were poor and unskilled; many of them could not speak English. They seemed to many American nativists to be alien, difficult to assimilate and threatening. Roman Catholicism had alarmed some Americans since the colonial era and native-born Protestants were not slow to point to what they took to be its inadequacies. Catholics, it was complained, substituted priestly authority for true religious conviction. The priest, and the Pope above him, represented a power that was potentially hostile to the Republic. Nativists focussed much attention on the confessional which, by absolving the sinner, it was argued, in effect offered him a license to sin afresh. According to one publicist, it was a "startling fact" that "the awful secrecy of the priest's closet supersedes and extinguishes all *moral obligations*, as well as every duty due from the citizen to the state". The confessional thus "ruins men and women – it ruins society – it ruins all it touches".[11]

[11] *Startling Facts for Native Americans* (New York, 1855), p. 109; *The Know Nothing and American Crusader*, 19 August 1854.

Hence Catholicism did not curb men's passions and appetites. It left them without the wholesome restraints that Protestantism fostered. As a result the foreign-born Roman Catholic, untutored in the exercise of the suffrage, was prey to the unscrupulous demagogue, who would appeal to his passions and encourage his licentiousness. The Catholic vote was thus fodder for the political party. Here nativists had in mind one party more than any other: the Democrats, who, as all observers recognised, received a disproportionate amount of support from Irish Catholics.

These general and, in some cases, long-standing concerns were fuelled in the 1850s by a series of specific events which seemed to dramatise the threat that immigrants now posed to the body politic. In 1846 Pius IX had become Pope and he quickly adopted a highly reactionary stance on almost every political and moral question. Adamantly opposed to all the revolutions of 1848, however moderate they might be, he also spoke out against liberty of conscience and of the press and even res-urrected the notion of papal infallibility. In short he did everything to confirm American suspicions.

Meanwhile in the United States a number of events or controversies combined to rouse the ire of nativists. American Catholic bishops in 1852 formally decreed that Roman Catholic children should be edu-cated exclusively in parochial schools but at the taxpayer's expense. Similarly there were attempts to prevent the reading in schools of the King James Bible, which the Catholic hierarchy viewed with suspicion but which, because of its greater accessibility, many Protestants believed indispensable. Finally there was a storm of protest as bishops sought to gain title to, and control over, the property of the Catholic church. These initiatives inevitably rekindled traditional Protestant fears of the temporal power of the church and at the same time revived traditional Protestant fears of papal power in Rome.

Partly to settle these disputes, Pius sent a fellow reactionary, Archbishop Gaetano Bedini, to the United States, who stayed a discon-certingly and, it seemed, suspiciously long time in the country. Around the same time President Franklin Pierce appointed a Roman Catholic to the position of Postmaster General, an office which itself had many patronage plums to dispense. By now Catholic leaders were even expressing their desire to make the United States a Catholic country. Since many of the American sects had similar expansionist ambitions, it was small wonder that Roman Catholicism and American Protestant evangelicalism frequently collided in these years.

Two additional features of nativist targeting should be noted. First the prioritising of Irish Roman Catholics created a perhaps unexpected problem in that it was not always easy for the nativist to find a principle on which to base his discriminatory practices or to make them consistent. If ethnicity were to be the test, then the Irish Catholic could certainly be condemned but so too could Irish Protestants. The nativist typically had no criticisms of these immigrants at all; indeed he applauded them for their long and distinguished history of opposition to the Catholic church. Moreover the Protestant Irish often came from more affluent backgrounds. On the other hand if religion were to be the key test then some of the old and often wealthy Roman Catholic families of the United States, concentrated in states like Maryland and Louisiana, would be caught by the ban. But the behaviour of these Catholics, like that of the Protestant Irish, did not attract the opposition of the nativist at all. In reality the problem was that the nativist sought to discriminate in good part on the basis of class but found it difficult to enunciate a principle which would allow him to do so.

Most of the criticism of immigrants focussed upon their religion or their ethnic loyalties. But there was another category of immigrant whom Know Nothings roundly condemned. These were the so-called Forty-Eighters, radicals who had entered the United States following the failed revolutions of 1848. By the early 1850s they had attracted attention by demanding fundamental changes in the political and social systems of the host nation such as the abolition of the Senate, the Presidency and even of landed property. As we shall see, nativists were highly conservative in their social and political outlook; it was therefore inevitable that the European radical should take his place alongside the Roman Catholic immigrant as a target of nativist hostility.[12]

Such hostility was not new in the 1850s. In 1843 the American Republican party had been created in New York City from where it spread to some other cities, primarily on the eastern seaboard, usually

---

[12] Bruce Levine, *The Spirit of 1848: German Immigrants, Labor Conflict, and the Coming of the Civil War* (Urbana, IL, 1992).

the focal point of nativist anxieties. In New York City too Thomas Whitney and James Harper established the Order of United Americans (OUA), while in Philadelphia Jacob Broom set up the United Sons of America. In 1850 Charles B. Allen founded the Order of the Star Spangled Banner, an organisation which attempted to maintain a high degree of secrecy. After a couple of years of very slow growth, its membership suddenly surged when the rank and file of the OUA joined in very large numbers. It was in late 1853 that this organisation became the Know Nothings and in 1854 entered politics with, as we shall see, extraordinarily rapid success. It was formally named the American Party but the Know Nothing label stuck, in recognition of the party members' tendency, when asked about the organisation, to reply that they knew nothing.

They did, however, know what they wanted, as far as major policy changes were concerned. Although they opposed the immigration of paupers and criminals, restricting immigrant numbers was not the Know Nothings' primary concern. Instead they wanted to lengthen the naturalisation period, the time between entry into the nation and eligibility for the franchise. They argued for in increase from the current figure of five years to twenty-one. This was the major plank in the Know Nothing platform. Some added a second demand, though this often failed to be adopted as official party policy, to the effect that the foreign born should be ineligible for political offices. "Americans", their slogan went, "should rule America".

There were several goals underlying these policy initiatives. One was to give an opportunity for Protestantism to compete freely with, and thus, nativists were confident, vanquish Roman Catholicism. Hence the importance of public schooling and hence the need for the extra years within which Protestantism would exert its benign influence prior to the exercise of the franchise. When he arrived in the country and while he was accustoming himself to the political freedoms available, the immigrant's prejudices should not be exploited by unprincipled politicians. If he were denied the vote for twenty-one years, unscrupulous politicians would lose the incentive to pander to him. And if he were ineligible for political office, the immigrant would lose the incentive to meddle in the politics of the new country. The Know Nothings were thus attempting not merely to reduce immigrant voting power but also to purify the nation's politics generally.

V

As we have noted, the Democratic party was a frequent object of nativist suspicion. Some Democratic spokesmen retaliated by denouncing the Know Nothings in equally unmeasured terms. The *National Democratic Review*, which purported to speak for Democrats throughout the nation, called the Know Nothing party "a foul and infamous blot upon the fair horizon of America"[13] and other newspapers and prominent statesmen often echoed these sentiments. The Democrats had traditionally offered a warm welcome to immigrants whatever their religious creed and the increase in their numbers gave an additional political motive for doing so. This is not to say, however, that Democrats lacked any principled opposition to the nativist movement; there is little doubt that their beliefs were, in many cases, sincerely held. Nevertheless not all rank-and-file Democrats maintained this tolerant attitude towards immigrants and a handful of leaders even made their peace with the nativists. In many localities former Democrats flocked into the Know Nothing lodges. Nevertheless it was upon the Whigs that the new organisation had its greatest impact. Many Whigs had flirted with nativism since the party's inception, and many of its senior figures had gone on record blaming the immigrant vote for the party's defeat in the presidential election of 1844, for example. But there were deeper forces at work too. On many issues Whigs and nativists, like Whigs and temperance reformers, thought alike.

Both groups believed that American society was inherently fair and just, offering extraordinary opportunities to the worthy citizen. Where Democrats had frequently assumed a conflict between labour and capital, rich and poor, farmer and manufacturer, Whigs and nativists alike believed these groups were utterly interdependent. If the poor labourer faced any insuperable problems, it was because he had to compete with immigrant pauper labour, to the exclusion of which the Know Nothings were, of course, committed. Moreover when the nativist observed what seemed to be an alarming level of crime in some of the nation's larger cities, he attributed it unhesitatingly not to any structural defect in the social system but rather to immigration. "To immigration alone", Thomas Whitney declared, "we are indebted for the

---

[13] *National Democratic Review*, I (1856), p. 16; II (1856), pp. 102–104.

vast excess of crime which so often startles the moral sense of our communities". Even when Whigs had not drawn the same nativist conclusion, their assumptions about American society had been remarkably similar.[14]

So with their assumptions about the American political system. Nativists and Whigs (especially conservative Whigs) were often highly sceptical of the claims made for the American democratic system. Whereas Democrats were wont to believe that the nation had staked out a new and glorious political course, one which made the experience of the past redundant, many nativists believed instead that American liberty was a delicate creation, the product of many centuries of experience in North America and in England. Some of them even denied that the United States had a democratic system at all. "Our system", John Sanderson declared, "is a *Republic*, as contradistinguished from *Democracy*".[15]

These nativists insisted that not everyone, even if adult, white and male, was fit to exercise political rights. The immigrant, and especially the Roman Catholic immigrant, was likely to be least fit. He had had no training in the exercise of self-restraint and thus was easy prey for the demagogue. Still less was he suitable for political office. Some nativists, in contrasting democracies with republics, argued, as Whigs had done in previous decades (and in direct opposition to Andrew Jackson's celebrated pronouncement two decades earlier), that the standards required for political officeholding were, or should be, extremely high.[16] Once again immigrants, and especially Roman Catholic immigrants, simply could not meet those standards.

It was therefore little wonder that the Whig party had frequently flirted with nativism. On the other hand there were reasons for the party to distance itself from the movement. To begin with it could be argued that the injection of ethnic hostilities into politics would threaten the very stability so prized by conservatives. Second some Whigs, like William H. Seward of New York, were sincerely and adamantly opposed to nativism. Third, and of even more immediate concern, was a troubling question: could the Whigs afford to alienate these

---

[14] Thomas R. Whitney, *A Defence of the American Policy* (New York, 1856), p. 183.
[15] John Sanderson, *Republican Landmarks* (Philadelphia, 1856), pp. 236–237.
[16] Jackson had argued that all "men of intelligence" could hold political office.

many thousands of new voters who might easily determine the outcome of many crucial elections?

In the presidential campaign of 1852, the party's leaders decided not and the party openly, though rather clumsily, courted the immigrant vote. Its presidential candidate, Winfield Scott, made a number of appeals to the Irish and German voters in a deliberate attempt to shed the party's nativist image. The strategy was a complete failure in that it attracted few immigrant votes while at the same time intensifying the resentment of nativist groups with the existing parties. It thus paved the way for the launch of the Know Nothing party.

VI

It remains to consider the Know Nothing attitude towards temperance and towards slavery. The first is easily disposed of. Many Know Nothings applauded the temperance movement. Nativists and temperance reformers, as we have observed, shared broadly similar goals and similar underlying assumptions about American society and the American political system. On the other hand there was no reason one could not both dislike immigrants and enjoy an alcoholic drink, and for this reason alone the two movements could never fuse.

As far as sectional questions are concerned, nativists not surprisingly espoused somewhat different attitudes in the different sections of the Union. Moreover, as we shall see, at the time of the Know Nothings' greatest strength these attitudes were different from those that had been held even a few months earlier or that would be displayed later. Nevertheless the core nativists, as they may be termed, were moderates on the sectional issue, distancing themselves equally from southern secessionists and northern abolitionists. They were convinced that the slavery question need not divide the nation. To the extent that it had already, by the early 1850s, succeeded in doing so, Know Nothings blamed foreign influence. Some of them even discerned a plot, orchestrated by the Pope from Rome, to subvert the Republic; others claimed instead that, in truckling to the immigrant vote, politicians had treacherously stirred up sectional animosities. Hence quite apart from its many other desirable effects, the implementation of the nativist programme, it was claimed, would inevitably reduce sectional tensions.

VII

By the middle of 1854 a sea change in American politics was imminent. The political system was now being subjected to unprecedented stresses and strains. The temperance movement was already making it difficult for each of the major parties to maintain its ranks. The Know Nothing movement, fuelled by the ethnic and religious tensions so apparent in the early 1850s, was about to erupt and create political havoc in many of the states of the Union. Meanwhile the Kansas–Nebraska Act, one of the most controversial pieces of legislation in the history of the Republic, was about to send an enormous shock wave throughout the nation. The ground had been prepared for the political upheaval of the mid-1850s, an upheaval that would mark a long step on the nation's road to civil war.

4

PREPARING FOR DISASTER

The Politics of Slavery, 1851–1854

I

At mid-century the United States had been in crisis, its very survival, many observers believed, under threat. After the Compromise measures of 1850 had been agreed and put into operation, there was a huge collective sigh of relief: the crisis, most now believed, had been resolved. They were wrong. The nation was still in crisis. The difference was that this time no one knew. This did not make the crisis any the less severe; on the contrary it made it still more dangerous.

A crisis may be defined as a situation that has reached an extremely difficult or dangerous point. In the aftermath of the Compromise of 1850, despite the relief felt by most Americans, the crisis had not in fact been averted. Those who perceived the problem thought they had a solution; those who rejected the solution believed the problem could be ignored. Both groups were mistaken.

The problem was the organisation of the nation's territory. Since the conclusion of the Mexican War, the United States had been a Pacific power. California in 1850 had been admitted into the Union. Despite southern resentment at the admission of another free state (and at the way in which it had been achieved), California, with her small population and infant economy, would henceforth play only a minor part in the struggle between North and South. But her entry into the Union created an extraordinary anomaly. The nation now consisted of states in the East and what would now be termed the Midwest, together with a state on the Pacific (with more projected there). But this left a huge gap, covering many thousands of square miles, between the two. This was the northern part of the Louisiana Purchase, still unorganised and generally referred to as the Nebraska territory. The crisis derived from the impossibility of organising this territory without creating a catastrophic conflict between North and South.

Some Americans in the 1850s, and many historians since, have denied the existence of the problem. But in denying any need to organise this territory, they have ignored what is surely an essential function of any viable government or regime. What are the fundamental tasks of government? One of them is the raising of revenue. In France before the Revolution the *ancien régime* was unable to govern because it was financially bankrupt; the attempt to find new ways of raising revenue then triggered the Revolution. In England an identical process resulted in the outbreak of civil war and revolution in the 1640s. The United States in the early 1850s had no major financial problems, still less ones which threatened the survival of the regime. But another, still more fundamental, feature of sovereignty is the capacity to administer and govern the territory over which the regime claims control. This was the problem for the United States in the early 1850s. As in France in 1789 and seventeenth-century England, the problem could be resolved, but only by ushering in a Revolution. The nation did manage to preside over the organisation of territory that now manifestly demanded it, but only by triggering a chain of events that would culminate in Civil War. Such was the effect of the Kansas–Nebraska Act of 1854.

The Kansas–Nebraska Act, creating two territories out of the Nebraska lands, decreed that slavery in this entire area could be established or rejected by the people who migrated there. The fate of slavery would thus be determined by "popular sovereignty". This meant the repeal of the Missouri Compromise of 1820–1821 (by which slavery had been banned from this area, since it lay to the north of the line of latitude at 36° 30′). Its principal architect was Stephen A. Douglas, Democratic Senator from Illinois.[1]

Those who initiated or supported the Act did not, of course, anticipate its disastrous consequences. They could see the problem, the need to organise the territory, but entirely misjudged the effects of their "solution".

---

[1] On the Kansas–Nebraska Act, see P. Orman Ray, *The Repeal of the Missouri Compromise* (Cleveland, 1909); William W. Freehling, *The Road to Disunion: Secessionists at Bay, 1776–1854* (New York, 1990); Roy F. Nichols, "The Kansas–Nebraska Act: A Century of Historiography", *Mississippi Valley Historical Review* 43 (1956), 187–212.

Meanwhile those who saw the dangers of the solution, a ruinous intensification of the sectional conflict, denied the problem. No one combined an understanding of the true depths of the problem with an appreciation of the dangers entailed by the solution. Herein lay the crisis.

In a deeper sense, however, even the territorial issue, intractable as it was, was merely a symptom of an even more fundamental problem. This was the antagonism between slavery and free labour. The settlement of 1850 had done nothing to remove the underlying causes of this antagonism. Nothing had happened to reconcile the slaves to their enslavement and this was the most powerful underlying cause of all. Moreover nothing had happened to arrest the social and economic changes in the North which had already made so many northerners critical of slavery. Indeed those changes were accelerating as the economy expanded. Economic growth meant that each side was increasingly committed to its social system, based upon free and, most critically, wage labour in the North, slave labour in the South. And the processes by which each side continued to adjust to the pressures placed upon it by its labouring classes and facilitate their integration would, beneath the surface, further the process of national disintegration.

II

Between what was in effect the (informal) ratification of the Compromise measures of 1850 and early 1854, the major source of overt conflict between North and South was the Fugitive Slave Act. Slaves fleeing from captivity were of course a conspicuous illustration of black resistance to slavery: contented slaves would simply not have run away. The Fugitive Slave Act of 1850 required all northerners to come to the aid of the slaveholder, or his agent, who was pursuing a runaway slave. But in so doing, it collided directly with another imperative to which many northerners felt themselves compelled to respond and which came from a still higher source: the need to follow the voice of conscience, planted in man by the Almighty. Northern abolitionists did not hesitate to announce that they would therefore disobey the law, however integral a part it might be of the Compromise of 1850, and whatever the consequences for relations with the South and for national unity. Meanwhile black leaders like Frederick Douglass urged their fellow African Americans to take up arms in order to resist the law.

The early 1850s thus saw a number of episodes concerning fugitive slaves, which attracted national attention. In Boston in these years, attempts were made to recapture a number of slaves. Slave catchers, backed by President Fillmore, who subsequently threatened to send in federal troops, attempted in 1850 to recover a couple, William and Ellen Craft, who had escaped to the city from Georgia. Abolitionists hid the couple and helped them flee to Britain. The following year a black waiter named Shadrach was seized by slave catchers but then snatched from them and placed on the underground railroad to Canada. In the same year the slaveholders were more successful in recapturing Thomas Sims but it took several hundred armed deputies and soldiers to overcome the opposition of local Bostonians. Then in September 1851 attention switched to the small town of Christiana, Pennsylvania, where a Maryland slaveholder was actually killed in a failed attempt to recover one of his slaves. The President sent out the marines but the blacks who had led the resistance fled to Canada, beyond the reach of federal authority. Finally in Syracuse, New York, a black cooper known as "Jerry" was spectacularly rescued from a jail where he had been held under the Fugitive Slave Act and smuggled across the border to Canada. In all these cases those helping the fugitives, with few exceptions, escaped conviction, to the delight of antislavery northerners, the chagrin of conservative northerners and the rage of virtually all white southerners.

Nevertheless the fugitive slave issue was not in itself fatal to national unity. Although it is very difficult to know how many slaves actually ran away to the North or Canada, a reasonable estimate might be several hundred a year. Many others were retrieved and recaptured. Moreover after 1851, interest in the issue declined somewhat. There were fewer cases attracting the nation's attention. To be sure, some southerners insisted that their continued loyalty to the Union was dependent on the North's willingness to return fugitives, and at the same time some northerners continued to denounce the law in the most unmeasured terms. But it was clear that, though it might deepen the division within the nation over slavery, the fugitive slave issue alone did not have the power to disrupt the Union.

Another symptom, as well as a cause, of the antagonism between North and South in these years was the extraordinary success of Harriet Beecher Stowe's famous novel and work of antislavery propaganda, *Uncle Tom's Cabin*, which appeared in book form in the spring of 1852. Stowe's novel

Here a Whig victory in the 1852 presidential contest is wrongly predicted. General Winfield Scott (Whig), pulls the "Presidential Chair" from under Franklin Pierce (Democrat). Pierce says: "Look out there! what you bout General? do you want to Knock a fellers brain out?" Scott replies: "Sorry to disappoint you Pierce; but *the people* wish *me*, to take *this chair*".

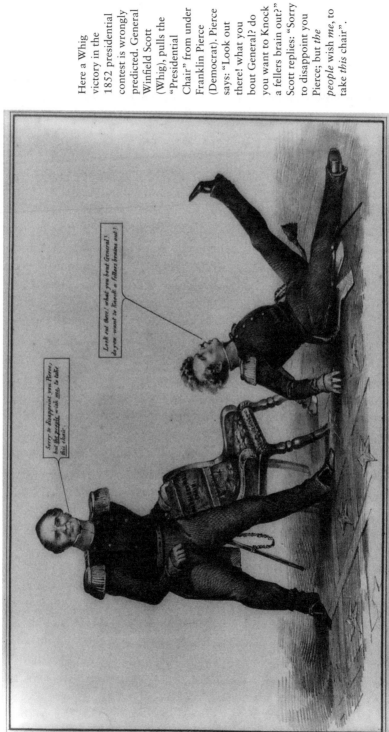

A CONTESTED SEAT.

had been inspired in good part by the Fugitive Slave Act and her depiction of the plight of the runaway slave, as well as the other evils of slavery, touched the hearts of thousands in the North and indeed throughout the book-reading world. Southerners of course denounced the novel, and some of them attempted to write literary rejoinders. But in the United States alone it sold three hundred thousand copies in its first year.

Despite this success, and despite the controversy generated by the Fugitive Slave Act, politics in the United States in the early 1850s betrayed no sign of the upheavals that were to come. In the presidential election of 1852, the Democrats nominated, to the surprise of almost everyone, Franklin Pierce of New Hampshire, who had never been a commanding figure within the party, but whose nomination, it was felt, would cause a minimum of offence throughout its ranks. Pierce and his party made much of their commitment to the Compromise of 1850 as a "final" settlement of the sectional controversy. The Whigs (whose fate as a national party we shall consider in a subsequent chapter) meanwhile also attempted to endorse "finality", as the phrase went, but found party unity more elusive. They nominated Winfield Scott, another military leader. In no sense did the party battle pit North against South, and as a result two other candidates took the field, representing the pro- and antislavery extremes. The election resulted in a huge Democratic triumph, as Pierce captured every state except two (Massachusetts and Vermont) in the North and all but two in the South (Kentucky and Tennessee). In terms of the popular vote Pierce obtained 1.6 million, ten times as many as the two sectional candidates combined. This seemed like a triumph for the forces of compromise and sectional moderation.

The following year, 1853, was, in terms of the sectional controversy, even quieter, indeed the quietest of the 1850s. Nothing happened to disturb the equilibrium apparently established by the settlement of 1850 and apparently confirmed by Pierce's overwhelming victory the previous year. The furore over the Fugitive Slave law had largely died down, the admission of California as a free state was now a fait accompli, and popular sovereignty was working much as had been hoped in New Mexico and Utah. Moreover with popular sovereignty now the established policy for the remaining territories acquired from Mexico, and the Missouri Compromise line at 36° 30′ established as the policy for dealing with the still unorganised lands in the Louisiana Purchase, there were now no territories capable of generating controversy and sectional conflict.

Or so it seemed. Accordingly extremists on both sides of the Mason–Dixon line were worried, precisely because, as far as the slavery question was concerned, there seemed little for the electorate to worry about.

These extremists need not have been so worried. A storm was approaching that would soon shatter the superficial calm of 1853.

III

Stephen A. Douglas had for many years wished to organise the Nebraska territory. His first attempt was made as early as 1844 but after 1850 he redoubled his efforts. Douglas knew what many historians and many of his contemporaries did not: as far as the territories were concerned, the status quo after the Compromise of 1850 was highly unsatisfactory and could not endure. Nebraska needed to be organised. How else, he asked, could the loyalty of the Pacific states be maintained? They must be integrated into the nation. Moreover like many Americans, Douglas's imagination was seized by the prospect of a transcontinental railroad. Though born a Yankee he had long identified himself with the interests of the West and these interests were his prime concern in 1854. If a transcontinental railroad were to become a reality and if the North West were to derive full benefit, the Nebraska territory needed a government. And for this it had to be organised.

His logic was compelling. When his enemies (correctly) pointed to the danger of upsetting the territorial equilibrium established in 1850, he (correctly) retorted by asking whether they supposed that "you could keep that vast country a howling wilderness in all time to come, roamed over by hostile savages, cutting off all safe communication between our Atlantic and Pacific possessions?" "You must", he reiterated, "provide for continuous lines of settlement from the Mississippi Valley to the Pacific ocean". The territory had to be organised. Though he did not put it in these terms, Douglas knew that this was an essential attribute of sovereignty. But if he was right in believing that something needed to be done, his critics were right in their predictions of the calamitous consequences of the action he proposed.[2]

Douglas was a staunch Democrat. As much as any Democrat in the nation, or even in the party's history, he believed in the Democratic

[2] *Congressional Globe*, 33rd Congress, 1st Session, p. 337.

party's fundamental principles. He believed that though their application might change in the light of changing circumstances, these principles were eternally valid. State's rights, limited government, the exclusion from politics of "moral" questions like temperance or slavery, "equal rights" for all adult white males – these were the principles that Democrats had defended since the party's inception, indeed since the time of Jefferson. They were synonymous with American democracy, with the nation itself.

It followed, or seemed to follow, that they were capable of steering the United States through any crisis. And if Douglas had believed this before 1850, there was still more reason to believe it in early 1854. The principle of popular sovereignty, though formulated only in the 1840s, was in its essence entirely consonant with the Democratic insistence upon a limited role for the federal government. In effect popular sovereignty applied the principle of state's rights to a territory. It took powers from the federal government and conferred them upon the settlers in a territory. And it was working quietly but effectively, in accordance with the terms of the Compromise of 1850, in the only places it had been tried: New Mexico and Utah. This only served to increase Douglas's confidence.

When in January 1854, as Chairman of the Senate Committee on the Territories, he made yet another attempt to organise the Nebraska territory, he did so at first in the hope of maintaining the provisions of the Missouri Compromise. Slavery would thus be excluded from this area. But once again it was clear that his bill would go the way of its predecessors, defeated in the Senate because it could not win enough votes from southerners. These southerners could see absolutely no reason to facilitate the creation of yet more free states in the North West whose representatives could then be mobilised against them in Washington.[3] Accordingly, and primarily under pressure from southerners, Douglas introduced several modifications to the bill. In the first place it now became a bill for Kansas and Nebraska. Second, and more important, it now incorporated the principle of popular sovereignty, so that in theory the settlers of either territory could decide to allow slavery within their borders. Finally, and most important of all, it thereby sensationally repealed the Missouri Compromise which had stood for a third of a century and which had forbidden slavery in these territories.

---

[3] We shall consider the southerners' motives much more fully subsequently.

Douglas had not expected this outcome when he introduced the bill in early 1854. Moreover he knew that the repeal of the Missouri Compromise would create a storm of controversy in the North. Here he was not mistaken. He also believed that the storm would quickly disperse. Here he was indeed mistaken. He even believed that, in the longer term, his action, and the principle of popular sovereignty upon which it was based, would ultimately confound the sectional extremists on both sides and thus preserve the Republic in perpetuity. Here he was still more fundamentally, and catastrophically, in error.

The mistakes, however, were deeply rooted in Democratic ideology and in Democratic experience; they were thus not mere individual aberrations. There had been many examples in the past of measures highly controversial when first introduced by the party but eventually winning widespread, often almost universal, acceptance. The destruction of the Bank of the United States was one, the Independent Treasury another, the lowering of the tariff a third. Even more important than these was the policy of territorial expansion over which Democrats had presided and to which their opponents had often initially objected.[4] Taken together, these examples established, or seemed to establish, a pattern. The principles of the Democratic party, once understood by the voters, would triumph. Douglas expected the Kansas–Nebraska Act to accord with this pattern.

The Act in no way established slavery in the territories in question. It merely created the possibility of its establishment. This, however, marked a triumph for the South: no chance had been replaced by a real chance. It was not Douglas's intention to spread slavery into Kansas. (Everyone agreed that for climatic reasons it could never go into Nebraska.) His priority was to organise the territory. He almost certainly would have preferred Kansas to become a free state and it is even more likely that he expected this to be the outcome. Nevertheless it is undeniably the case that his action furthered the interests of slavery.

How had this happened? His enemies in the North accused him of being a pliant tool of the slaveholders, a northern "doughface" who could be manipulated by the Slave Power and made to do its bidding.[5]

---

[4] Democrats here included Jefferson's purchase of Louisiana in 1803 within their party's history.

[5] The Slave Power, it will be recalled, was the term used by slavery's enemies to describe those slaveholding southerners who, it was held, sought to control not merely the South but the nation itself.

His enemies were mistaken here. Nevertheless they were correct in noting that the interests of the slaveholders had indeed been furthered and correct too in refusing to believe that this could have been an accident.

How then had it happened? To understand this process we must recur to Democratic ideology. As previously noted Democratic ideology, from the very inception of the party under Thomas Jefferson, had borne the imprint of the slaveholding interest. To maintain its traditions was therefore to promote that interest. This process operated via many of the cardinal tenets of the Democratic faith. Douglas, in common with the vast majority of northern Democrats, believed slavery to be a matter of dollars and cents; if and only if it were profitable in an area would it be established. He was blind to the moral dimension just as so many of those northerners who had supported Jefferson many decades earlier had been blind to the Virginian's ownership of slaves. Moreover Jefferson had embraced what might be termed a moral individualism by which each adult white male (other individuals were here ignored) was deemed to be "free" to reach his own decision about slaveholding (or other moral questions). There must therefore be no coercion on the part of the federal government.

Such a doctrine might have operated to promote antislavery had the rights of non-whites been similarly safeguarded. But in conjunction with the racism that was, and always had been, an equally fundamental feature of the Democratic tradition, the effect was the opposite. The tradition operated to blunt the force of antislavery. One white man must not question the right of another white man to own black men (and women).

So with state's rights. Democrats believed in the rights of the states. This was in no sense reducible to a defence of slavery in that there were powerful reasons for defending local power that were unconnected with slavery. But the doctrine inevitably promoted the defence of slavery, since southerners recognised that the threat to their peculiar institution would come not from within their own states but rather from the federal capital.

State's rights, racism, moral individualism – these were key tenets of the Democratic faith. Each of them could be defended without reference to slavery. Each of them attracted supporters throughout the nation, sometimes without reference to slavery. But the Democrat who subscribed to these doctrines was all too likely to be simultaneously furthering the interests of the slaveholders, whether he knew it or not.

This was the process by which Douglas came to the aid of the slave-holders in 1854. He believed in all these tenets of the Democratic faith; he was not seeking to further the slaveholding interest. But it was no accident that he ended by doing exactly that.

IV

The Kansas–Nebraska Act was the child of Stephen A. Douglas. But it was nevertheless deeply influenced by southerners who, as we have seen, managed to persuade him to incorporate within it the repeal of the Missouri Compromise. This marked, or seemed to mark, a triumph for the South, and especially for those southerners who worried about the threat of anti-slavery emanating from the North. As a result the Act became almost, if not quite, universally popular in the South. By the time it became law at the end of May 1854, southern expectations were extraordinarily high.

Why did so many southerners support the measure and what did they expect to gain from it? There were many attractions. Some of them flowed from the possibility of establishing slavery in Kansas. Others would be derived from the precedent that would be set: even if slavery did not go to Kansas, its expansion elsewhere would be facilitated. Finally even if slavery did not expand anywhere at all, the principles contained in the Act would, it was almost universally assumed, be beneficial for the South.

Some southerners believed Kansas could become a slave state. Others doubted it, while still others inclined first one way then the other. But if slavery could indeed be established there, then the benefit would be obvious. Southerners had been for many years keenly aware of the danger of additional free states augmenting northern power within the federal government. The stakes were, of course, very high here, since, as southerners were all too painfully aware, with a three-fourths majority of the states, the North would be able to amend the Federal Constitution so as to permit a direct assault upon slavery in the states where it already existed. An additional slave state in Kansas would obviously help counter this process. No southerner who supported the Kansas–Nebraska Act needed to be reminded of this fact.

Moreover some of those who doubted whether slavery could be established in Kansas were nevertheless extremely keen to see it expand elsewhere, either into the South West or into Latin America. But how was this to be achieved? Northerners had in the late 1840s voted down all attempts to extend the Missouri Compromise line at 36° 30′. And since the North had control of the House of Representatives (as well as a small majority in the Senate), it was difficult to see why this power would not be used again and again in the future to prevent the spread of slavery anywhere and everywhere. But the formula of popular sovereignty might remove the difficulty. Rather than secure a majority in Congress in favour of a new slave state, southerners need only secure a majority that was so inclined in a territory, a territory perhaps relatively close to the South and from which antislavery "fanaticism" could be excluded. So the principle of popular sovereignty, whether or not it produced a slave state in Kansas, was extremely appealing to southern expansionists.

Some of these expansionists stressed the need for more slave territory not merely on political grounds (the need for more states to offset northern power in Washington DC), but also because of the economic pressures to which they thought the slave system was subject. For decades some southerners had fretted that the natural growth of the slave population would mean, within a generation or two (they found it difficult to be precise in their predictions), an excess of slaves within the current boundaries of the South. Slave values would fall to uneconomic levels and many masters would be impelled to resort to manumission. In these circumstances a race war, according to some southerners, might even break out. In any event the South, men like Senator Albert Gallatin Brown of Mississippi insisted, needed an "outlet" for her potentially surplus slaves. Cuba and other parts of Latin America beckoned. And the principle of popular sovereignty, if it could only be established as the basis of federal policy for the territories, would facilitate their incorporation into the Union as slave states.

Thus the Kansas–Nebraska Act appealed strongly to expansionists, whether or not they believed slavery could expand into Kansas itself. But the attractions did not end there. Virtually every southern supporter of the measure, whether he wanted expansion or not, believed in one of the key principles enshrined in the Act. The vital provision was the withdrawal of congressional control over slavery, in this case in the territories. Almost since the creation of the Federal Constitution, the most ardent defenders of slavery had feared federal power being brought to bear upon the peculiar institution. The Kansas–Nebraska Act, however, meant a renunciation of federal power over slavery. It would thus help promote a true understanding of the relationship between federal and state power, from which the South might derive incalculable benefit. And this gain would accrue, whether or not slavery spread into Kansas or anywhere else. Although there had been no movement prior to 1854 for the repeal of the Missouri Compromise (partly since southerners thought the project hopeless), many of them had long been on record against it. These southerners had viewed it as a disastrous concession to the North, a dangerous precedent from which the enemies of the South might in the future derive enormous advantage. Douglas was now offering them a heaven-sent opportunity to rectify the problem.

These constitutional, political and economic arguments in favour of the Kansas–Nebraska Act were extremely compelling. But they did not exhaust its appeal. Another set of arguments could be adduced for favouring it. These had to do with the key state of Missouri.

Missouri contained relatively few slaves, a mere 90,000 in 1850. They produced hemp and tobacco, many of them in the western counties, adjoining the now-to-be-created territory of Kansas. Missourians were divided in their views of slavery. Some like Senator David Rice Atchison were utterly determined to retain it; others like Thomas Hart Benton were on record as regretting its introduction into the state. Still others actually planned, in the 1850s, to remove it from the state. This was a wider spectrum of opinion on the subject than could be found in any other state in the Union.

A further feature of Missouri was its need to attract new settlers. This, it was generally agreed, would be facilitated by the opening up of Kansas, for which Atchison's constituents were pressing. But if Kansas came into the Union as a free state, as the Missouri Compromise stipulated, then Missouri would be bordered not on one or even two but on three sides by free states. It would then, slaveholders concluded, become impossible to retain slavery in the state. Claiborne Fox Jackson, a prominent Missouri Democrat and future Governor, wrote that if Kansas were to become "'free nigger' territory, Missouri must become so too, for we can hardly keep our negroes here now". Atchison himself announced that he would "rather see the whole of Nebraska [including Kansas] in the bottom of hell, than see it a Free State".[6]

---

[6] Freehling, *Road to Disunion: Secessionists at Bay*, p. 549; Allan Nevins, *Ordeal of the Union: A House Dividing* (New York, 1947), p. 93; Weston Platte *Argus*, 26 December 1856.

What was the solution? The solution was to open up Kansas, but with the Missouri Compromise repealed. Perceiving this, Atchison became one of the prime shapers of the Kansas–Nebraska Act. Along with fellow southerners, dedicated defenders of slavery all, he put pressure on Douglas. The pressure told; the Missouri Compromise was duly repealed.

Southerners like Atchison were confident that in strengthening slavery in Missouri, they were strengthening it throughout the South. For some years they had feared that antislavery pressure and agitation would produce a domino effect, whereby pressure on Missouri, for example, would weaken states further south. Atchison himself cited Arkansas and Texas as being vulnerable to this process. "We are playing", he announced, "for a mightly [sic] stake".[7]

It was therefore little wonder that the Kansas–Nebraska Act was so enormously popular in the South. It was indeed full of promise, offering, or so it seemed, an extraordinary number of possible advantages. Some southerners hoped it would strengthen slavery in Missouri; some believed the creation of a new slave state would at least reduce the impact of new free states; others found in it reason to believe that it would facilitate territorial expansion elsewhere if not in Kansas; almost everyone thought it would overturn an odious restriction that set a dangerous constitutional precedent. Moreover these aspirations were not contradictory. None seemed to rule out the others. The more general effects could be expected to ensue even if the more specific ones did not. The South, it seemed, had nothing to lose and everything to gain.

V

The Kansas–Nebraska Act had assumed its final form because of southern power exerted directly over Douglas and indirectly via the ideology of the Democratic party. But in a more profound way, the Act reflected not the strengths but the weaknesses of slavery, its inability to match the free-labour system of the North. Thus the need to create new slave states was present only because the South could not match the North in the race to develop the West. Southerners might fear an excess of slaves

---

[7] David Rice Atchison to R. M. T. Hunter, quoted in James A. Rawley, *Race and Politics: "Bleeding Kansas" and the Coming of the Civil War* (Lincoln, NE, 1969), p. 81.

in their midst, but northerners meanwhile had in most years an insatiable demand for additional labour (in the form of immigrant labour, for example). Southerners might require a strict construction of the Federal Constitution in order to protect slavery from a hostile majority, but northern employers had no comparable fears for their wage workers. Missouri's slave-labour system might need to be shored up; free labour required no such support in any state of the North.

Southerners could not of course see matters in this light. When the Act was passed, most of them rejoiced. But the Act was ultimately powerless to overcome the weaknesses of slavery. For this reason, among others, it would prove an unmitigated disaster for the South.

VI

This was in part because of the opposition it aroused in the North. When he heard of the plan to allow slavery into the Nebraska territory (which then included Kansas), Salmon P. Chase of Ohio seized his opportunity. Chase, now a Senator, destined to be a member of Lincoln's cabinet and Chief Justice of the Supreme Court, was an implacable enemy of slavery. He was genuinely outraged at the prospect of the Missouri Compromise being set aside (as Douglas first planned) or repealed outright (the final outcome), and he wrote one of the most famous political tracts of the 1850s in response. It was entitled *The Appeal of the Independent Democrats in Congress,* and it appeared over the signature of a half a dozen Senators or Congressmen. But it was essentially Chase's work. It was nothing if not direct. The Bill was "a gross violation of a sacred pledge", "a criminal betrayal of precious rights", "part and parcel of an atrocious plot to exclude from a vast unoccupied region, immigrants from the Old World and free laborers from our own States, and convert it into a dreary region of despotism, inhabited by masters and slaves". Douglas's plan was "doubtless", Chase continued, "to extinguish freedom and establish slavery in the States and Territories of the Pacific, and thus permanently subjugate the whole country to the yoke of a slaveholding despotism". "Shall a plot against humanity and democracy", he asked, "so monstrous, so dangerous to the interests of liberty throughout the world, be permitted to succeed?"[8]

---

[8] Salmon P. Chase et al., *An Appeal of the Independent Democrats* (Washington DC, 1854), pp. 1, 6–7.

The Kansas–Nebraska Act

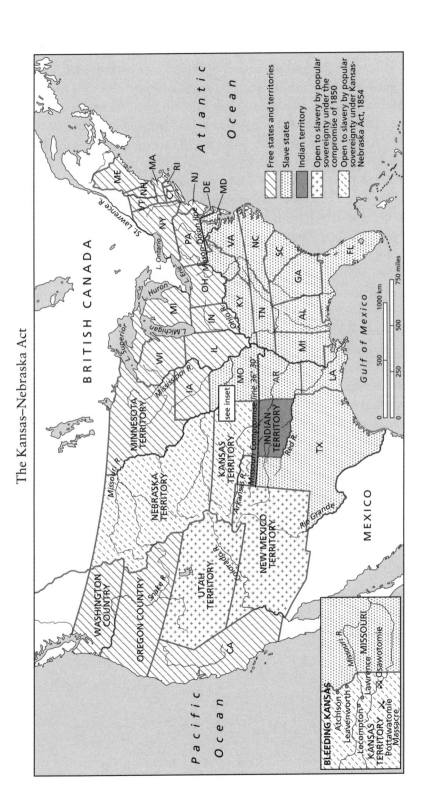

Free states and territories

Slave states

Indian territory

Open to slavery by popular
sovereignty under the
compromise of 1850

Open to slavery by popular
sovereignty under Kansas–
Nebraska Act, 1854

BLEEDING KANSAS
Atchison
Leavenworth
Lecompton
Lawrence
Osawotomie
Pottawatomie
Massacre

The most determined enemies of slavery took their cue from Chase's appeal. But other northerners, who had been much more moderate on the slavery question, were also hostile to the Kansas–Nebraska Act. These men could see no reason to rekindle the sectional controversy which, they noted, had died down following the settlement of 1850. Many of them had not wanted the nation to expand to the Pacific anyway and thus felt able to ignore the need to organise the Nebraska territory.

Between them these two groups were able to mobilise an extraordinary degree of opposition to the Kansas–Nebraska Act. They were even joined by some northern Democrats. The Democratic administration of Franklin Pierce had come down in favour of the Act; indeed Pierce determined to make it a test of party orthodoxy. But some northern Democrats simply could not stomach it. The measure was thus opposed in the North by all Free Soilers and Abolitionists, the great majority of Whigs and a significant number of Democrats.

Not surprisingly therefore it proved difficult to steer through Congress. But the administration offered carrots and sticks in an attempt to rally the Democratic troops, while Douglas and other leading Democrats spared no effort in trying to persuade the waverers. Eventually, at the end of May 1854, helped by the votes of southern Whigs, the measure became law.

Democrats rejoiced. But William Seward, the antislavery Whig Senator from New York, on its passage offered what should have been a chilling warning to southerners. Since the future of Kansas was to be determined not by Congress but by popular sovereignty, slavery could now only be barred by those who migrated to Kansas. The lesson was clear. "Gentlemen of the Slave States", Seward said, "I accept your challenge....We will engage in competition for virgin soil of Kansas, and God give the victory to the side which is stronger in numbers as it is in right". Many of the southerners who heard his words probably believed they could win this struggle. They were to be proved hopelessly and catastrophically wrong.[9]

[9] *Congressional Globe*, 33rd Congress, 1st Session, Appendix, p. 769.

5

POLITICAL MAELSTROM, 1854–1856

I

The middle years of the 1850s saw a profound transformation in American politics. As 1854 opened, sectional animosities were at a low point and the two-party system pitted, as it had for twenty years, Democrat against Whig, with each party able to recruit from each side of the Mason–Dixon line. By the time the results of the presidential election of 1856 were known, a transformation had occurred. One of the two parties, the Whigs, had ceased to exist, the other, the Democrats, had suffered an extraordinary reversal of fortune across almost the entire North, and sectional tensions were greater than at any time in the nation's entire history. As if all this were not enough, by the end of 1856 the temperance cause, once so full of disruptive potential, was in headlong retreat while the Know Nothings had, as a political force, experienced a meteoric rise and an equally spectacular fall. Finally a new party, the Republicans, had come into existence and had done remarkably well in the presidential election that had just been held. An observer could have been forgiven for wondering how such dramatic and bewildering changes could have taken place in so short a period of time.

These were years of political confusion and even chaos. In 1854 several processes converged. First there was a general dissatisfaction with party politics; Whig and Democrat seemed to have little to argue about. The result was to prepare the ground for other issues, ones with which the party system might not be able to cope. Second some of those new issues, which historians often refer to as "ethnocultural", were themselves acquiring new vitality. The temperance crusade was having its impact upon politicians and voters alike; the Know Nothing movement would play a still more dramatic role. Both would inflict damage on the second party system. Finally, and most important, events in Kansas would bring sectional issues, those that pitted North against South, bubbling to the very top of the political agenda. These were the issues that would ultimately destroy the second party system and then, within a few short years, the unity of the nation.

II

The political upheaval of 1854–1856 took place against the background of events in Kansas. As we have noted, northerners, having lost the battle to prevent the repeal of the Missouri Compromise, now faced the possibility that Kansas would become a slave state. To those who refused to tolerate this possibility, it now seemed essential to take action in Kansas itself. Accordingly in April 1854, Eli Thayer of Massachusetts obtained a charter for the Massachusetts Emigrant Aid Society (later renamed the New England Emigrant Aid Company). The Society was both a money-making venture and an attempt to ensure that Kansas became free territory. Thayer sent perhaps two thousand settlers into the territory.[1]

The result among the slaveholders of neighbouring Missouri was intense panic. Fearing that a free Kansas would make slavery in Missouri itself utterly unviable, Missourians, led by David Rice Atchison, determined to take action. Not once but repeatedly over the coming months and years, they would cross into Kansas, intimidate free-state settlers and vote illegally in the elections that would either directly or indirectly determine the fate of slavery in the territory. Not surprisingly the free-soil settlers also engaged in violent and illegal activities.

Electoral fraud on a large scale ensued. Nevertheless a proslavery territorial legislature was established first at Shawnee, then at Lecompton,

---

[1] On events in Kansas, see Nichole Etcheson, *Bleeding Kansas: Contested Liberty in the Civil War Era* (Lawrence, KA, 2004); Craig Miner, *Seeding Civil War: Kansas in the National News, 1845–1858* (Lawrence, KA, 2008); Allan Nevins, *Ordeal of the Union: A House Dividing* (New York, 1947); David Potter, *The Impending Crisis, 1848–1861* (New York, 1976); James A. Rawley, *Race and Politics: "Bleeding Kansas" and the Coming of the Civil War* (Lincoln, NE, 1969); Gunja SenGupta, *For God and Mammon: Evangelicals and Entrepreneurs, Masters and Slaves in Territorial Kansas, 1854–1860* (Athens, GA, 1996).

which passed draconian measures in support of slavery. Anyone denying the legality of slavery in Kansas, for example, was subject to imprisonment. Moreover only those in favour of slavery were eligible for office. In response the free-soil settlers established a competing assembly at Topeka, which then set about prohibiting slavery throughout the territory. When this enactment was submitted to a popular vote, it was overwhelmingly approved, but this time the election was boycotted by the proslavery elements on the grounds that the entire Topeka movement was treasonous. President Pierce meanwhile, a northerner who had always been inclined to side with the South on slavery-related issues, also condemned the Topeka government as illegal and revolutionary. By the end of 1855 the disorder in Kansas had already resulted in the dismissal of one governor, and there were now rival governments, each with its own armed supporters, and each heaping derision upon the other.

These events meant that the sectional question would not go away. If the settlement of Kansas had proceeded as the originator of the Kansas–Nebraska Act, Stephen A. Douglas, and all its supporters had hoped and anticipated, the controversy stirred up by its passage might have abated, as they had also hoped and anticipated. But wave after wave of dramatic news from Kansas kept the subject alive and proved no less than the main factor in the collapse of the second party system.

III

It was, however, by no means the only factor. Other longer-term processes were at work. These processes combined to weaken the party system, and especially the Whig party. Ironically the death of the Whig party owed something to the successes of the American economy. Still more ironically, these successes, especially in the North, conformed to the Whig rather than to the Democratic blueprint for economic growth.

By the mid-1850s the capitalist world was in the midst of a period of remarkable economic expansion. It would last, with a number of short-lived interruptions, into the early 1870s, and it owed much to the huge increase in international trade and international investment, as the capitalist world created a new network of global interdependencies. In the first forty years of the century, world trade had not even managed to double; between 1850 and 1870 it increased by 260 per cent.[2]

The United States was deeply involved in these processes, even though its economic revival started somewhat earlier and was seriously affected by the domestic upheavals of 1861–1865. This was the age of the railroad boom, in which the United States again participated fully. Economic growth brought a new stability to the nation's banking system. At the same time the discovery of gold in California (and elsewhere) fuelled the growth process still further, and, as specie flowed freely into the banks, stabilised the financial system and thus weakened anti-bank radicalism at its very source. The United States, as late as the early 1840s, had shown many of the signs of an underdeveloped economy with chronic shortages of capital for much-needed infrastructural projects. But the new prosperity of the banks, together with the increased willingness of overseas investors to support American commercial ventures, brought a new maturity and a new stability to the nation's economy.

The effect was steadily to remove the rationale for the Whig economic programme. The Whigs had stood for a public–private cooperation exemplified in the charter of the second Bank of the United States, and reflecting the shortage of private capital in the economy as a whole. In the same way the party had stood for a protective tariff which would allow undercapitalised and therefore small-scale manufacturing establishments in the United States to compete with more fully capitalised and thus larger scale ones in Europe. Now, however, banks and manufactured goods no longer needed this kind of support, either politically or economically. The new fiscal stability and commercial expansion blunted Democratic radicalism and threatened the Whigs' raison d'être.

This was a curious outcome in that the developing economy corresponded much more closely to Whig than to Democratic visions. But it had been achieved without the Whig policies that party members had believed indispensably necessary. Instead it was Democratic policy that became bipartisan orthodoxy.

Banking offers a clear example. By the mid-1850s the Democratic policy of an Independent Treasury (which would allow the government

---

[2] Eric Hobsbawm, *The Age of Capital, 1848–1875* (London, 1975), p. 49.

to keep its funds entirely separate from the nation's banks) had taken root. Meanwhile in the great majority of the states the Democrats had retreated from their anti-bank radicalism, partly because the banks had been reformed, but essentially because the economic environment meant that banks were able to operate much more safely. By 1850 there was a widespread agreement on banking, once the most divisive of all issues that separated Whig from Democrat. There would be, and there needed to be, no national bank, but banks within the states were to be preserved. In a sense this settlement within the states owed as much to Whig priorities as to Democratic ones, but as far as federal politics were concerned it was Democratic policies that had triumphed.

An analogous process occurred with the protective tariff. This had been second in importance only to a national bank in Henry Clay's American System, itself the embodiment of Whiggery's economic programme. The Walker tariff of 1846, however, had not brought about the economic catastrophe and the ruin of the nation's manufacturing system that the Whigs had predicted. Instead American manufacturing entered upon a period of unprecedented progress, led by the farm machinery sector where the United States in any case had a technological lead and where there was thus little need for a protective tariff.

The situation in the South was somewhat different, but equally damaging to Whig fortunes. Traditionally the tariff had been popular with sugar and hemp growers in states like Louisiana and Kentucky; it had been popular elsewhere only when it had been possible to point to the evils of an undifferentiated, monocultural economy. In a sense, therefore, southern Whiggery needed a weak southern economy in which there was pressure for diversification.

As we have seen, by 1848 the Whigs were retreating from the tariff. President Taylor actually announced (privately) that he believed such issues dead and buried, while the Whig campaign of 1852 made few references to it. Once again economic recovery had proved disadvantageous to the Whigs.[3]

The third leg of the American system was a carefully planned network of federally sponsored internal improvements. This, however,

[3] Michael F. Holt, *The Rise and Fall of the American Whig Party: Jacksonian Politics and the Onset of the Civil War* (New York, 1999), p. 272; David N. Young, "The Mississippi Whigs, 1834–1860" (unpublished Ph.D. thesis, University of Alabama, 1968), pp. 114–132.

had been largely abandoned in the 1830s, another casualty of Andrew Jackson's and the Democratic party's belief in a limited central government. In the 1850s a Pacific Railroad was high on the agenda of many Americans, but it was a bipartisan project, enthusiastically supported by many Democrats and indeed, as we have seen, a major concern of Stephen A. Douglas when he introduced the Kansas–Nebraska Act. Within the states a similar pattern was manifest. Economic recovery brought a fresh surge of interest in internal improvements, this time focussing upon railroad building, but once again there was no clear party division. Often the projects were either bipartisan and uncontroversial or they pitted one locality, rather than one party, against another. Moreover the railroads of the era were essentially private corporations rather than the public or public–private enterprises of previous decades which the Whigs had championed. Like the other economic issues of the 1830s and 1840s, internal improvements now ceased to generate much partisan interest except in a minority of localities. As Meredith Gentry of Tennessee, himself a Whig, acknowledged, the issues that had formerly divided the parties were, by 1852, "practically obsolete".[4]

Two issues that were not obsolete, however, were temperance and immigration. But as we have noted, neither could revitalise the party system. As far as temperance was concerned, each of the parties was split and could not offer the voters a clear choice. On immigration there was no longer a wide gap between them, since, as we have seen, in 1852 the Whigs had made a deliberate attempt to court the immigrant vote. The way was now clear for another organisation to profit from the antagonism towards the foreign born that was mounting in the early and mid-1850s, largely, as we have also seen, in consequence of the unprecedentedly large influx of immigrants now taking place. The stage was now set for the political transformation of the mid-1850s.

IV

The longer-term causes of the political upheaval now converged with the immediate precipitating factors. With the gap between the parties on both economic and political questions narrower than at any time

---

[4] *Speech of M.P. Gentry of Tennessee, Vindicating His Course in the Late Presidential Election…Delivered…at Franklin, Tennessee, Nov 20, 1852* (Washington DC, 1853), p. 28.

in two decades and anti-immigrant sentiment about to explode, the Kansas–Nebraska Act supplied the final spark.

The problem was of course its sheer divisiveness. To the vast majority of northern Whigs, it was utterly unacceptable. Even the more conservative of them found it extremely difficult even to contemplate the repeal of the Missouri Compromise. Such an action seemed like the most wanton disregard of the prescriptive wisdom of the past: a statute that had been in force for a third of a century was now being torn up at the behest of the South. Those northern Whigs who had spent many years pleading for compromise with the South and rejecting the northern antislavery militant's claim that a Slave Power ruled the nation now had the ground cut from beneath them. By the same token those who had argued in 1850 (and earlier) that concessions to the Slave Power would merely encourage further aggressions had, it seemed, been triumphantly vindicated. When the Bill was finally passed, it had the support of not a single northern Whig in either house.

Nor, of course, were these northerners slow to express their feelings of outrage. Such sentiments were almost certainly perfectly genuine, but in any case northern Whigs were themselves under pressure from antislavery elements affiliated to other parties or to none. Even more than antislavery Whigs, Liberty men, Free Soilers and Garrisonians had had their predictions and warnings fully borne out. And these groups did not have a southern wing to conciliate.

In fact conciliation was not the goal of northern Whigs. Instead they placed pressure on their southern Whig allies, traditionally the more moderate party in the South, to vote the Kansas–Nebraska Act down. Otherwise, they warned, the party would be destroyed as a national force.[5] But these southerners were themselves trapped. As we have seen, the Act was enormously popular in the South. It seemed to offer the South so much with so little risk. John Bell of Tennessee was a leading southern Whig. A moderate on the sectional question, Bell cast his vote against Douglas's Bill. But even he recognised that he had risked his entire political future in doing so. Others refused to take the gamble. They either genuinely welcomed the Bill or, unable to withstand the charge of disloyalty to the South, with varying degrees of reluctance, voted for it. In the Senate, Bell was the only southern Whig to vote nay;

---

[5] Holt, *Whig Party*, p. 814.

in the House he was joined by only seven others. In the House the final vote was quite close, and the thirteen southern Whigs who voted "aye" provided the margin of victory.

This placed Whig unity under enormous strain. It is worth repeating that, if Kansas had then been settled quietly and uncontroversially, the party might indeed have survived the pressure. But the constant strife in the territory, assiduously reported by the nation's newspapers, meant there could be no respite. Here was the main factor that finally destroyed the Whig party.

The party's destruction was not, however, a simple or linear process. For a time the Know Nothings complicated matters. In 1854 it has been estimated that the total Know Nothing membership was a mere fifty thousand. But the Kansas–Nebraska Act, coinciding as it did with some of the factors that themselves promoted nativist sentiment, produced a huge accession of strength for the new organisation. Its most spectacular gains came in Massachusetts where the Know Nothings in 1854 won the entire congressional delegation, every single seat in the state senate and ninety-nine per cent of those in the lower house. Massachusetts had long been one of the strongest Whig states in the entire Union. Clearly this was no longer so.[6]

In other states the Know Nothings made impressive gains too, though not on the scale of those in Massachusetts. But it is important not to misinterpret these successes, as some historians have. It has been tempting to argue that since the Know Nothings (rather than the nascent Republican party) were initially the primary beneficiaries of the upheaval of 1854, anti-immigrant sentiment was more important than antislavery in bringing it about. This is a non sequitur. In fact in the North (and particularly in a state like Massachusetts), the Know Nothings were adamantly opposed to the Kansas–Nebraska Act. Indeed it soon became apparent that most northern Know Nothings, partly because of the constant drumbeat of events in Kansas, were more strongly committed to antislavery than to nativism. As a result the process was the opposite of the one sometimes discerned. Nativist strength in the North was in part testimony to the appeal of antislavery.

[6] John R. Mulkern, *The Know Nothing Party in Massachusetts: The Rise and Fall of a People's Movement* (Boston, 1990), p. 76.

It is clear that more than one factor was responsible for the collapse of the Whig party. Longer-term trends combined with short-term factors and specific events to destroy the party. But the primary factor was clearly the sectional controversy.[7]

V

The same pressures that inflicted the coup de grace on the Whig party operated, and with similar effects, on the Know Nothings themselves. At first, however, slavery did not pose a problem for the Order. In its structure it was highly decentralised and at first there was neither a need nor even an opportunity to adopt a consistent stance. But as the Know Nothings went into politics, it became more difficult for them to avoid taking a stand on sectional questions and, after the passage of the Kansas–Nebraska Act, actually impossible.

With few exceptions they agreed that the repeal of the Missouri Compromise had been an error. However, once repeal had occurred, it was difficult for them to respond. At the first significant Know Nothing convention of November 1854, the party instituted what was termed a Third Degree, which required all members to defend the Union against its enemies. But who were its enemies and who its friends? William Lloyd Garrison and his supporters could be termed an enemy of the Union, as could an out-and-out secessionist like Robert Barnwell Rhett of South Carolina. But between these extremes lay virtually everyone who supported any of the major parties, including the infant Republican party. Abraham Lincoln was a committed unionist. Jefferson Davis meanwhile could and did argue in all sincerity that only by resisting the antislavery movement could the South make the Union safe for slavery and thus durable. The Third Degree therefore, if it were to have any value, must be made more specific.

This, however, was impossible, if Know Nothing unity were to be maintained. Once again the problem was that, owing to events in Kansas, the sectional issues still would not go away. At the end of 1854 elections were held in Kansas and more than a thousand Missourians crossed the border and voted illegally. It was clear that frauds had taken

---

[7] This may strike some readers as a familiar conclusion. It is indeed the traditional interpretation. But it has been challenged in recent years.

place on a large scale. Northerners who had for years complained about the Slave Power, and its nefarious effects upon white as well as black liberties were vindicated; northerners who had resisted such claims were highly embarrassed.

In this context another national Know Nothing convention met in June 1855. It was now almost impossible for the Order to avoid taking a stance on sectional issues. But some northerners, who clearly placed antislavery ahead of nativism, demanded a highly radical programme against the South; southerners could not even agree that the Missouri Compromise line should be restored (on the grounds that restoration would add further fuel to the flames). In other words it was far easier for the Order to assert the need for neutrality on the sectional questions than to find a policy that all members could agree was truly neutral in its impact. The convention ended by adopting a platform which corresponded to the wishes of southern Know Nothings. It reaffirmed the Kansas–Nebraska Act as a final settlement of the slavery question and denied that Congress could prohibit slavery in either a territory or the District of Columbia. To a large majority of the northern members of the Order, this was simply unacceptable.

In much the same way, however, southerners resented the attitudes of their northern colleagues. Within the northern states Know-Nothing-controlled legislatures passed antislavery resolutions and implemented antislavery policies that pleased their local electorates but which deeply embarrassed their southern allies, themselves under constant pressure to demonstrate their loyalty to slavery and to the South. In Virginia, for example, Democrat Henry Wise rode to victory in the gubernatorial election of May 1855 by condemning the Know Nothings as a party dominated by northern "abolitionists" and accordingly disloyal to the South. In this respect, as in so many others, the experience of southern Know Nothings replicated that of southern Whigs.

Under these circumstances southerners could not countenance the repeal of the Kansas–Nebraska Act, even if they had so wished. In retaliation, the Know Nothing State Councils of several northern states repudiated the national policy and in some cases even severed ties with the national organisation. By now the Know Nothings were as divided over slavery as the Whigs had ever been. Even when the party ran well in the North, it was because the national policy on slavery was either repudiated or ignored. In November 1855 northern Know Nothings met at

Cincinnati and concluded that they would try to persuade southerners to agree to a restoration of the Missouri Compromise. In February 1856 another national convention met, this time charged with the task of finding a presidential nominee. By now the divisions within the party were beyond repair. Southerners were threatening to bolt if the Order sought to restore the Missouri Compromise; northerners did bolt when it became apparent that it would not seek to restore it. With most northerners gone, the nomination went to former President Millard Fillmore. By now in most of the states of the North, Know Nothings were entering the Republican party in droves; those that remained were conservative Whigs, like Fillmore himself, for whom maintenance of the Union took primacy over nativism and antislavery alike

Once again events in Kansas provided the crucial backdrop, ensuring that consideration of sectional issues could not be suspended. By 1856 David Rice Atchison, still determined to make Kansas a slave state (essentially to safeguard slavery in Missouri), was appealing to other southern states for aid, in the form of additional manpower. Northerners were by now also calling for weapons – the famous Sharps rifles – to be sent into the territory to defend free-state settlers against the so-called Missouri ruffians. There was even bloodshed, though on a small scale. In May 1856 came one of the most celebrated events of the entire Kansas saga: the "sack of Lawrence". The city of Lawrence was attacked by a posse of proslavery Missourians on the grounds that it was an abolitionist stronghold. Again there was relatively little bloodshed though much destruction of property. By now violence was occurring on both sides, there were widespread guerrilla activities as well as burning and pillaging and, as a direct result of the sack of Lawrence, John Brown, the militant abolitionist, brutally murdered five men at Pottawatomie in Kansas. It has been estimated that between November 1855 and December 1856, perhaps two hundred lives were lost and perhaps two million dollars worth of property destroyed.[8]

Not surprisingly Congress became increasingly preoccupied with events in the territory. When, in response to the actions perpetrated by the proslavery forces in Kansas, Charles Sumner of Massachusetts denounced slavery in general and South Carolina and one of her

---

[8] Rawley, *Race and Politics*, p. 160. Other estimates put the total lower, at fewer than one hundred.

Senators, Andrew Butler, in particular, Preston Brooks, a relative of Butler, retaliated with a physical assault upon Sumner which kept him out of the Senate and unable to resume his duties for several years. The result was a further polarisation of opinion, with southerners sending Brooks canes to replace the one broken in the affray, and northerners denouncing the assault as fresh evidence of southern barbarism. The election of 1856 was thus played out against the background of "Bleeding Kansas" and "Bleeding Sumner". These were the direct or indirect effects of events in Kansas, and they were fatal to the prospects of the Know Nothings.[9]

By now sectional animosities had destroyed any prospect of victory for the new party in the coming presidential election. While almost all northerners condemned the assault on Sumner unreservedly, southern Know Nothings defended the actions in Kansas of the Missouri "border ruffians" and most refused even to censure Brooks. The problem for those in the new party was that both north and south of the Mason–Dixon line, they were in constant danger of being outflanked by opponents who were more radical on sectional issues. Slavery thus divided the Know Nothings at what should have been their moment of greatest triumph.

VI

In the North the bulk of Whig and Know Nothing reverses became gains for the newly created Republican party, as it strove to become the main focus of opposition to the Democrats. After the introduction of the Kansas–Nebraska Act, a meeting had been called of opponents of the measure in May 1854. The name "Republican" was adopted. By November 1856 in good part as a result of the constant stream of shocking information that came from Kansas, the new party had clearly become the principal vehicle through which opposition not only to the Kansas–Nebraska Act but also to the extension of slavery in general was to be conveyed. In one sense this had perhaps been extremely rapid progress for a party that had been in existence for so short a time, but the process was anything but neat and uniform across the

[9] Newspaper reaction to the Sumner beating can be conveniently found at http://history. furman.edu/editorials/see.py?menu=sumenu&sequence=sumenu&location=%3E%20 Sumner%20Caning

North. Instead almost every state followed a distinctive path as the realignment of the mid-1850s unfolded. Whilst it is not necessary to trace this development in each state, it is important to note the patterns that emerged. At least five tendencies transcending state boundaries can be discerned.[10]

First, in a majority of states, the Know Nothings grew considerably in popularity and entered politics in the later part of 1854 or the first months of 1855. Only in one state (Massachusetts) did they manage to win independently, though they controlled the elections in others (Indiana and Pennsylvania). Second antislavery sentiment proved to be more intense in the Upper North than in the Lower North (as it had been for many years and would continue to be after 1856). Thus elections in the Upper North tended to result in a victory for strongly antislavery candidates (Maine, New Hampshire), whereas in the Lower North (Pennsylvania, Indiana) lack of antislavery zeal delayed the formation of the Republican party.

Differences between East and West produced a third pattern. In the states of the West (Michigan, Wisconsin), concern over the extension of slavery tended, other things being equal, to be more pronounced than in the East, and for this reason, in part, the formation of the Republican party occurred more quickly than in the East. By contrast nativist sentiment tended to be stronger in the East (where most Irish Catholics were located) and this both strengthened the Know Nothings and delayed the formation of the Republican party (Massachusetts, Connecticut, New Hampshire, New Jersey, Pennsylvania). This sectional pattern was sometimes visible even within a single state. Southern and eastern Pennsylvania, for example, displayed relatively less interest in the

[10] As we have already noted, the realignment had in reality already begun in the early 1850s in the Deep South. Some of the better works on this theme are Dale Baum, *The Civil War Party System: The Case of Massachusetts* (Chapel Hill, NC, 1984); John F. Coleman, *The Disruption of the Pennsylvania Democracy, 1848-1860* (Harrisburg, PA, 1975); Robert Cook, *Baptism of Fire: The Republican Party in Iowa, 1838-1878* (Ames, IA, 1994); Stephen L. Hansen, *The Making of the Third Party System: Voters and Parties in Illinois, 1850-1876* (Ann Arbor, MI, 1980); James L. Huston, "The Demise of the Pennsylvania American Party", *Pennsylvania Magazine of History and Biography* 109 (1985), 473–497; Stephen E. Maizlish, *The Triumph of Sectionalism: The Transformation of Politics in Ohio, 1844-1856* (Kent, OH, 1983); Joel Silbey, "'The Undisguised Connection': Know Nothings into Republicans: New York as a Test Case", in Silbey, *The Partisan Imperative: The Dynamics of American Politics before the Civil War* (New York, 1985), pp. 127–165; Kevin Sweeney, "Rum, Romanism, Representation and Reform: Coalition Politics in Massachusetts, 1847-1853", *Civil War History* 22 (1976), 116–137.

slavery issue, relatively more in nativism, than the northern and western parts of the state.

A fourth factor that transcended state boundaries concerned the prior strength of the Whig party. Where the Whigs had been strong (Massachusetts, New York), they were able to block the formation of the Republican party in a way their colleagues in traditionally weaker states (Maine, Indiana) could not. And finally there was a tendency for Whigs, as their party faced unprecedented challenges from other groupings, to divide according to the liberal/moderate split that had existed in most states virtually since the party's birth. In some states (Massachusetts) the more conservative among them remained longer within the party, though in New York the opposite happened as they en masse joined the Know Nothings.

These were the principal factors transcending state boundaries that influenced state politics in these years of extraordinary flux. But of course some other factors were unique to particular states. Thus in New York William Seward came up for re-election to the Senate in early 1855 and his manager and alter ego Thurlow Weed did not want to disband the Whig party (if it were to be disbanded at all) until that re-election had been secured. This almost certainly delayed the formation of the Republican party in New York. In other states other unique considerations also made themselves felt. Nevertheless it is clear that these factors were more likely to accelerate or retard the pace of realignment rather than decisively to affect the final outcome, by which the Republicans emerged as the major anti-Democratic force in the North.

As the election approached, the new party sought a presidential candidate and found one in former Democrat John C. Frémont. As we have seen, the Know Nothings, or the American party as it now wished to be known, nominated Millard Fillmore who had never been a committed nativist and whose chief appeal was as a moderate on the slavery question who had helped broker the compromise measures of 1850. The Democrats meanwhile nominated James Buchanan of Pennsylvania, a hugely experienced statesman who had, like Pierce before him, proved a faithful servant of the South.

Each party adopted a platform. The American party rehearsed its standard claims about the need to curtail the political power of immigrants and lamented the repeal of the Missouri Compromise, though without proposing to reinstate it. The Democrats meanwhile reiterated their traditional ideals, stressing as always the need to maintain the rights of the states, and added a defence both of the rights of immigrants and of the administration's territorial policy especially towards Kansas. Most interesting perhaps was the Republican platform which denounced slavery as, along with polygamy, one of "those twin relics of barbarism" and denied that Congress or a territorial government or any individual could give it "legal existence...in any Territory of the United States". Much of the platform was devoted to a listing of the outrages that had taken place in Kansas.[11]

Fortune favoured the Republicans during the campaign in that the explosive events in Kansas ("Bleeding Kansas") together with the unprecedented attack upon Charles Sumner in the U.S. Senate ("Bleeding Sumner") ensured that sectional issues would predominate. The Republicans benefited enormously from the disgust northerners felt at the repeal of the Missouri Compromise and the disastrous chain of events that had followed in Kansas and finally in Washington DC. Many southerners in turn made it clear that they would not tolerate a Republican victory; here they were merely reiterating their response to the Wilmot Proviso ten years earlier. But the existence of the Republican party was the new element in the mix. Many northerners, though not Republicans, took southern threats extremely seriously and took fright at them. A Republican victory, they feared, would indeed jeopardise the existence of the nation.

There were several results. One was the further squeezing of the American party vote. Voters were now being asked to adjudicate between two major parties, one of which condemned the North for its antislavery fanaticism, the other of which condemned the South for its undemocratic assault upon northern freedoms, economic and political. As a result it was difficult for the Americans to avoid the charge that a vote for them would play into the hands of the enemy, however he might be defined. Fillmore himself warned that the South would secede following a Republican victory, but many of his erstwhile supporters probably concluded that this outcome was best avoided by supporting Buchanan.

The actual election results were striking. Fillmore carried only a single state: Maryland. But the Republicans ran extremely well in

---

[11] The platforms may be found in Donald Bruce Johnson and Kirk H. Porter, *National Party Platforms, 1840–1972* (Chicago, 1975).

A Republican cartoon, showing Fillmore, the American candidate (left) and Buchanan (the Democrat) crushed by an avalanche of giant balls inscribed with the names of northern and western states. "Border Ruffianism", "Kansas Bogus Laws", "Polygamy & Slavery", and so on refer to Republican charges against the Pierce administration. Note that Buchanan is squashed beneath the Democratic convention's "Cincinnati Platform", while Fillmore holds two documents, one of which is the "Fugitive Slave Bill". At the top of the picture are the names of the Republican candidates (Frémont and Drayton) and their campaign slogans. On the right a burning town in Kansas is depicted.

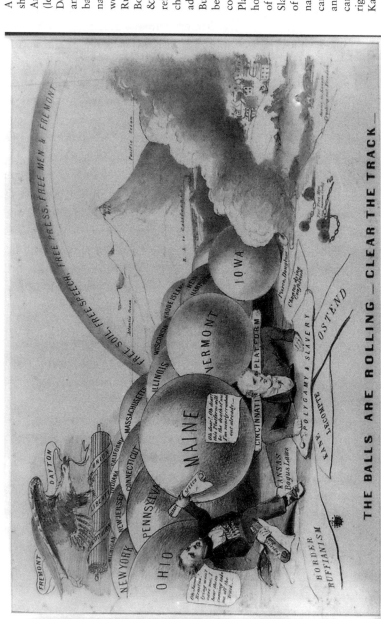

THE BALLS ARE ROLLING — CLEAR THE TRACK

The Presidential Election of 1856 (Electoral College Votes)

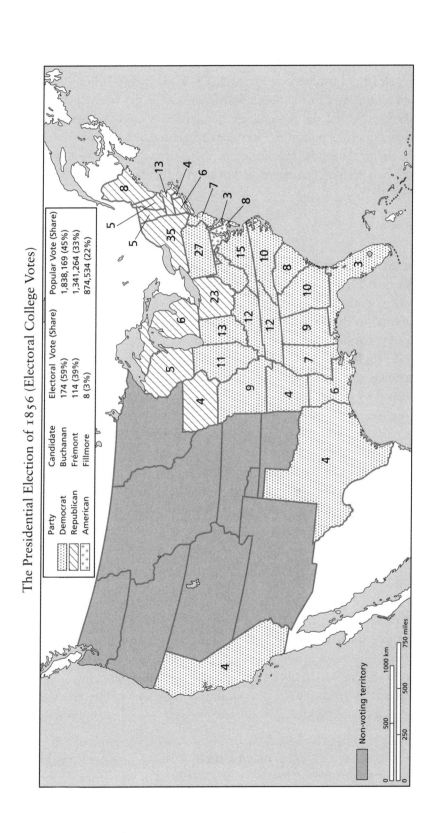

Party	Candidate	Electoral Vote (Share)	Popular Vote (Share)
Democrat	Buchanan	174 (59%)	1,838,169 (45%)
Republican	Frémont	114 (39%)	1,341,264 (33%)
American	Fillmore	8 (3%)	874,534 (22%)

Non-voting territory

the North, capturing every state except Pennsylvania, Illinois, Indiana and California. In the South Buchanan swept the board (except for Maryland), and the Republicans received not a single electoral vote. The nation was polarising. Sectional differences were now at the top of the political agenda. The second party system was no more and a long step had been taken towards the cataclysm that would erupt four years later.

VII

In the election of 1856 temperance had been almost an irrelevance. What had happened to this crusade once, it seemed, so full of promise and potential? There were many causes of its decline, some of them internal to the movement itself, others related instead to the gripping events that dominated the politics of the mid-1850s.

To begin with although antislavery had clear affinities with the temperance movement, not all who joined the nascent Republican party wished to rid the nation of alcohol and especially not by the use of coercive legislation. Former Democrats within the Republican coalition remained as hostile to such a strategy as ever. More generally party members recognised that they simply could not afford to adopt such a divisive issue: antislavery needed all the support and all the votes it could muster. As a result from the mid-1850s onwards in areas where it had once been a plank in their platform, Republicans generally abandoned Prohibition.

In part the problem was that slavery had simply overshadowed Prohibition, as it had overshadowed nativism and every other issue. There were, however, other factors at work. Some of them were problems that came to light only after Prohibition had been enacted. The Maine Laws usually conferred wide powers upon officials charged with finding violators of the law. In some states the courts struck down these laws.[12] Even when this did not happen, they proved very difficult to enforce. This was partly on account of public opposition, but it was also the case that many states and localities simply lacked effective policing agencies. Nor could the law prevent interstate trading in liquor, and this

---

[12] Ian R. Tyrrell, *Sobering Up: From Temperance to Prohibition in Antebellum America, 1800–1860* (Westport, CT, 1979), pp. 282, 290–293.

continued or even increased in extent. Even more important was the disorder that sometimes accompanied Prohibition. Although its supporters had insisted that alcohol posed a major threat to public order and decency, there were riots in places like Maine and Chicago caused by the attempt to enforce Prohibition; this was most emphatically not the orderly society that temperance crusaders had promised.[13]

These local confrontations, however, were a symptom rather than the fundamental cause of Prohibition's failure. The real problem was that temperance had promised what it could not deliver. The idea that the banning of alcohol could conquer poverty, for example, was itself an intoxicating idea but one which almost certainly mistook causes for consequences. Those who doubted whether Prohibition could bring either the material or the moral rewards it promised formed a powerful opposition whose mere existence prevented the movement from producing the harmony and tranquillity for which its supporters yearned.

As a result the Republicans abandoned Prohibition on the grounds that it would, on balance, both lose them votes and deflect attention from the antislavery cause, which alone united all elements within the party.[14] By 1857 the crusade for the Maine Law was over. Two decades later only three states were still dry. All were in New England.[15]

VIII

If the struggle to excommunicate the drinker was virtually over, that in Kansas was not. It had already taken a huge toll on national unity. As we have observed, the collapse of parties that sought to maintain a moderate or even-handed course on the slavery question (Whigs and Americans) had been hastened by events in the territory, which made it difficult or even impossible not to take sides. Northerners were apt to conclude that the "border ruffians" were to blame; southerners were equally likely to conclude that the blame lay elsewhere.

The southern view requires further consideration. The incursions by the Missourians were prompted by fears for slavery in their home state

[13] Tyrrell, *Sobering Up*, pp. 293–307.
[14] On the Republican abandonment of prohibition, see Eric Foner, *Free Soil, Free Labor, Free Men: The Ideology of the Republican Party Before the Civil War* (New York, 1970), pp. 241–242.
[15] Tyrrell, *Sobering Up*, pp. 307–316.

as well as in Kansas. It was at this point that the vulnerabilities of slavery as an exploitative system made themselves felt.

In defence of the actions of the Missourians in Kansas, southerners offered some extremely interesting arguments, more interesting indeed than they themselves knew. They began by denouncing the northern Emigrant Aid societies as abolitionist in intent. Next they insisted that, faced with this antislavery agitation in Kansas, the Missourians had had no choice. They thus in effect conceded that in such circumstances, a slave regime could only maintain itself by adopting the most savage, anti-democratic and lawless actions. In this way they unwittingly acknowledged the weaknesses of slavery.

In 1855 a Pro-Slavery Convention was held at Lexington, Missouri, in which this argument was spelt out. The Emigrant Aid societies, the delegates agreed, would not shrink from the use of violence and would not hesitate to stir up servile insurrections. This would of course, as one of them put it, "be fatal to the peace and security of the neighboring State of Missouri", as well as that of Kansas. Another speaker announced that Missouri's slaveholders would not "wait until the torch is applied to our dwellings, or the knife to our throats, before we take measures for our security and the security of our firesides". Inaction would mean the loss of "twenty five million dollars worth of [slave] property".[16]

So action was essential. But what action should be taken? From the premise that a "negro-thief" was no better than a horse-thief or a burglar, it followed that "slaveholding communities have just the same rights to take all *necessary measures of defence, whether legal or extra-legal, judicial or extra-judicial* [emphasis added], against a negro-thief, or an organized band of negro thieves, as they have a right to take, and are universally acknowledged to have a right to take, against horse-thieves, or house thieves". Otherwise the danger was of a "servile war". At all costs slaveholders must prevent this possibility, "peaceably if we can, forcibly if we must". Thus the right of self-defence was invoked.[17]

Slaveholders were acutely aware of the dangers of their slaves running away, with consequent financial loss to themselves. But this was

[16] *Address to the People of the United States, Together with the Proceedings and Resolutions of the Pro-Slavery Convention of Missouri, Held at Lexington, July 1855* (St. Louis, MO, 1855), pp. 7, 23.

[17] [James Shannon], *An Address Delivered Before the Pro-Slavery Convention of the State of Missouri…July 13, 1855, on Domestic Slavery* (St. Louis, MO, 1855), pp. 27–28.

not the worst evil. For "other slaves are thereby induced to make like attempts" and "a hatred for their masters, whom they begin to regard as their oppressors, is thus begotten; and this, too, often is followed by arson and murder". Moreover antislavery agitation in Kansas, especially if it were successful, would stimulate and bring into the open those within Missouri who had abolitionist goals but "who now from policy hide their hellish designs". In these circumstances such niceties as due process and the rule of law must be discarded. Since no laws existed to prevent the lethally dangerous talk of the abolitionist, the law must be set aside. For "in a slaveholding community the expression of such sentiments is a positive act more criminal, more dangerous, than kindling the torch of the incendiary, mixing the poison of the assassin". Once again the right of self-defence was invoked. This time a comparison was made with bloodthirsty Indians. The New Englanders sent by the Emigrant Aid societies were "to us as would be a band of Blackfeet or Camanches who should encamp upon our borders for the avowed purpose of stealing our cattle and horses, of plundering our farms and villages". It followed that "we are not bound to wait until they have 'stolen our negroes', 'burned our slaveholding towns'". Was it not obvious that "robbers and murderers have no right to call upon the law for protection"? Faced with these dangers the Missourians professed astonishment that their conduct should have elicited any criticism whatever.[18]

These arguments were advanced by highly eminent Missourians. David Rice Atchison, leader of the "border ruffians", was a former U.S. Senator and equally prominent in the group were a former Attorney-General of Missouri and a Justice of the Missouri Supreme Court. Moreover defences were also made in Congress of the actions of the Missourians. Senators from Virginia and Mississippi attributed the problems of the territory to the character of the northerners who had moved there. The Missourians had merely acted in self-defence.[19]

[18] *Negro Slavery, No Evil: or the North and the South: A Report Made to the Platte County Self-Defensive Association* (St. Louis, MO, 1854), pp. 4–8; William W. Freehling, *The Road to Disunion: Secessionists at Bay* (New York, 1990), p. 549; Peter G. Camden, *A Common-Sense, Matter-of-Fact Examination and Discussion of Negro Slavery in the United States* (St. Louis, MO, 1855), p. 14.

[19] *Congressional Globe*, 35th Congress, 1st Session, Appendix, p. 78; M. W. Cluskey, ed. *Speeches, Messages, and Other Writings of the Hon. Albert Gallatin Brown, A Senator in Congress from the State of Mississippi* (Philadelphia, 1859), pp. 497–498, 545.

Nor was the recourse to extra-legal action in Missouri out of line with practice in other slaveholding states. The slaveholders of South Carolina, for example, prided themselves on their cultivation and refinement, fostered within a community radically different from anything that could be found on the frontier. But their attitude towards abolitionists, or suspected abolitionists, was very similar. Throughout the South extra-legal actions were recommended to combat the abolitionist threat and they were seen as entirely appropriate, fully justified by reference to the fundamental and unchallengeable right of self-defence.[20]

In this way, therefore, slavery's weakness had resulted in recourse to extra-legal activities, the abandonment of due process and the repudiation of civil liberties.

The events in Kansas were so dramatic, controversial and powerful in their impact because of the attitudes of the Missourians who felt themselves driven to act in the way they did by what we can now recognise as the weaknesses of slavery. In this way those weaknesses, making themselves felt on this occasion in Missouri but characteristic of slavery throughout the nation, generated the deep conflict seen in Kansas.

Much of what the Missourians did, and which other southerners either excused or applauded, was in response not so much to what the slaves had done or were doing but rather to what they *might* do. It was the potential for resistance on the part of the slaves, rather than simply the resistance itself, which southerners responded to. But whether actual or potential and whether the slaveholders recognised the fact or not, that resistance stemmed from one basic fact: the slaves did not want to be slaves. The ensuing conflict as it erupted in Kansas in the mid-1850s destroyed the second party system and transformed national politics.

[20] See, for example, *Governor Hammond's Letters on Southern Slavery: Addressed to Thomas Clarkson* (n.p., n.d.), p. 7; Steven A. Channing, *Crisis of Fear: Secession in South Carolina* (New York, 1974), pp. 31, 38–42; [John Townsend], *The South Alone, Should Govern the South* (Charleston, SC, 1860), p. 43; Lynda Lasswell Crist et al., eds. *The Papers of Jefferson Davis* 11 vols (Baton Rouge, LA, 1971–), V, p. 84.

6

NORTH AND SOUTH, REPUBLICAN AND DEMOCRAT

I

The Pierce and the Buchanan years were dominated by first the Kansas–Nebraska Act then the subsequent developments in Kansas itself. They were not, however, the only events of these years, nor even the only attempts made at this time to strengthen slavery in the South. Pierce's victory in 1852 immediately heralded the return of at least one highly controversial policy of the 1840s, one which had had both a partisan and a sectional dimension. In the 1840s the Democrats had sought to expand the nation's territory; in the 1850s under first Pierce then Buchanan, the same goals were apparent.

In his inaugural Franklin Pierce declared that his administration would "not be controlled by any timid forebodings of evil from expansion". According to the new President, "our attitude as a nation and our position on the globe render the acquisition of certain possessions not within our jurisdiction eminently important for our protection". Within two years the policy bore fruit. James Gadsden had been sent to Mexico to negotiate the purchase of yet more territory from that hapless nation. Somewhat to Pierce's disappointment, Gadsden managed to obtain only the small (by the standards of previous American acquisitions) area around the Gila River. Even this, however, proved more than many northern Senators were prepared to accept, given that the administration's objective seemed to entail the expansion of slavery. The area covered by the Gadsden purchase was accordingly reduced still further.[1]

---

[1] James D. Richardson, ed. *A Compilation of the Messages and Papers of the Presidents 1789–1897* (Washington DC, 1899), V, p. 198.

This, however, was only the start of the administration's expansionist plans, though it proved to be the end of its expansionist successes. Pierce, like many other Democrats, also had his eye upon Cuba, currently a Spanish colony. Many Americans, especially southerners, believed that it was indeed the "manifest destiny" of the United States to annex Cuba and there were filibustering attempts almost every year in the 1850s.[2]

The lure of Cuba resulted in one of the most extraordinary documents in the history of American foreign policy. The Ostend Manifesto was an initially confidential memorandum, drawn up in October 1854 by Pierre Soulé of Louisiana, James Mason of Virginia and James Buchanan of Pennsylvania, ambassadors representing the nation at Madrid, Paris and London respectively. Following leaks, however, it had to be made public. It urged the annexation of Cuba with all possible speed, partly on the grounds that the island "naturally" belonged to the United States. Spain should thus sell it forthwith. But what if Spain should foolishly refuse to do so? The three Ministers then explained that the United States should take Cuba by force and, moreover, had a clear moral right, if not a duty, to do so. To those who failed to discern any such right, the Ministers cited the right of self-preservation.

Here the vulnerability of slavery, deriving once again from the fact that the slaves did not want to be slaves, again came decisively into play. The Ministers made it clear that they feared that slavery in Cuba was under threat. Cuba might "become a second St. Domingo with all its attendant horrors to the white race". This, however, would mark only the beginning of the problem, since the danger was that "the flames" would "extend to our own neighboring shores, seriously to endanger or actually to consume the fair fabric of our Union". Indeed "the Union can never enjoy repose, nor possess reliable security, as long as Cuba is not embraced within its boundaries".[3]

---

[2] See Robert E. May, *The Southern Dream of a Caribbean Empire* (Gainesville, FL, 2002), pp. 26, 29. See also, on a related issue, Edward Rugemer, *The Problem of Emancipation: The Caribbean Roots of the American Civil War* (Baton Rouge, LA, 2008). Filibustering is the process by which adventurers seek to overthrow regimes by force, without the explicit or legal backing of another government.

[3] The Manifesto may be found in *House Executive Documents*, 33rd Congress, 2nd Session, X, pp. 127–136 or alternatively at http://www.historyofcuba.com/history/havana/Ostend2.htm. The reference to Santo Domingo was of course to the bloodshed that had characterised the slave uprising of 1791 in Haiti.

The Ostend Manifesto, since it urged a resort to naked force in the event that Spain refused to sell Cuba, was immediately denounced by Republicans (and those who were soon to become Republicans) and others as a disgrace to the nation. Yet his support for it did nothing to prevent James Buchanan from receiving the Democratic nomination for President a little more than a year later. Indeed it probably helped his cause. And during his presidency Buchanan too called for negotiations to purchase Cuba. Finally in 1860 both the northern and the southern wings of the Democratic party urged annexation of the island. But all these efforts proved utterly futile. As far as the United States was concerned, Cuba at the time of the Civil War remained an object of desire rather than a possession.

The attempts to acquire Cuba, whether by force or purchase, were not the only examples of a widespread craving for further territorial expansion. William Walker of Tennessee was the most prominent, and for a time the most successful, filibuster in American history. Walker was one of several Americans who led filibustering attempts on parts of Mexico but his most remarkable success came in Nicaragua where he actually managed for a time to install himself as its head of government. In May 1856 his regime was even recognised by President Pierce. In a successful bid to recruit southern support, Walker legalised slavery in Nicaragua. For a time he was able to bask in the adoration of slavery expansionists throughout the South, but his triumph was short-lived. In 1860 he met his end at the hands of a firing squad.

It is important to note the links between these expansionist initiatives and both the Democratic party and slavery. Not only was the Ostend Manifesto impeccably Democratic in its authorship (though an embarrassment even to many confirmed expansionists in the party), Democrats frequently applauded filibusters like Walker, who received a ringing endorsement from the party's national convention in 1856.[4]

Some of those who supported expansion into Cuba (and elsewhere) did so without reference to slavery, citing the traditions of "Manifest Destiny", the need to maintain the agrarian republic and the importance of spreading "democracy" and "liberty" throughout the western hemisphere. Nor did all southern proslavery spokesmen support expansion. South Carolinians in particular as well as southern militants like

---

[4] May, *Southern Dream of Caribbean Empire*, p. 100.

William Lowndes Yancey of Alabama questioned the desirability of further territorial annexations, partly because of their racially inspired doubts about the indigenous populations who came with the territory. So territorial expansion in the 1850s cannot be equated with the desire to strengthen southern slavery.

Nevertheless this desire was what gave the movement its momentum. The fear that slavery would be assailed in Cuba was, as we have noted and as many southerners freely acknowledged, a key, and probably the key reason the island was coveted. Other southerners stressed that more territory was needed to strengthen slavery economically. Even more important, in the eyes of many of them, was the familiar need to acquire more territory and thus more slave states in order to combat northern political power. As ever southerners were acutely aware of the growing imbalance between North and South in the federal government. And this imbalance, of course, as they also did not hesitate to warn their fellow southerners, opened up the possibility of the abolition of slavery throughout the South, carried out in accordance with the terms of an amended Federal Constitution.

The links with the Democratic party reveal once again the party's symbiosis with slavery. The Ostend Manifesto with its overt references to the dangers of abolition in Cuba revealed once again the extent to which democratic and Democratic ideals were being subordinated to, or reshaped and modified by, the need to protect slavery. In the 1840s it had been possible to furnish a patriotic appeal to northerners and southerners alike on behalf of "Manifest Destiny". By the 1850s this was no longer possible, partly because northerners, it was realised, having had to stomach the Kansas–Nebraska Act, were disinclined to welcome other projects that might result in the extension of slavery.

Similarly the desire for additional territory in the 1850s revealed the failure of Democrats to understand the nature of the sectional controversy that now threatened to overwhelm them. By the mid-1850s an alternative perspective on the nation's territorial expansion might have suggested itself. The Louisiana Purchase had, after all, generated a deep sectional crisis over the admission of Missouri. In the 1840s the Mexican cession had brought the nation closer than it had ever been to dissolution. In the mid-1850s the attempt to organise another area of the Louisiana Purchase, Kansas and Nebraska, had raised sectional animosities to a still higher pitch. Yet as late as 1860 Democrats continued to believe that territorial acquisitions would strengthen nationalistic feeling and even serve as an antidote to sectional animosity. By the 1850s a huge weight of evidence to the contrary had accumulated. Experience counted for little when it challenged the orthodoxies, or perhaps we should say the dogmas, of the Democratic faith.

II

If the drive for additional territory, whether in Kansas or in Latin America, on which to plant or protect slavery, was a major concern of southerners in the 1850s, it was not the only sign of their anxieties about their future within the Union. From the 1840s onwards many southerners began to fret about the dependence upon, or even, as some of them would have it, their economic inferiority to, the North. We have already noted that the South by 1850 lagged far behind the North according to all the principal indices of economic development. In the 1850s although the southern performance did improve in absolute terms, the lag in most respects became still more pronounced. By 1860 the North had more than twice as many miles of railroad per square mile of territory or per capita than the South. In that year the South had only one sixth of the nation's total manufacturing capacity. Immigrants continued to shun the region so that in population too, the South was falling far behind.

What was to be done? In the late 1840s and early 1850s there were frequent calls for industrialisation in the South. Southern commercial conventions were held in which the gospel of industrial development was preached. In 1846 J. G. B. De Bow launched *De Bow's Review*, intended to voice these aspirations. But once again, the success of cotton, as prices recovered then rose in the 1850s, encouraged southerners to cling to the familiar ways of agriculture. Many of them continued to harbour fears of immigrants in their midst, to view large cities with trepidation and to believe that slaves were, for a variety of reasons, best suited to agriculture. The result was that by the mid-1850s there were fewer voices calling for diversification in the South.

Overall the 1850s were years of rapid economic growth throughout the nation. But in August 1857 this process was suddenly interrupted. News that an Ohio insurance company was about to collapse triggered a sudden financial crisis as stocks fell, banks failed, land and commodity prices collapsed. In effect a speculative bubble that had been forming for some time suddenly burst.[5] If the economic effects had been as significant as those that had followed the Panic of 1837, the political ramifications might have been momentous. But the nation recovered comparatively quickly. Moreover the South escaped especially lightly, more lightly than the North, where in some states (such as Pennsylvania) the effects were somewhat more prolonged, though still not on the scale of the early 1840s. Southerners were delighted; it strengthened their confidence in slavery and in cotton. "Cotton is king", boasted James Hammond of South Carolina a few months later. Without it, he predicted, Britain would collapse and carry with her the entire civilised world – except the South. In these circumstances, why should the South seek to diversify?[6]

Reflecting these changes, the southern commercial conventions of the late 1850s began to consider other topics. If the calls for diversification were prompted by a feeling of economic inferiority, enhanced prosperity now opened up a new possibility, equally disturbing to many southerners. Reflecting the flush times, the price of slaves had soared in the 1850s, and the result was that a decreasing number of southern families, now only about one in four, could afford them. Here was a powerful potential threat to slavery. The slaveholders had always known that their regime depended utterly upon the acquiescence of the non-slaveholding whites. If high slave prices threatened to exclude those whites from the benefits of slave ownership, then could their loyalty be maintained? Many southerners doubted it, and the southern commercial conventions of the late 1850s were dominated by a new proposal: the demand for the reopening of the African slave trade, closed since 1808.[7]

This was probably the most extreme demand made by southerners during the entire history of the sectional conflict. The horrors of the "Middle Passage" (the journey across the ocean to the Americas) had been recognised even by southern proslavery apologists. But in the 1850s

---

[5] Allan Nevins, *The Emergence of Lincoln: Douglas, Buchanan and Party Chaos, 1857–1859* (New York, 1950), pp. 187–197; William Shade, *Banks or No Banks: The Money Issue in Western Politics 1832–1865* (Detroit, 1972), p. 201.

[6] *Selections from the Letters and Speeches of the Hon. James H. Hammond of South Carolina* (New York, 1866), pp. 311–322.

[7] On the movement to reopen the trade, see Ashworth, *Slavery, Capitalism and Politics in the Antebellum Republic* vol 1, *Commerce and Compromise, 1820–1850* (Cambridge, England, 1995), pp. 262–279.

as in increasing numbers they trumpeted the virtues of slavery, they were driven forward by their own logic. If slavery were good for the slaves, then why not extend its benefits to tens of thousands more Africans, whose material and moral welfare would thus be promoted? Indeed was it not hypocritical, even sinful, to have closed the slave trade?

Even northern Democrats drew the line here. Moreover the drive to reopen the African slave trade divided the Lower from the Upper South. Slaveholders in the Upper South wanted a high price for slaves, not only so that they could sell their slaves further south should the need arise, but also because they feared that low prices might make the institution unviable in their states and thus promote manumission on a large scale. Moreover the logic of the proslavery position pointed in opposite directions. If the slaves in the South had indeed been "civilised", then what would be the effect of unleashing several hundred thousand "uncivilised" blacks, fresh from Africa, among them? Some slaveholders, however militant they might be, shuddered at the thought. For these reasons, the campaign to reopen the slave trade, even though it received support from some highly eminent southerners, did not manage to unite the South let alone the nation, and the ban on slave importations remained in place.

III

The movement to reopen the African slave trade, together with the demand for additional territory for slavery, were both products, as well as additional causes, of the escalating sectional conflict. They both bore testimony to the deepening divide between North and South. This divide was also finding expression in the patterns of trade within and between the different regions of the nation.

In the 1840s and especially the 1850s, the economies of the North East and North West were becoming increasingly interdependent, in both absolute and relative terms. At the same time the economies of North and South were becoming, at least in relative terms, less interdependent.[8] Thus the canals that were built in these and the preceding decades were not only overwhelmingly concentrated in the North,

---

[8] For a different view, see James Huston, *Calculating the Value of the Union: Slavery, Property Rights and the Economic Origins of the Civil War* (Chapel Hill, NC, 2003).

they also tended to carry freight from west to east. The Erie Canal for example, had long been an example of this but by the end of the 1850s it was, for the first time, matching the amount of trade carried down the Mississippi and Ohio rivers. And while the South remained largely self-sufficient in foodstuffs, the North East was by now heavily dependent on food brought in from the North West. The railroads played a huge role here. And when north-eastern manufactured goods left the region, they went, for the most part, not to the South but instead overwhelmingly to the North West. In effect a highly productive interaction between an agricultural North West and a rapidly industrialising North East was developing.[9] This was reflected in the character of northern industrialism. The vanguard sector in the northern industrial revolution was not textiles, in which southern cotton played a huge role, but rather agricultural machinery, where the role of the South, in terms of both production and consumption, was virtually negligible. Hence the agricultural implements industry, which produced ploughs, reapers, mowers, threshing-machines and the like, was of enormous importance on the American path to industrialism. The sector was highly dynamic and it facilitated great productivity gains in western agriculture. According to one estimate, the value of agricultural implements manufactured in the West quadrupled in the 1850s, whereas in the same decade the value of those produced in the South declined absolutely.[10]

What was the political effect of these changes in interregional trade? In fact they operated to strengthen antislavery sentiment in the North. But this effect was not achieved directly by the creation of a narrowly economic imperative to dismantle slavery in the South. Instead the process operated indirectly by removing an impediment to the growth of

---

[9] Jeremy Atack and Peter Passell, eds. *A New Economic View of American History* (2nd ed., New York, 1994), p. 151; Albert Fishlow, "Antebellum Regional Trade Reconsidered", *American Economic Review* (1964) 352–364; Colleen Callahan and William Hutchinson, "Antebellum Regional Trade in Agricultural Goods: Preliminary Results", *Journal of Economic History* XL (1980) 25–32; Douglas North, *The Economic Growth of the United States, 1790–1860* (New York, 1961); North, "Location Theory and Regional Economic Growth", *Journal of Political Economy* LXII (1955) 243–258; Lawrence A. Herbst, "Interregional Commodity Trade from the North to the South and American Economic Development in the Antebellum Period", *Journal of Economic History* XXXV (1975) 264–270.

[10] Gavin Wright, *The Political Economy of the Cotton South: Households, Markets and Wealth in the Nineteenth Century* (New York, 1978), pp. 108–109; Nevins, *House Dividing*, pp. 165–166, 256; Charles Post, "The American Road to Capitalism", *New Left Review* 133 (1982) 30–51.

antislavery in the North. As we have seen, the spread of wage labour generated a series of ideological shifts in the North, as a result of which slavery increasingly seemed, on political, moral and economic grounds, profoundly unsatisfactory and alien, and its extension unacceptable. Here was a complex process that involved the relations of wage workers to their employers, the relations of slaves to their masters, and, as it were, the relations between the relations. This network of relationships and interests was a disruptive force, a centrifugal tendency within the Republic. But the economic ties between North and South had traditionally operated as a counter-tendency. The growth of northern antislavery sentiment had been constrained by the economic ties between North and South which gave many northerners a stake in the continued success of southern slavery. But as those ties became less important relatively and the northern interests which depended upon them lost ground politically, a barrier to the further growth of antislavery in the North was removed. The increased integration between North East and North West and the diminishing importance of northern trade with the South would find political expression in the decline of the "Cotton Whigs" and the rise of the Republican party.

IV

At the same time as northern antislavery sentiment was deepening, increasingly extreme defences of slavery were being made in the South. In the 1850s they went even beyond the claim that African slavery was a better foundation for a society and an economy than free labour.

The most celebrated, or notorious, though not the only, exponent of these views was George Fitzhugh of Virginia. Fitzhugh wrote a number of influential articles in *De Bow's Review* and elsewhere, together with two remarkable books in which he took extreme proslavery ground. Whilst the vast majority of southern defenders of slavery argued that slavery for blacks was not only compatible with, but actually a guarantor of, freedom for whites, Fitzhugh instead argued that slavery was appropriate for whites as well as blacks. Although he did not go so far as to suggest that in the United States at present there was a need to enslave whites, he explicitly challenged, and even mocked, the idea that slavery was solely for those of a different race. After all, he reminded southerners, they were eager to cite the precedent of slavery in biblical times as a justification for contemporary chattel slavery. But slavery in antiquity had not entailed the enslavement of one race by another. Fitzhugh's fate was that often experienced by a fearless though impractical logician: he scored many points against his adversaries (the defenders of an exclusively race-based slavery) but could scarcely convince them of the practicality of his favoured alternative.[11]

V

Meanwhile in the North, the slaveholders' allies were encountering greater difficulties than ever before. Northern Democrats in the 1850s were, as they had been since the time of Jefferson, their principal defenders. As such these northerners were not required to approve of slavery in the abstract, still less to advocate measures like the reopening of the African slave trade. Least of all were they expected to defend slavery in accordance with the doctrines of George Fitzhugh, that is to say, without regard to race. Nevertheless the demands that were made of them by southerners in the 1850s ultimately destroyed the party's dominant position in the North. What then was the basis of the party's appeal from the mid-1850s onwards?

As we have noted, Democrats had traditionally been opposed to the intrusion of moral questions into politics. As we have seen, they had therefore been more resistant to the temperance crusade than any other major grouping in the North, though it would be wrong to assume that they were totally impervious to its appeal. So with immigrants. Democrats had traditionally defended immigrants throughout the nation and in the 1850s, when the Know Nothings politicised immigration as never before, northern Democrats, though again making compromises in some states and on some issues, continued to play this role. In effect they stood for cultural and ethnic pluralism in the North.[12]

---

[11] Fitzhugh's main works were *Sociology for the South, or the Failure of Free Society* (New York, n.d.) and *Cannibals All! or, Slaves Without Masters* (new ed. C. Vann Woodward, Cambridge, MA, 1960). For a critique of Fitzhugh, see Eugene D. Genovese, *The World the Slaveholders Made: Two Essays in Interpretation* (rev. ed., New York, 1988), pp. 115–244. For a critique of Fitzhugh and Genovese, see Ashworth, *Slavery, Capitalism and Politics*, I, pp. 228–246.

[12] The northern Democrats in the 1850s have received too little attention from historians. See Ashworth, *Slavery, Capitalism and Politics in the Antebellum Republic* vol 2, *The Coming of the Civil War 1850–1861* (Cambridge, 2007), pp. 339–470;

At the same time as they defended the immigrant, however, they heaped scorn upon the nation's racial minorities. By the 1850s little attention was paid to the Native Americans, now largely relocated beyond the Mississippi. But the place of free blacks in the North, and of course, of slaves and slavery throughout the nation, was under scrutiny as never before. Democrats were responsible for most, though not all, of the racist utterances made by northerners in the years preceding the Civil War. Northern Democrats sought to frighten northern voters, especially after the advent of the Republican party, by raising the spectre of millions of freed slaves moving north and stealing their jobs, their wives, their daughters. Democratic racism was unqualified and unashamed. According to the *National Democratic Review* the black race was unlike any other: it was always in servitude when in contact with another race. "The cause...of this unvarying condition of the African, through every age, can only be found", the editor concluded, "in *an inherent, ineradicable mental inferiority to every other people*" (italics in original). Nor were these utterances confined to the lower echelons of the party. Leaders like Pierce and Douglas entertained very similar sentiments. In the 1850s as northern Democrats offered a warm welcome to Caucasian immigrants, they shunned blacks, whether free or enslaved.[13]

This rejection of the nation's racial minorities was central to the party's image and its rhetoric in the 1850s. It was not, of course, its only appeal. Northern Democrats, as we have seen, were keen to embrace territorial expansion, usually without reference to the expansion of slavery. At the same time the party continued to stand for state's rights and limited government. In the immediate aftermath of the Panic of 1857, there was a flurry of interest in the economic questions that had traditionally separated Democrat from Whig. Some Democrats, including President Buchanan, now opened fire on the nation's banking system. But for a variety of reasons the party battles of the 1830s and 1840s could not be re-enacted. In the first place the Republican party, comprising both former Whigs and former Democrats, did not (and probably could not,

---

Jean H. Baker, *Affairs of Party: The Political Culture of Northern Democrats in the Mid-Nineteenth Century* (Ithaca, NY, 1983); Bruce W. Collins, "The Ideology of the Ante-Bellum Northern Democrats", *Journal of American Studies* XI (1977) 103–121; Yonatan Eyal, *The Young America Movement and the Transformation of the Democratic Party, 1828–1861* (New York, 2007).

[13] *National Democratic Review* I (1856) 185–193.

given its composition) defend the banking system as wholeheartedly as the Whigs had done in previous decades. In the second place the rapid economic recovery meant that the issue of slavery, with all its ramifications, continued to dominate the political agenda. Thus although the Panic might have given the Democrats an additional set of policies with which to appeal to the northern electorate, its effects were too limited in both scale and duration.

As a result northern Democrats were left in an unenviable position. Saddled with responsibility for the passage of the Kansas–Nebraska Act, they were easily blamed for all the disturbances and departures from standard democratic practice that characterised that territory's early years. More generally, as Republicans denounced the Slave Power with increasing vehemence, northern Democrats found themselves squeezed. The demands made by southerners gave them a cruel dilemma: to acquiesce risked huge and increasing unpopularity in the North; to resist meant alienating their principal allies and, in effect, destroying their hopes of victory in federal politics. From this dilemma there could be no escape.

The need to conciliate the South had still more profound effects. Whereas the Republicans, as we shall see, developed a vision of northern society which catered to the ambitions and aspirations of the northern electorate, by the 1850s northern Democrats lacked an analysis of the northern labour system. Whereas Republicans talked of social mobility, of the dignity of labour, of incentives as key features of a free-labour system, Democrats had little to say on these matters. Their tolerance for slavery in the South was both cause and effect of their lack of understanding of, or even interest in, these subjects. Unlike the Republicans they were unable to articulate a vision of northern society which would focus upon its strengths and upon what it offered to large numbers of northerners. As a result northern Democrats missed a development in the North whose significance can scarcely be exaggerated. Northerners were coming to believe, in ever-increasing numbers, not merely that the values of free (and wage) labour were of great importance but that they were the values of the nation as a whole. In effect the legitimation of northern society was, for these northerners, increasingly in terms of free labour. If its values were those of the nation, then the spread of slavery into new territories was a subject of the profoundest importance to every American, and not merely, as Democratic devotees of popular sovereignty argued, to those who lived in those territories. Indeed, as we shall see, many northerners were coming to identify democracy itself with the values of free labour.

Northern Democrats, however, continued to view the enemies of slavery as Jefferson had done a generation earlier: they were unreconstructed Federalists in disguise, precisely as the Whigs and the National Republicans had been in previous decades. But this was a profound error. Republicans were instead the representatives of an emergent northern social order, one which celebrated free labour in the North and which was profoundly hostile to slavery in the South. Far from being anti-democrats, they were the spokesmen for a newly emerging American democratic ethos, one which threatened to overwhelm the party of Franklin Pierce, James Buchanan and Stephen A. Douglas.

VI

As northern hostility to slavery deepened in the final years of the antebellum Republic, a subtle shift occurred. In the past the Democratic party had successfully discredited and disabled antislavery sentiment.[14] In the 1850s, however, a tipping point was reached as antislavery increasingly discredited and disabled the Democratic party. The party's southern orientation became ever more apparent and ever more of a liability as the southern wing, desperate to find a way of reconciling slavery and the Union, asked more and more of its northern allies. Thus what had been an implicit or covert defence of slavery and the South now became increasingly explicit and overt. One consequence was the dramatic haemorrhaging of electoral support in the North. In 1852 Pierce had carried every northern state but two; in 1856 the Republicans won every northern state but five (out of sixteen). In 1858 the woeful state of the Democratic party in the North was confirmed; the party elected only thirty-two Congressmen. The Republicans had 116.

VII

What did the new party stand for? The Republicans were not a single-issue party, opposed merely to the spread of slavery into the territories.

---

[14] Democrats had traditionally denounced antislavery agitators as enemies of the Constitution and of the Union; this had served to discredit them and largely disable their cause.

Nor were they monolithic. Before examining their principles and their electoral appeal, we should note the party's composition. Four groups of Republicans can be discerned. First of all were the radicals, men like Charles Sumner, Benjamin Wade or Owen Lovejoy. Then there were conservatives like Edward Bates, Orville Browning and William Evarts (some of whose attachment to the party was often only lukewarm). Between these two groups stood moderates like Abraham Lincoln of Illinois or William Pitt Fessenden of Maine. Finally there was a self-conscious contingent of former Democrats, known as Democratic-Republicans, in the party, among whom were numbered David Wilmot, Preston King and William Cullen Bryant. Each group brought its own specific set of concerns and its own priorities to the new party.[15]

The late 1850s was in part the story of the conversion of large numbers of northerners, especially those residing in the Lower North, to the Republican party. Thus the party underwent some changes even in the few years between its inception and its momentous triumph in 1860. Nevertheless its core principles can easily be delineated.

To begin with, nativism had some impact on the new party, though not as much as some historians have claimed. Despite their strong showing in 1856, the Republicans clearly needed to broaden their appeal, especially to those of a conservative disposition who had feared the divisive effect of a Republican victory and who might accordingly have supported the Know Nothing (or American) candidate Millard Fillmore. Thus Pennsylvania was something of a nativist stronghold and it was also a state that Republicans believed they would need to carry in 1860. In 1857 and 1858 they coalesced with other groups to combat the Democrats and displayed mildly nativist sympathies. But in terms of policies the Pennsylvania Republicans had to concede very little to their nativist allies. As one historian puts it, Republicans "avoided open expressions of hostility to foreigners". In Massachusetts the situation was somewhat different. Given the success of the Know Nothings earlier in the decade, many nativists hoped to enact their principal proposal, an extension of the naturalisation period to a full twenty-one years. But by 1858 they had to settle for two years, and the Republicans

---

[15] This is the typology employed in Eric Foner, *Free Soil, Free Labor, Free Men: The Ideology of the Republican Party before the Civil War* (New York, 1970). I have discussed Republican ideology at some length in *Slavery, Capitalism and Politics*, II, pp. 173–336.

were, as a party, unwilling to tolerate any longer period, though they were prepared to support a literacy test for voting. This was a genuine indication of the persistence of nativist principles within the Republican party.[16]

Elsewhere, however, even this modest concession to nativism was more than the Republicans were prepared to make. The Massachusetts two-year amendment elicited a chorus of disapproval from large numbers of western Republicans, who viewed nativism as not merely unprincipled but also electorally calamitous, given the numbers of immigrants resident in the West.[17] It was not adopted in any other state. Nevertheless in some other states, primarily in the East, nativists continued to display strength. In New York, for example, the Republicans consented to a registry law, intended to prevent illegal voting by immigrants. But apart from the registry law and a few offices, nativists got little from the Republicans and by 1860 had been swallowed up by them. And even the registry law was an extremely mild measure, falling well short of the old nativist demand for a twenty-one-year naturalisation period. By 1860 the situation in New York was typical of that in the North as a whole: nativism was no stronger than it had been a decade earlier, before the Know Nothing upsurge. Its real influence on the Republican party is suggested by the fact that the leading Republican in the 1850s, William Seward of New York, was as hostile to nativism as any politician in the land. When Abraham Lincoln replaced Seward as the party's effective leader, it was now headed by another confirmed, though perhaps less ostentatious, opponent of the Know Nothings. Finally the Republican platform of 1860 contained a clear repudiation of nativist principles.[18]

If nativism played only a minor role in the Republican appeal, the party was nevertheless identified with some economic policies that acquired prominence in some parts of the North. Following the Panic of 1857 Republicans were under renewed pressure to present a coherent

---

[16] Tyler Anbinder, *Nativism and Slavery: The Northern Know-Nothings and the Politics of Antislavery* (New York, 1992), pp. 247–253, 261–64; Michael F. Holt, *Forging a Majority: The Formation of the Republican Party in Pittsburg, 1848–1860* (New Haven, CT, 1969), p. 288; Dale Baum, *The Civil War Party System: The Case of Massachusetts* (Chapel Hill, NC, 1984) pp. 11, 45.

[17] These included Lincoln, Chase, Trumbull together with important Republican newspapers like the *Chicago Tribune* and the *Ohio State Journal* – Foner, *Free Soil, Free Labor, Free Men*, p. 251.

[18] Anbinder, *Nativism and Slavery*, pp. 237, 253–259.

economic programme to the electorate. To some extent this challenge was met. Thus the party stepped up its demands for a Homestead Act, which would give free land to settlers in the West. This measure pre-dated the emergence of the Republicans, but the party seized upon it with enthusiasm. It reflected the changing patterns of inter-regional trade, specifically the greater integration between North East and North West, and it was almost certainly a significant vote-winner, especially in the West. Northern Democrats too tended to support the measure, but they were encumbered by their southern wing, which objected to it as a device for spreading free labour across the West. Republicans accordingly made much of the fact that President Buchanan, acting at the behest of southern Democrats (to whom he owed his position), vetoed a Homestead bill in the final months of his presidency.

Along with the Homestead Act, Republicans moved some way towards endorsing a protective tariff. Again the Panic of 1857 prompted renewed interest in the subject. In 1860 the party endorsed the protective principle but in very vague terms and without even using the word "protection". In Pennsylvania the party was presented as staunchly protectionist, but in that state even the Democrats had presented themselves in similar terms for a generation. True advocates of protection were privately disappointed by the Republican stance on the issue, and in some parts of the North it was even claimed that the party was committed to free trade.[19]

The reason for this ambiguity was straightforward. The former Democrats in the party came from a tradition that viewed the tariff as a device for transferring wealth from farmers to manufacturers and opposed it accordingly. Given its composition the Republican party in reality could not afford to take a strong line either for or against the tariff. Fortunately for the party's prospects in 1860, the economic recovery that took place in the late 1850s meant that except in the Middle Atlantic states, the tariff remained a secondary issue.

The final items of financial legislation favoured by the Republicans were internal improvements. The party strongly advocated the construction of a Pacific railroad together with river and harbour improvements that were "of a national character". Once again these measures were almost certainly vote-winners for the party, but the Pacific railroad

[19] Foner, *Free Soil, Free Labor, Free Men*, pp. 175–176.

commanded bipartisan support (though there was often disagreement as to the route it should take) and river and harbour improvements, though important in some localities, were never a central concern in the North as a whole.

VIII

Though not the sole issue on which it took a stand, slavery was nevertheless the primary concern of the Republican party before the Civil War. Republicans were, in effect, pledged to preventing its spread into the West (or into territories to the south not yet acquired). In 1856 and in 1860 the party officially committed itself to this policy, denying (in 1860) "the authority of congress, of a territorial legislature, or of any individuals, to give legal existence to slavery in any territory of the United States". As we shall see, there were many reasons for this hostility. But it is important to note that the non-extension of slavery meant different things to different Republicans. The more conservative among them resented in particular the fact that southerners, in pressing for the expansion of slavery, were distracting the nation from its true purposes. They believed that other issues should predominate in the federal government, issues connected with banks, tariffs, internal improvements, homesteads and the like. The federal government should be brought back to what ought to be its true concerns. A Republican victory would thus administer a rebuke to the South and to southerners' pretensions and would remove slavery from the national agenda. (Some of these conservatives might even have been content merely to see the Missouri Compromise restored and the Kansas–Nebraska Act thus repealed, but they accepted in the interests of party unity the more thoroughgoing demand for the prohibition of slavery in all territories.) This achieved, these Republicans would have been satisfied; they would then have left slavery as it was.

At the opposite extreme lay the radicals within the party. For them the prohibition of slavery in the territories was merely one measure, though assuredly an extremely important one, directed against the South. The radicals were political abolitionists; their programme was specifically intended to produce the abolition of slavery in the South. This would not happen immediately; it might take some considerable time. Nor would it be accomplished by a direct assault upon slavery, which the radicals acknowledged, often ruefully, would be unconstitutional. However, the same result could be achieved indirectly by divorcing the federal government from slavery. If restricted to the states in which it already existed, then slavery would ultimately, radicals were convinced, wither away. (Many of their southern enemies, it is important to note, shared this assumption.) Hence non-extension would ultimately mean abolition. "To restrict Slavery within its present limits", according to the New York *Tribune*, greatest of all antebellum newspapers, "is to secure its speedy decline and ultimate extinction".[20]

According to the radicals, moreover, the federal government could and should take other steps against slavery. Abolition in the District of Columbia should be undertaken, the Fugitive Slave law should be repealed or at least negated and, even more dramatically, the interstate slave trade should be prohibited. More than any other Republican, Salmon P. Chase of Ohio was the architect of the radical programme. "With these principles established", Chase announced, "and an administration based upon them, Slavery would come to a speedy end".[21]

As if this were not enough, the radicals argued strongly that if federal policy towards slavery were altered, then a tremendous impetus would be given to the antislavery movement within the South itself. "Who", Chase asked, "does not see that the divorce of the General Government from slavery...would exert a great moral influence for Freedom in those States?" As a result "the People of those States, encouraged by the example of the General Government, and stimulated by its legitimate influence", he predicted, "would themselves take up the work of enfranchisement; and slavery would disappear speedily, certainly, peacefully, from the whole land". Whether this would indeed have happened is something that historians can, of course, never know. However, the process that Chase and the radicals described was precisely the one that southerners themselves predicted and dreaded. Each group believed it would culminate in the abolition of slavery in the states. Thus by indirect and direct means, and gradually rather than immediately, abolition would be secured.[22]

This was an agenda that was far-reaching and truly radical in the most literal sense of the term. Not all Republicans shared it. What of the

[20] New York *Tribune*, 15 October 1856.
[21] Chase quoted in Foner, *Free Soil, Free Labor, Free Men*, p. 117.
[22] *Politics in Ohio: Senator Chase's Letter to Hon A. P. Edgerton* (n.p., n.d.), p. 15.

moderates, who held the balance of power within the party? Abraham Lincoln was the archetypal moderate. Though he did not advocate the repeal of the Fugitive Slave law and did not propose to prohibit the interstate slave trade, he fully shared the radical goal. The non-extension of slavery would, he argued, doom the institution, in the long term. In his famous "House Divided" speech of 1858, he stressed the need to place slavery where "the public mind shall rest in the belief that it is in course of ultimate extinction". Lincoln was extremely vague on the details and the timing of this process, but he wanted and expected slavery to die in the states of the South and was committed to policies which, he believed, would bring about that result.[23]

He and other Republicans were similarly vague when it came to the ultimate fate of the freed slaves. In common with many others in the party, Lincoln himself was, and remained for many years, committed to colonisation, essentially on the grounds that his fellow Americans were too prejudiced against the black race to allow full integration to take place. Some African-American leaders denounced this policy in unmeasured terms, insisting that the United States was their country as much as anyone's. Many abolitionists and some Republicans also rejected colonisation and were able to point to the enormous practical difficulties the scheme faced, as well as its moral shortcomings. But the antebellum Republican party essentially bequeathed this problem to the future.

The vital point, however, is that for those in the centre of the party the non-extension of slavery was sought not only as an end in itself but also as a means to a far more dramatic end: the destruction of slavery in the United States. This was not the goal of everyone in the party, but it was the goal of those who controlled it.

Why was slavery so objectionable? There were many reasons. It is convenient to place them into three categories: the economic, the political and the moral, though we should note that these categories are not watertight. We must also remember that the different groups within the party often placed different degrees of emphasis upon the different sets of criticisms.

---

[23] Roy F. Basler, ed. *The Collected Works of Abraham Lincoln* 9 vols (New Brunswick, NJ, 1953–1955), II, p. 515; Eric Foner, *The Fiery Trial: Abraham Lincoln and American Slavery* (New York, 2010).

For the radicals, the moral objections were uppermost. Their critique of slavery in this respect strongly resembled that put forward by abolitionists of the Garrison stripe. Radical Republicans, like Garrisonians, focussed upon the sufferings of the slaves themselves. They viewed slavery as nothing less than a monstrosity, an abomination in the eyes of God. Foremost among its nefarious effects, perhaps, was its impact upon the slave family, which lacked any legal foundation. "What rights", asked Horace Mann, "are more sacred or more dear to us than the conjugal and the parental?" When Charles Sumner in summary form listed the five main objections to slavery, no fewer than two concerned its impact upon the family.[24]

Radical Republicans also took their cue from Garrisonians in their emphasis upon the individual conscience. Slavery subjected the slave to the will of another and thus prevented him from following the dictates of his own conscience. Hence "slavery", again in the words of Horace Mann, "is an unspeakable wrong to the conscience". Moreover radical Republicans insisted that the Fugitive Slave law of 1850 should be repealed partly on the grounds that it required all citizens to aid in the recapture and return of fugitives, contrary to the promptings of their individual consciences. In this sense it was, according to Charles Sumner, a "detestable, Heaven-defying Bill".[25]

Here was the moral case against chattel slavery. Radical Republicans, like Garrisonians, were convinced that they were part of a crusade to end slavery in the Americas, and ultimately in the entire world. Transcendent moral forces were at work, against which legislative enactments such as the Fugitive Slave law of 1850 would ultimately prove futile and temporary. History, the radicals were convinced, was on their side.

IX

Conservative Republicans, although disliking slavery, did not dwell upon its moral shortcomings and indeed remained suspicious of moral crusades and moral crusaders. Democratic-Republicans similarly came from a tradition which frowned upon the intrusion of moral issues

---

[24] *Congresisonal Globe*, 30th Congress, 1st Session, Appendix, p. 841; *Works of Sumner*, IV, pp. 207–208.

[25] *Congressional Globe*, 30th Congress, 1st Session, Appendix, p. 841; *Works of Sumner*, II, p. 404.

into politics. Moreover the Democratic heritage was one that viewed the African American with considerable suspicion, even contempt. Democratic-Republicans like David Wilmot thus made no secret of their lack of compassion for the slave. Though Wilmot looked forward to a time when slavery would be abolished throughout the nation, he confessed that he was not motivated by a humanitarian concern for its victims.

The economic case against slavery, by contrast, united all Republicans, indeed virtually all Americans who expressed any hostility towards the institution. A tactic employed almost universally by party spokesmen in the 1850s was the comparison between pairs of states, one northern one southern, designed to demonstrate the relative merits of free and slave labour. The conclusion was always the same. As one Republican put it, "in schools, in churches, in manufacturers, in roads, in canals, in commerce, in domestic peace and security, in agriculture and in wealth, (upon soil where the natural advantages are equal), the free States uniformly excel".[26]

What explained this northern superiority? Republicans argued that slavery degraded labour. In a slave society, it was claimed, manual labour was all too often held in contempt. The result was to demoralise the labouring man. Republicans insisted that the non-slaveholding whites of the South were lazy and shiftless, not because of inherent moral or physiological shortcomings, but because southern society failed to honour labour. In the North by contrast, Republicans contended, all (or virtually all) forms of labour were esteemed. For this reason alone it was imperative that the territories be settled by free labour: their economic growth would be fatally stunted if slavery were allowed to pollute them.

Similarly slavery destroyed incentives. Republicans argued that free labour was inspired by hope, the hope of economic betterment. Many Republicans stressed the importance of social mobility and in so doing testified to the importance of the wage labourer in their thought.[27] But in a slave society this process was absent. Neither the slaves, who had no hope of rising in society, nor the non-slaveholding whites, to whom economic opportunity was systematically denied, would be inspired

[26] *Congressional Globe*, 35th Congress, 1st Session, Appendix, p. 273.
[27] See the final section of the conclusion to this volume.

to labour productively. Here was the reason the South lagged so far behind the North. Here too was a major reason for excluding slavery from the territories. The West must operate as a safety valve for the North, offering renewed economic opportunities to the labouring man, if and when conditions in the East became difficult. But for this safety valve to operate, slavery must be excluded. It was therefore not the case, as Democrats like Stephen A. Douglas liked to claim, that only the inhabitants of a territory were interested in the existence of slavery in their midst. Republicans instead emphasised that all northerners had a deep stake in the spread of free labour throughout the West. Little wonder that they wanted to offer free land to western settlers. A Homestead Act would ensure that slavery obtained no new foothold in the region.

X

Despite their many differences all the groups within the Republican party agreed on the economic indictment of slavery. Radicals (like Garrisonian abolitionists) were every bit as convinced of slavery's economic weaknesses as conservatives, moderates or former Democrats within the party. The main difference was that the radicals (again like Garrisonian abolitionists) did not attach as much importance to this economic critique. They believed that the moral arguments must be kept uppermost so that an appeal above all to the conscience of the nation could be made.

So with the political critique of slavery. This too was all but universal within the party, though once again the radicals subordinated it to the moral indictment. What then was the political case against slavery? It was encapsulated in one of the Republicans' key phrases, though one they had borrowed from the abolitionists: the Slave Power. According to Republicans slavery produced an aristocracy that controlled the South and which had already taken long strides towards achieving control over the entire nation. The Slave Power thus posed a profound threat to American democracy itself.

According to Republicans the Slave Power was "a vast material interest" that comprised all the slaveholders, or perhaps all the large slaveholders, of the South and that had begun to control the nation in recent decades. Republicans were struck by the way in which debate over slavery in the South, and especially the Deep South, had been curtailed or even completely silenced. Within their own states the slaveholders held unchallengeable sway. Almost without exception the non-slaveholders were kept out of high office. But the evils did not end there. Republicans also stressed southerners' power within the federal government. A favourite tactic here was to examine the historical record in order to demonstrate the disproportionate power wielded by southerners at Washington. They had held far more than their share of the major offices of state, from the presidency downwards.[28]

It was, however, in terms of federal policy that the damaging effects of slaveholder control had been most severe. Republicans remembered the gag rule, which had operated to prevent northerners from discussing antislavery petitions in the House of Representatives. They remembered too the annexation of Texas and the Fugitive Slave Act, both undertaken at the behest of the Slave Power. They recalled the threats of disunion, frequently employed to extort concessions from the North. Most of all, perhaps, they did not need reminding of the Kansas–Nebraska Act, whose passage was testimony to the slaveholders' ability to control even northerners as eminent as Stephen A. Douglas, together with all the evils that had flowed from its introduction, culminating in 1856 with "Bleeding Kansas" and "Bleeding Sumner".

The task of the Republican party was thus to check slaveholder aggressions and to preserve and purify the American democratic experiment. Once again the motives of the different groups of Republicans were distinct. Radicals believed that to destroy the Slave Power would be to destroy slavery itself. They were certain that the slaveholders desperately needed the Union. If the North ceased to comply with their excessive demands, and instead administered the federal government as the founders had intended, slavery, now denied federal support, would wither and die. Conservative Republicans, on the other hand, believed that a salutary check on southern aggressions would lead southerners to cease agitating the slavery issue. The nation would then be able to concentrate on more important issues. Nevertheless almost all Republicans believed that the Slave Power was a threat; the political indictment of slavery united virtually all of them.[29]

---

[28] *Congressional Globe*, 36th Congress, 1st Session, p. 593.
[29] Ashworth, *Slavery, Capitalism and Politics*, II, pp. 244–264.

XI

It is vital to recognise the importance of wage labour in generating Republican opposition to slavery. Some Republicans advocated policies like the Homestead Act in the hope that they would reduce the numbers of northerners who were employed for wages. This, however, was far from the typical Republican view; it was held by only a small minority within the party. Another minority of Republicans, probably a larger one, with Abraham Lincoln among them, extolled the wages system provided that the wage labourer was able to climb into the ranks of the self-employed or become an employer of others in his turn. These Republicans had a certain suspicion of the labourer who remained a labourer for life. Nevertheless they held that wage labour, even though it should be a temporary condition, was indispensably necessary to American democracy.[30] The majority of Republicans took still another view. They often equated free labour with wage labour and argued that even the wage worker who remained a wage worker throughout his life was in no sense degraded as a result. This was a ringing repudiation of the traditional view of wages. It was, moreover, an implicit repudiation of the Jeffersonian assumption that the ownership of productive property, and especially landed property, was essential to the maintenance of freedom, equality and American democracy. More than any previous major party in the nation's history then, the Republicans accepted, welcomed or extolled the wage system. Their antislavery convictions derived in good part from a sometimes implicit often explicit comparison between slavery and wage labour.

Moreover the Republicans were probably correct in their assessment of the importance of the wages system. Although this is not a question that economic historians have addressed, it is virtually certain that the gap that was widening every decade between North and South in terms of economic development and diversification reflected the spread of the wages system. To take only the most obvious example, manufacturing, in which the North, to the delight of Republicans, excelled, depended utterly on wage labour. It had no existence without it. The Republicans' economic critique of slavery was in good part the product of a society in which the wages system was coming to predominate.

[30] See the final section of the conclusion to this volume.

Finally we should note that the moral critique of slavery itself owed much to the spread of the wage system. The traditional assumption that the wage labourer was not a fit citizen for a republic was challenged by the sheer increase in their numbers. If the possession of productive, and especially landed, property was no longer necessary to anchor the individual in society and to maintain his loyalty, what was? The answer was not only economic opportunity and political freedoms (both threatened by slavery) but also the possession of a family and the right to act according to the dictates of the conscience. As northerners came to prize these qualities as the defining features of citizenship in the Republic, so slavery looked increasingly unacceptable.

It remains to summarise the party's governing idea, to rank Republican criticisms of slavery in order of importance and finally to identify and explain some of the errors in that world view. The core idea can be restated easily: it was that *slavery was an unnatural and inherently disorganising force.* It disorganised a community economically by disrupting what would otherwise be, in a free-labour society, the natural processes of growth and development. It disorganised a community politically by generating a ruling class, an aristocracy which, in order to maintain its control, was inevitably tyrannical. All Republicans shared these assumptions. Some, but not all, added that slavery disrupted a community morally too, not only because of the inhuman treatment accorded to the slave, but also because the inherent immorality of enslavement polluted the morals of the slaveholder as well as of those who were required to do his bidding.

Which of these criticisms was most important? Some historians have argued that this distinction belongs to the political critique.[31] Yet this conclusion is unwarranted, partly because the economic criticisms commanded equally wide acceptance within the party. More fundamentally, however, one must seek to explain the emergence and the spread of Republican ideas; this is the key question for all who seek to understand the origins of the Civil War.

How had the political critique emerged? Resentment of southern power had occasionally flared up prior to the 1830s, but at most times

---

[31] William E. Gienapp, "The Republican Party and the Slave Power", in Robert H. Abzug and Stephen E. Maizlish, eds. *New Perspectives on Race and Slavery in America* (Lexington, KY, 1986), pp. 51–78; Michael F. Holt, *The Political Crisis of the 1850s* (New York, 1978), pp. 189–190.

it had provoked relatively little controversy. In the 1830s, however, a new era opened. Southerners now sought to prevent discussion of slavery both in Congress via the Gag Law and in the States by restrictions on freedom of speech. They also sought to prevent the circulation through the federal mails of antislavery pamphlets in the South. Why did they take these actions? They were taken in response to three underlying fears: fears of the slaves themselves (who might be induced to rebel or flee), fears of the non-slaveholding whites of the South (who might challenge the privileged role of the slaveholder), fears of northern antislavery sentiment (which had entered a new and menacing phase with the emergence of the abolitionist crusade). Southerners believed that the threat from the North underlay the others. We now know, however, that they were mistaken. In reality the primary threat came from their slaves who refused to embrace their chains and passively accept their own enslavement.

Thus the initial southern actions, which gave rise to the Slave Power charge, were themselves the product of the weaknesses of southern slavery (which was vulnerable to the opposition of the slaves in so many ways) and the growth of abolitionism (which, it should be noted, stressed the moral rather than the political case against slavery). As a result, in the 1840s and 1850s, as we have seen, southerners took a further series of actions intended to protect themselves against the threats which surrounded them. The demand for Texas, the proposal to reopen the slave trade and the pressure to plant slavery in the territories – all were attempts to compensate for slavery's weaknesses. All, moreover, reflected not merely the growing strength of antislavery sentiment in the North, but also the obvious fact that the South was being outpaced by the North, in terms of both population and states. At this point, therefore, the economic weaknesses of slavery play a key role – in generating the political critique. For if the South had been able to keep pace with the North, then the growth of northern antislavery sentiment would have been of far less importance, and the actions taken to combat it – actions which fuelled the fear of the Slave Power – would not have seemed so necessary.

Thus the political critique was derivative of the other criticisms slavery attracted and of the weaknesses of slavery itself in the South. We should note, moreover, that one cannot reverse this equation; it is a mistake to assume that these different factors, because interdependent, should be weighted equally. The weaknesses of slavery, its vulnerability to the resentment of the slave and its failure to keep pace with the free-labour system of the North did not derive from the political objections raised against it.

What of the moral criticisms? Even though not all Republicans endorsed them, they were in fact more important than might be assumed. Southerners reacted so angrily to this moral assault not least because they believed that compromise with fanaticism was entirely futile. The moral absolutism of abolitionists and radical Republicans thus had an impact that was disproportionate to their numbers. Moreover the initial actions taken by southerners in the 1830s, the actions which fuelled the accusations concerning the Slave Power, were taken in response to the abolitionist critique of slavery, a critique in which moral considerations were uppermost. This too suggests a greater role for the moral critique than might at first be assumed.

Yet these moral arguments, which revolved around the violence that slavery did to both the individual conscience and the family, were themselves a function of the changes taking place within northern society and the northern economy. Southern slavery had not become in itself more immoral as the years passed, and even its enemies did not make this claim; rather northern society became increasingly intolerant of its long-standing moral shortcomings. As we have already observed, within northern society the increasing separation between work and home generated a view of the home as a refuge from the wider world and of the family as an irreplaceable, almost sacred, source of virtue and stability. Meanwhile the growth of wage labour (itself a prerequisite of the separation between home and work) meant that increasing numbers of northerners lacked the ownership of land or other means of production that had previously been thought necessary for inclusion in a republican or democratic polity. Abolitionists and radical Republicans, however, insisted that the individual conscience could instead perform this role. The conscience would operate as an anchor for individual morality and a guarantor of social harmony. The implications for slavery, which scorned the conscience of the slave and denied him the right to a family, were obvious: slavery was simply intolerable and must be abolished, by means of an appeal to the conscience of the nation, or at least of the North.

Thus if we are explaining the growth of antislavery in the North, we should certainly not ignore the political critique of slavery that found expression in the concept of the Slave Power. Nor should we fail to note the almost certainly disproportionate impact of the minority of northerners, within Republican and abolitionist ranks, for whom the moral indictment was paramount. Nevertheless this should not obscure the fact that economic and class factors were of primary significance. Economic changes in the North operated in a number of ways. First they produced the belief, universal among Republicans and abolitionists alike, that the northern economy was superior in productive potential and in the opportunities it provided to individual citizens. As we have observed, this was a cardinal tenet of the Republican political faith. Second they played a decisive role in generating the moral critique of slavery which focussed upon the impact of enslavement upon the family and the conscience. Third they gave rise to an increasing imbalance in political power between North and South. Faced with this moral and economic challenge from a region whose political power, both relative and absolute, seemed to be ever increasing, southerners took, in the political arena, what they hoped would be preventative action and in so doing fuelled the fears of the Slave Power

At this point the weaknesses of the slave regime itself, and the conflict between master and slave that was at its core, were, in their turn, decisive. Unable to diversify economically (and thereby weaken the northern economic critique of slavery), unable to match the growth of the northern free-labour system (and thus ignore the threat from the free states) and unable to loosen the controls they held over their slaves by, for example, legalising slave marriage (and thus begin to blunt the moral critique), southerners, as we have seen, took a series of actions in the 1830s, 1840s and 1850s that were intended to make the Union safe for slavery. These actions, however, merely served to fuel the political critique of the institution, the claim that the nation was being ruled by a Slave Power.

It is clear, therefore, that a whole series of factors, some economic, some political and some moral, generated the antislavery movement, a movement which culminated in the creation of the Republican party. It is also the case, however, that not all these factors were of equal importance. There is every reason to believe that the economic and class forces were primary.

XII

Given its history in the antebellum Republic, Republicans were perhaps correct in viewing slavery as an unnatural, disorganising force in the nation. But this view in turn rested on a still more fundamental assumption: that northern society itself was "natural" and in harmony with the basic aspirations of humanity. Republicans did not necessarily claim that the North was currently free of social abuses and evils. Radicals amongst them in particular were involved in other movements intended to improve the quality of life in the North, and it would be quite wrong to claim that the crusade against slavery was intended to divert attention from these other concerns. But what Republicans, including radical Republicans, did believe was that northern society, whether as it actually was, or as it potentially might be, did cater to the most fundamental human needs. Slavery by contrast did not and could not. From this many critically important conclusions followed; they would become apparent in the final climactic years that followed the election of James Buchanan in 1856.

7

POLITICAL
POLARISATION,
1857–1860

I

On 4 March 1857 James Buchanan was inaugurated as President of the United States. In his address the new president expressed his hope and belief that the agitation of the slavery question would soon be at an end. The electorate, he argued, had delivered a resounding verdict in approval of the Democratic policy towards the territories. Congress could not and should not intervene; the matter should be left up to the inhabitants of the territory itself. Buchanan recognised that there was some difference of opinion as to the point at which this decision should be made. He himself, he announced, believed that it should be at the time of entry into the Union, rather than at the time the territorial legislature came into existence. But he also declared that the matter was of little practical consequence and that the Supreme Court would soon offer a ruling on the matter. To this decision not only he but "all good citizens", the President was convinced, would "cheerfully submit".[1]

Buchanan's words combined truth with error. The Supreme Court would two days later indeed pronounce upon this, and other questions in its famous, or perhaps one should say notorious, *Dred Scott* decision. But Buchanan's hope that this would quell the slavery agitation was unfounded. Instead of the Supreme Court discrediting the cause of antislavery, in the North at least the antislavery cause would discredit the Supreme Court. And "good citizens" in the North, even within Buchanan's own party, would seek ways of circumventing the Court's conclusions. During the new president's term of office, the slavery

[1] Buchanan's inaugural is conveniently available at http://www.bartleby.com/124/pres30.html.

agitation would become still more intense, and four years later it would plunge the nation into the deepest crisis it has ever encountered.

II

Dred Scott was a slave who in the 1830s had been taken to Illinois and to the northerly part of the Louisiana Purchase, both areas in which slavery had been forbidden. In the 1840s and in 1850 Scott brought suit in St. Louis, Missouri, on the grounds that these periods of residence made him a free man. After a sequence of trial, retrial and appeal, the matter eventually came before the United States Supreme Court.[2]

There were now several issues at stake, and the task of the Court was not merely to rule upon them but also to determine which it should rule upon and which it should ignore. For a variety of reasons the Court, under Chief Justice Roger Taney of Maryland, decided to offer a wide-ranging judgement. The principal reason was probably that politicians, and especially Democratic politicians, had been hoping for some time that the Court would rule on the question of slavery in the territories, partly to remove all doubt and uncertainty. Their assumption was identical to that of the new President: a Supreme Court ruling would end all controversy.

The Court reached two momentous conclusions. First the majority opinion, as expressed by Taney, was not only that Scott was not entitled to bring suit at all but that neither slaves nor free blacks were, or could ever be, citizens of the United States. This was controversial enough, though in one sense Taney merely echoed the racism in which especially Democrats (of whom he was one) so frequently indulged. Beyond this, however, the Court now pronounced, again in a majority opinion, on the legality of the Missouri Compromise and the prohibition of slavery north of 36° 30'. This prohibition, Taney affirmed, had been unconstitutional. The effect of this bombshell was literally to outlaw the main policy of the Republican party, which stood for congressional prohibition of slavery in the territories, and which had carried in the recent presidential contest a large majority of the free states of the Union.

[2] On the *Dred Scott* judgement, see Don E. Fehrenbacher, *The Dred Scott Case: Its Significance in American Law and Politics* (New York, 1978); Mark A. Graber, *Dred Scott and the Problem of Constitutional Evil* (Cambridge, MA, 2006); Earl M. Maltz, *Dred Scott and the Politics of Slavery* (Lawrence, KA, 2007).

The controversy did not end there, however. For if Congress did not, after all, possess the power to rule on slavery in the territories, then surely it could not delegate that power to a territorial legislature. This seemed to make unconstitutional the Douglas version of popular sovereignty, by which the territorial legislature, well before the point of the territory's admission into the Union, could allow or forbid slavery. As we shall see, Douglas himself implicitly recognised this consequence of the ruling, even as he tried to circumvent its effects. The Court had tried to end the slavery agitation, but now that agitation rose to heights not even seen during the election of 1856.

Opposition to *Dred Scott* from the Republicans was as intense as might have been predicted. However, much of the time the party tried to argue that the ruling, and especially that part relating to slavery in the territories, was on issues not before the court. It was thus obiter dictum and consequently not binding. This allowed Republicans to avoid having to challenge the authority of the Court itself, whilst maintaining their favoured policy towards the territories. At the same time, however, some of them now discerned a conspiracy designed to spread slavery even into the North. Abraham Lincoln himself asserted that the circumstantial evidence in favour of this plan was conclusive. Lincoln argued that Douglas, Pierce, Taney and Buchanan were systematically preparing the way for a legalisation of slavery everywhere. His reasoning was that since 1854 these Democrats had denied first that Congress, then territorial governments, had the power to outlaw slavery. The administration's own newspaper, the Washington *Union*, had hinted that slavery might be legal even in the states of the North. This would be the culmination of the plot: the Slave Power would then have spread slavery into the North.[3]

Lincoln and the other Republicans who made this charge were mistaken; there was no conspiracy to spread slavery into the North. It is important to ask, however, why they made this error. The misperception is readily intelligible when one recurs to Republican ideology. The entire Republican campaign against the Slave Power exaggerated the unity and the farsightedness of southerners who themselves, rather than controlling events according to some carefully arranged master plan,

---

[3] Washington *Union*, 17 November 1857; Roy F. Basler, ed. *The Collected Works of Abraham Lincoln* 9 vols (New Brunswick, NJ, 1953–1955), II, pp. 465–466.

were reacting, often hastily and sometimes desperately, to the unfolding of events. But Republicans were driven to misinterpret southern actions because of their most fundamental beliefs about slavery and southern society. They did not merely believe that slavery was bad or inferior to free labour, by however wide a margin. As we have noted, they believed it was inherently disorganising, and thus in the most literal sense *unnatural*. A free-labour system, by contrast, was both natural and, potentially at least, harmonious. From this assumption many Republican misperceptions followed. As we shall see, these misperceptions would be enormously significant in the final years of the antebellum Republic. As far as *Dred Scott* and the alleged plot to spread slavery into the North were concerned, the assumption led them to conclude that only concerted action by the Slave Power could explain the success of a system that so clearly ran counter to the most basic human needs and aspirations. To spread slavery into Kansas, for example, as the Slave Power had almost succeeded in doing, represented such an extraordinary deviation from the nation's natural course, which was to establish free labour and democracy there, that only a deliberate conspiracy could account for it. Thus the circumstantial evidence in favour of a plot to extend slavery into the North was enough, along with a single editorial from the Washington *Union*, to convince so sober and thoughtful a statesman as Abraham Lincoln.

These Republican misperceptions should not encourage us to conclude that blundering statesmen were responsible for the deepening sectional conflict of the 1850s (or earlier). Those who have made this case have generally tried to argue that the errors of a "blundering generation", rather than intractable economic (or moral) differences between North and South were at the heart of the sectional conflict.[4] This itself, however, is a major blunder. It was not that Republicans made no errors; assuredly they did. Nor were these errors inconsequential; on the contrary they were of enormous importance. But they were rooted in Republican ideology. And that ideology was itself grounded in the lived experience of millions of northerners. It had vitally important social and economic roots and performed a major function within the northern social order. Although there was no conspiracy here either, in extolling their free-labour system and insisting

---

[4] This is the so-called "revisionist" interpretation of the Civil War.

that it corresponded to the deepest needs of humanity, Republicans were effectively helping to reconcile northerners to the far-reaching changes taking place in their own midst. To note Republican errors, therefore, is thus not to argue that they were part of a "blundering generation" which stumbled into war when no major economic issues were at stake. In this case (and many other cases), statesmen's errors proceeded from their world views. And those world views were structured by the social, political and economic conditions from which they sprang.

III

Lincoln and the Republicans were particularly mistaken when they included Stephen A. Douglas in the conspiracy to spread slavery. Not only was Douglas not party to any plan to resolve the territorial question along the lines of the *Dred Scott* decision, he was actually embarrassed by the ruling. Faced with Republican denunciations of northern Democrats as "doughfaces" (northerners with southern sympathies), Douglas had for some time clung all the more tightly to his version of congressional non-intervention (which empowered a territorial legislature to exclude slavery). This had allowed him to offer southerners a principle that they welcomed, the renunciation of federal power over slavery in the territories, whilst offering northerners the substance of what they demanded: free states in the West. *Dred Scott*, however, threatened this delicate balancing act.[5]

Douglas now came up with an ingenious response. He accepted the ruling but claimed that even if the territorial legislature could not directly exclude slavery it could indirectly achieve the same result by refusing to pass the policing laws that were essential in any slaveholding community. He had argued for this before, but without the point being accorded much significance.

In the summer of 1858 it achieved nationwide attention. Douglas's term of office in the United States Senate was about to expire. As a candidate for re-election, he was faced by Republican nominee Abraham Lincoln, a single-term congressman who had held no major executive

---

[5] An excellent biography of Douglas is Robert W. Johannsen, *Stephen A. Douglas* (New York, 1973).

office and who was relatively unknown outside Illinois. Lincoln proposed a series of debates and Douglas agreed. Seven were held in the prairie towns of the state, and they were attended by Illinoisans in their tens of thousands. They have become the most celebrated political debates in U.S. history.

In fact neither candidate said much that was new. Lincoln charged Douglas, as he had before, with polluting the fountains of public opinion by refusing to condemn slavery on moral grounds. He also denied Douglas's accusations that he was an abolitionist who favoured equality for blacks. At the most famous of the debates, held in Freeport, he asked his adversary how the *Dred Scott* decision could be reconciled with popular sovereignty. Once again Douglas replied with his argument that a local majority could indirectly but decisively exclude slavery in the territorial phase by refusing to pass the necessary policing laws. This now became known as the Freeport Doctrine.

In one sense the Freeport Doctrine was highly successful in that it allowed Douglas to maintain his home support in Illinois and throughout the North. Moreover he won the contest with Lincoln in that the legislators of Illinois chose him to represent them.[6] But Lincoln had done well: he had held his own in debate against the most formidable Democrat in the nation.

Moreover, however popular it might be in the North, the Freeport Doctrine spelt disaster for Douglas's standing in the South. Many southerners now concluded that they had been duped. Douglas had constantly promised that he would abide by the decision of the Supreme Court regarding slavery in the territories. Now that decision had been made but Douglas had evaded its real consequences. He had been a hero in the South when the Kansas–Nebraska Act had been introduced and passed. Now he became a villain.

This effect was multiplied many times over by events in Kansas themselves, which continued to absorb the nation's attention. The real fruits of the Kansas–Nebraska Act were now tasted by southerners. In 1854 the Act had seemed an extraordinary triumph for them. It now became apparent that it was instead an extraordinary disaster.

---

[6] At this time U.S. Senators were elected not directly by the people but indirectly by a state's legislators.

IV

By the commencement of the Buchanan administration, if not much earlier, it was clear that in Kansas there was a clear majority of free-soil settlers. But the southern dominated Lecompton legislature remained as determined as ever to make Kansas a slave state. Accordingly it drew up plans to facilitate this outcome. By 1856 Kansas had its third governor in place, each of his predecessors having failed to calm the territory. John W. Geary came increasingly into conflict with the Lecompton legislature, vetoed some of its actions, had his vetoes overridden and finally, after an unsuccessful appeal to President Pierce for federal troops, resigned.

Buchanan now chose a fourth governor, Robert J. Walker. Walker doubted whether slavery could go into Kansas, given its climatic conditions, and publicly aired these doubts. Elections to a constitutional convention were now scheduled and Walker advised the free-soil settlers to participate in them. But the elections produced yet another fraudulent outcome and the ensuing Convention did all it could to safeguard the rights of slaveholders. The new constitution reaffirmed the right to hold slaves already in the territory, and it called for a referendum on the future admission of yet more slaves. Was this a real choice? Critics, both in Kansas and throughout the North, argued that it was not: two proslavery options were on offer; the voters were not allowed to reject the constitution in its entirety.[7]

The referendum seemed to provide a ringing endorsement of the proslavery constitution. Those in favour of "the constitution with slavery" defeated those in favour of "the constitution without slavery" (which in fact guaranteed the possession of slaves already in the territory) by a wide margin. But the free-soil settlers had boycotted the referendum entirely and it was subsequently found that more than a third of the votes cast had been fraudulent. This now struck Walker as absurd and unacceptable.

More important was the reaction of Stephen A. Douglas, and the great majority of northern Democrats. They too refused to accept the Lecompton constitution. But many southerners insisted that it be accepted and that Kansas enter the Union as a slave state. President

---

[7] On this and related points, see especially David Potter, *The Impending Crisis, 1848–1861* (New York, 1976), pp. 296–327.

Buchanan, mindful as ever of his dependence on southern support, succumbed to this pressure and endorsed Lecompton. Walker resigned and Douglas now broke with the Democratic administration, not, he was careful to explain, on the grounds that the Lecompton constitution would make Kansas a slave state but rather because it had not been drawn up in a properly democratic manner. For the Democratic party in the nation, this was a catastrophe. The most popular Democrat in the North, Stephen A. Douglas, was now hopelessly at odds not only with the party's leader in the White House but also with the southerners upon whom it depended for victory in federal elections.

In February 1858 in a message to Congress, Buchanan formally urged the immediate admission of Kansas under the Lecompton constitution. He also poured scorn upon the free-state Topeka government which he denounced as treasonous and revolutionary (as Pierce had). Kansas, according to the President, was now as much a slave state as Georgia or South Carolina. By now tempers were running high. Some in the Deep South went so far as to threaten secession if Kansas did not enter the Union as a slave state. The administration did everything possible to get the Lecompton constitution through Congress. But the opposition of not merely the Republicans but also the Douglas Democrats was too much. Lacking popular support in the North, the administration resorted to bribery and corruption.[8] But the constitution was finally submitted for approval to the voters of Kansas, and in what was, by the standards of 1850s Kansas, a remarkably fraud-free election, the voters rejected the Lecompton constitution in August 1858 by 11,200 to 1,788. This spelt the end of southern dreams of the territory becoming a slave state and some two-and-a-half years later Kansas entered the Union – as a free state.

The entire history of Kansas in its territorial phase was, from the perspective of the South, or at least of those southerners who sincerely wished to stay in the Union, a series of disasters, culminating in outright catastrophe. In 1854, when the Kansas–Nebraska Act was passed, hopes and expectations, as we have observed, had been extraordinarily high. An entire range of possible gains had been expected. None had materialised.

---

[8] Mark Summers, *The Plundering Generation: Corruption and the Crisis of the Union, 1849–1861* (New York, 1987), pp. 249–255.

Some southerners had expected Kansas to become a slave state. Initially their numbers had been small but the actions of the Lecompton legislature and the support it received from Presidents Pierce and Buchanan encouraged more of them to believe that Kansas was, after all, suitable for slavery. This had, of course, proved not to be correct, in that the free-state settlers, determined to make Kansas a free state, had ultimately triumphed. Southern fears of northern political power constantly being augmented by the admission of new free states had thus been intensified rather than relieved.

The consequences were felt far beyond Kansas. Southerners had hoped that the principle of congressional non-intervention, incorporated in the Kansas–Nebraska Act, would facilitate the creation of additional slave states elsewhere. So even if Kansas were not acquired for slavery, other territory, perhaps in the Caribbean or in Central America, would be. Southerners could then ensure that a local majority would form and establish or retain slavery in these areas. But the problem was that the Kansas–Nebraska Act, together with the tumultuous events that had ensued in the territory of Kansas, had so antagonised northern opinion and so discredited the policy of popular sovereignty that it was now impossible to obtain additional territory for slavery anywhere. In effect a huge amount of political capital had been squandered in the struggle for Kansas.

The result was that those who feared either for the political or the economic health of slavery and who accordingly demanded the creation of new slave states had even deeper cause for concern. There was now little prospect of any new slave state ever. Meanwhile additional free states were being created. As we have seen, some southerners were preoccupied with the political consequences of an ever-growing northern majority at Washington. Others argued that slavery needed additional territory for economic reasons. Both groups had their prospects shattered by the events connected with Kansas.

Constitutionally, too, the effect was the opposite of that which had been expected. The Kansas–Nebraska Act had amounted to a rolling back of federal power, which southerners welcomed wholeheartedly. But the attempt to resolve the constitutional questions concerning federal power in the territories had intensified rather than resolved the sectional conflict. The *Dred Scott* decision had not brought southerners the repose they had expected. Although it had confirmed the view of congressional power that most of them believed had underlain the Kansas–Nebraska Act from the start, the effect had been to arouse a chorus of condemnation from the North. The creation of the Republican party and the catastrophic split in Democratic ranks owed much to the southern urge to establish constitutional safeguards for slavery. The backlash in the North left the South more vulnerable than ever.

Finally in Missouri the effects were again directly antithetical to those that had been anticipated. Far from strengthening slavery in that state, the clash between slavery and freedom in neighbouring Kansas promoted the cause of antislavery and plans for the ending of slavery in Missouri were actually submitted. In 1860 the Republicans would run strongly in some parts of the state, and this confirmed fears (or hopes) that the state would soon become free.[9]

The gulf between what southerners had expected from Kansas and what they actually obtained is thus so vast that it cries out for explanation. Once again there were errors involved of course; southern hopes were, it transpired, built upon an erroneous reading of the situation. But once again these errors revealed underlying, structural weaknesses, this time the inherent weaknesses of slavery.

The problems in Kansas arose ultimately because southerners could not in fact compete with northerners in settling the territory. There were two reasons. First southern slaveholders were not particularly attracted to Kansas. Even if, as some claimed, slavery would prove as viable there as in Missouri, this was not saying very much. In Missouri after all the institution was not particularly robust, as southerners themselves frequently acknowledged. For slaveholders there were far better opportunities elsewhere in the South, notably in Texas and Arkansas, each of which was developing rapidly in the 1850s.

Even more important were the structural weaknesses of slavery itself. The key problem for southerners, as far as Kansas was concerned, derived from the weaknesses of slavery in any community where antislavery sentiment existed. Here was the reason the Missouri "Border Ruffians" had come into the territory again and again and voted fraudulently. Here too was the reason for the draconian measures in support

---

[9] See B. Gratz Brown, *Extracts from a Speech of B. Gratz Brown of St. Louis, Delivered in the Missouri House of Representatives, Feb. 12, 1857* (Philadelphia, n.d.); Richard H. Sewell, *Ballots for Freedom* (New York, 1976), pp. 318–320.

of slavery that were passed and the repeated violations of northerners' civil liberties. It is vital to recognise that southerners believed that the rule of law could and should be set aside wherever the safety of slaveholders was at risk. As a result they and their supporters took a whole series of actions in Kansas which outraged northern opinion and which made the entire Kansas imbroglio such a disaster. In a sense the events in Kansas, though in a way quite unique, recapitulated in miniature the ruinous process that frequently characterised the sectional conflict. Northern antislavery opinion derived from and also revealed the weaknesses in slaveholding societies; southerners reacted vigorously and even violently and the effect was to generate even deeper hostility in the North to slavery and the slaveholders. This sequence of events would be replayed again, as the nation finally collapsed in 1860–1861.

At the heart of the problem was the attitude of the slaves themselves. Although southerners were oblivious to the fact, the slaves did not want to be slaves. Here was the reason antislavery activity in Kansas was so unacceptable to southerners. As historians now know, contented slaves could not in fact have been "tampered with" by antislavery agitators. But southerners as always misread the situation. They believed antislavery elements would turn inherently loyal slaves into rebellious ones. But in fact antislavery activity was so potent precisely because the slaves yearned for their liberty. Unable to understand this longing for freedom on the part of their slaves, the slaveholders nevertheless attended to its consequences and in so doing fuelled the sectional conflict.

V

However defective their understanding of their slaves, the slaveholders nevertheless did understand the critical importance of the non-slaveholding whites in their midst. Without their support or at least acquiescence, slavery could not continue. Most of these whites possessed the vote; they could thus, in theory, vote slavery down. In more immediate, practical terms, their cooperation was needed to help return fugitive slaves, to man slave patrols and to maintain, as far as was possible, the racially based caste system upon which the entire system was based. It is of course true that, had the slaves been genuinely contented under slavery, the attitude of the non-slaveholding whites would have been infinitely less important. But, as always, southerners were blind to this fact.

Instead they reacted vigorously, often violently, to anyone who suggested that the interests of the slaveholder conflicted with those of the non-slaveholding whites. The reaction was all the more intense if that suggestion came from within the South itself. In the border states there had long been pockets of antislavery activity. Cassius Clay in Kentucky, the Blairs in Missouri and Maryland, Benjamin Gratz Brown in Missouri – these individuals and their relatively small coteries of supporters sometimes risked life and limb when campaigning against slavery. The most conspicuous of them, however, was a native son of North Carolina. He was Hinton Rowan Helper.

Helper was from a family of North Carolinian yeomen. He came to an important conclusion about the South, one that Republicans and abolitionists shared: slavery retarded its economic development and social progress. The casualties of the system, Helper announced, were not so much the slaves, nor even the slaveholders but rather the non-slaveholding whites, the very class from which he had himself sprung. According to Helper, their prospects for advancement were blighted, their labour was not respected, and they were constantly belittled by the slaveholding aristocracy. Helper wasted little time on the sufferings of the slaves; his indictment of slavery was political and economic rather than moral. But it stung the southern leadership none the less for that.

In 1857 Helper achieved sudden fame when he published his attack on the southern social system in a book entitled *The Impending Crisis of the South*. It provoked a storm of controversy. Much of the volume consisted of reams of statistics, many of them taken from the census of 1850, and all of them intended to demonstrate the absolute superiority of the northern, free-labour economy. Helper seemed to call for a revolutionary upsurge in the South, directed against the slaveholding elite. His book was endorsed by many Republicans, who agreed with his verdict on the southern economy, if not with the means by which he proposed to transform it.[10]

Immediately the book became caught up with congressional politics. In the Congress that convened in December 1859, no party had a

---

[10] Hinton R. Helper, *The Impending Crisis of the South* (New York, 1857).

majority in the House of Representatives, though the Republicans had a plurality. Their candidate for Speaker, John Sherman, had hoped to attract the votes of enough southern moderates to carry the election, but when it was found that he, like many other Republicans, had endorsed Helper's book (though without having read it, he claimed), his candidacy was doomed. Eventually a more moderate Republican, William Pennington, who had not endorsed the book, won the election, though only after the deadlock had persisted for two months. But by now tempers were running so high in Congress that many members came to the halls armed. No serious incident occurred but it was yet another sign of the polarisation that was taking place.

VI

In the presidential election of 1856 the Republican candidate, John C. Frémont, had carried all but five of the sixteen free states. Buchanan had been successful only in Indiana, Illinois, California, Pennsylvania and New Jersey. In the course of the Buchanan administration, the Republicans extended their control over the North. By 1860 only Pennsylvania and Indiana had non-Republican governors. The stage was already set for the great triumph that would occur in the presidential election of that year.

How did the Republicans enhance their appeal in the North between 1856 and 1860? After 1856 it was clear that the crucial battleground in 1860 would be the Lower North. In particular the state of Pennsylvania was vital. (To win in the electoral college the party needed to retain the states it had carried in 1856 and add to them Pennsylvania plus Illinois, Indiana or New Jersey.) In some of these states, including Pennsylvania, the Know Nothings had been a significant force; the Republicans thus needed to recruit heavily among those who had supported Fillmore in 1856.

We have already noted that the party did very little to appeal to these voters on the basis of nativism. In one or two states some extremely mild nativist policies were endorsed, but on the whole the Republicans fought shy of any clear identification with nativist principles. This was for reasons of political expediency (there were simply too many immigrants, especially in the West, who might be alienated) as well as of principle.

Instead the party recruited new converts on the basis of its core appeal. As we have noted, their fundamental principle was that slavery disorganised a community, politically, economically and, some added, morally. This principle was the one that now allowed them to recruit former Fillmore supporters and thus secure virtually full control of the North.

For these newly converted Republicans, as for many others who had been longer in the party, the essential task was to deliver a stern rebuke to the slave interest, to prevent it continuing to exert a disorganising influence on the nation. These Republicans, joining those already on the conservative wing of the party, acknowledged that the slavery question had, contrary to their wishes, overwhelmed everything else (including nativism). "All other questions", one of them conceded, "of principle or governmental policy have shrunk into insignificance, and it alone has become the issue of a presidential campaign". For these former Know Nothings, as for other conservative Republicans, the task of the party would not be to end slavery. On the contrary it would be to end slavery agitation, for which they ultimately held the South almost entirely responsible. They recalled with some anger that while northern Know Nothings had tried to suppress the slavery question, their southern colleagues had not allowed them to do so. Now southerners, it seemed, were even trying to spread slavery into the North. For the sake of sectional peace it was essential to resist these and other southern attempts to engross yet more power, at the expense of northern freedoms. "We have been crying peace, peace", one of them lamented, "but", he added in a phrase which signalled his adoption of the principal Republican motif, "there is no peace". There could be none until the aggressions of the Slave Power had been decisively checked. Slavery would be left where it was within the states where it currently existed, but able to go no further and henceforth unable to disturb the tranquillity of the nation. Ironically therefore, these Republicans urged northerners to seek an immediate confrontation with the South – in order to put an end to confrontations with the South.[11]

VII

A comparable polarisation was occurring in the South. Although Buchanan in 1856 had carried every slave state apart from Maryland

---

[11] *Proceedings of the American Mass Meeting, And the Speeches of Hon. James O. Putnam, and Roswell Hart, Esq., Sept. 7, 1860* (Rochester, NY, 1860), pp. 9–10; *The Duty of Americans; Speech of Gen. G.A. Scroggs, and of Hon. Geo. B. Babcock, also of Hon. James A. Putnam* (n.p., n.d.), pp. 3–4, 14–15.

(which went to Fillmore), this outcome perhaps masked the continuing strength of the Know Nothing or American party in what had always been the southern Whig heartland, the Upper South. During at least some of the Buchanan years, Delaware, Maryland and Kentucky all had Know Nothing governors. More important, after the collapse of the Whigs and Know Nothings in much of the Upper and Border South, former Whigs began to call themselves an "Opposition" party. By 1860 they held no fewer than twenty-three seats in the House of Representatives. Most of their strength remained in states where the Whigs had been strong: North Carolina, Tennessee and Kentucky. But even in Virginia in 1859 the Opposition polled almost half of the votes cast in that year's gubernatorial election. These Opposition parties, like the Whigs before them, typically espoused a strong, though usually by no means unconditional, Unionism. They were not slow to condemn some of the more extreme demands, such as the call for the reopening of the African slave trade, emanating from southern militants at this time. Even more significantly perhaps, some of them were prepared to voice their objections to the Lecompton constitution, however unconditionally some of their fellow southerners might defend it.[12]

As a result there was, for a time, the possibility that some of these southerners might ally or even unite with the Republicans in what would effectively be a rejuvenated Whig party. Some prominent former Whigs and the newspapers supporting them even voiced a preference for the Republicans over the Democrats. On this basis it seemed as though the Democratic party might not after all control an effectively undivided South.

Yet there were pressures operating to produce the opposite effect. As they observed the ever-increasing dominance of the Republicans in the North, some southerners reached a very different conclusion: only by supporting the Democratic party could the South resist. This was the attitude of both Robert Toombs and Alexander H. Stephens of Georgia, once the two most prominent Whigs in the entire Deep South. Others, like Judah P. Benjamin of Louisiana and Henry Hilliard of Alabama, voiced similar opinions. In this way the alarming growth

---

[12] Daniel Crofts, *Reluctant Confederates: Upper South Unionists in the Secession Crisis* (Chapel Hill, NC, 1989), pp. 52–54, 63.

of the Republican party in the North produced a backlash within the South, from which the Democratic party benefited considerably.

Moreover the very successes of their party in the North left many Republicans with the impression that they did not need to court the southern Opposition parties. Why should they consent to the dilution of their antislavery principles that any successful attempt at fusion would require? Most Republicans could see no reason. Finally the Opposition party in the South was itself vulnerable to the polarisation which was occurring on its own turf. These moderate southerners were always open to the charge that they were insufficiently loyal to slavery. And John Brown's raid of October 1859 gave this charge still greater, indeed almost irresistible, potency.

VIII

John Brown was a militant abolitionist. He believed that slavery must be abolished and, if necessary, by bloodshed. In Kansas he had been responsible for the massacre at Pottawatomie, where five proslavery settlers were cold-bloodedly murdered. He had been provoked into action, he subsequently explained, by rage at southern aggressions both in Kansas, specifically the "sack of Lawrence", and in Washington, specifically the assault on Charles Sumner. Now he conceived a plan to enter the South itself and foment a slave insurrection. Brown won the backing of a coterie of well-to-do northerners, the so-called "Secret Six", all of whom shared his abolitionist goals.[13]

He planned to capture the federal armoury and arsenal at Harpers Ferry, Virginia. From there he expected large numbers of slaves to rise up. He would then arm them. The plan was hopelessly flawed from the start. The slaves had no notice of his intentions; even if they had had, the odds against success were overwhelming. It is even possible that before he embarked upon it, Brown knew that his raid would fail and that he knew his true role would be that of martyr.

So it proved. With a band of some twenty men Brown launched his strike on 16 October 1859. They stopped a train but then allowed it to proceed, whereupon the alarm was sounded. The following day a

---

[13] See Jonathan Earle, *John Brown's Raid on Harpers Ferry: A Brief History with Documents* (Boston, 2008); and David S. Reynolds, *John Brown, Abolitionist: The Man Who Killed Slavery, Sparked the Civil War, and Seeded Civil Rights* (New York, 2005).

company of U.S. marines arrived. Brown was wounded and captured. The raid was over.

John Brown was hastily tried and convicted of both murder and fomenting insurrection. What had been the effect of his raid? In the South there was initially a feeling of shock and horror. But the ease with which the attempt had been thwarted and the "loyalty" that the slaves had demonstrated (in that they had not risen up in armed rebellion) offered southerners some reassurance. In the North the raid was initially condemned by all Democrats and almost all Republicans. But Brown played his role as martyr to a glorious cause with consummate skill, showing a courage that even won the respect of some of his captors. On 2 December 1859 he was hanged. In the North on execution day, bells tolled, guns were fired and sermons were preached in which Brown featured as a hero if not a saint.

This reaction dismayed and outraged southerners. Stephen A. Douglas had already asserted that the Brown raid, diabolical as it was, was in fact the inevitable consequence of Republican antislavery agitation. Now it appeared that Republican denials of sympathy for the project were shallow and unconvincing. Could southerners be expected to remain in a Union in which the Republican party was dominant? Notwithstanding Douglas's utterance, could they even continue to trust their northern Democratic allies, most of whom had denied them the fruits of victory either in Kansas (with the Lecompton constitution) or in regard to the *Dred Scott* decision? These anxieties were very much to the fore when the Democratic party met to choose its presidential candidate for the election of 1860.

IX

In April 1860 the Democrats convened in Charleston, South Carolina, a city not renowned for its temperate approach to the sectional controversy. The majority of southerners were determined to destroy Douglas's prospects now and forever. They were incensed at his betrayal of their cause in regard to both the Lecompton constitution and the Freeport Doctrine. If it was now too late to do anything about Kansas, it was still possible, they felt, to consign the Freeport Doctrine to oblivion. They now demanded a federal slave code for the territories, by which during the territorial stage slavery would be protected by the federal government. Thus a local majority would not in fact be able to block the policing regulations that all agreed were necessary for slavery to take root. Douglas would thus be prevented from evading the full implications of the *Dred Scott* decision, the Freeport Doctrine would be effectively annulled and slavery would finally receive the constitutional protection to which it was entitled.

Douglas had insisted even before the convention met that he could not accept a federal slave code; it would have confirmed every Republican charge that he and his supporters were mere pawns in the hands of an all-controlling Slave Power. The result, as his supporters announced time and again, would have been electoral annihilation for the party in the North. Moreover southerners knew that he could not accept it. They nonetheless refused to recede an inch, even when it became apparent that the price would be a disastrous split in the Democratic party.

Why were southerners so intransigent? A small number of them actually desired secession and thus were quite happy to see the Democratic party break up. But this was not the attitude of most southerners at this time. What they wanted were iron-clad guarantees for their slave property. If possible these guarantees would be provided within the Union, if not they would be found outside it. But this was precisely what Douglas was not offering. Although he was willing and eager to denounce the Republicans, and even prepared to blame them for the Brown raid, he also espoused, on many occasions at least, an unqualified Unionism. In other words, southerners noted, he expected the South to submit to rule by a party (the Republicans) which, by his own reckoning, would actually precipitate slave rebellions throughout the South. Clearly he was not merely an untrustworthy ally but one whose support would merely disarm the South and expose slaveholders to yet more deadly assaults. In effect, therefore, William H. Seward or Abraham Lincoln were no more dangerous to the South than Stephen A. Douglas, since, as the Richmond *Enquirer* put it, while "the former would rob him, regardless of the Constitution, of his means of subsistence", "the latter would shoot him if he had the courage to resist". Douglas had betrayed the South over the *Dred Scott* decision and shown his faithlessness to the Constitution. And his Freeport Doctrine would exclude the South from the territories just as assuredly as the Republican's doctrine of congressional prohibition. "Of what advantage", asked one contributor to *De Bow's Review*, "is it to the South to be destroyed by Mr Douglas through territorial sovereignty to the exclusion of Southern institutions, rather than by Mr

Seward through Congressional sovereignty to the same end?" According to another southerner, Douglas differed from the Republicans only "in making insidious, instead of open, war upon the South".[14]

Some southerners insisted upon a federal slave code because they hoped to acquire more land and create more slave states in the future. For others it was the abstract principle that was involved. This was the principle of equality, equality of treatment for southern property. For southerners this meant the clear right to take slave property into the territories where it would be fully protected. Otherwise slaveholders would not go there and their equal rights in the territories would be violated. And if they could not claim equality under the Constitution, they could not remain in the Union.

A further set of issues, however, was involved. For Douglas and his supporters also believed in equality of treatment for southern property. For them this equality was to be preserved by keeping the federal government out; a territorial legislature would choose whether or not to protect slave property just as it might choose whether or not to protect property in rum or wine. Ironically, therefore, each side in the debate believed that it was contending for equality for northerners and southerners alike in the territories. But there was a profound paradox: a benign environment for slavery, the essential precondition for southern equality, seemed to result, as the experience of Kansas amply demonstrated, only in a denial of the equal rights of non-slaveholders, whose freedom of (antislavery) expression and (antislavery) opinion had to be severely and, if necessary, violently curtailed. Thus both sides demanded equality; each approach necessarily violated it.

The root of the problem lay in the unique characteristics of slave property. It was not like other forms of property. As Douglas was fond of reminding his supporters and opponents alike, if the rum seller did not convince his fellow citizens of the desirability of liquor, he ran the risk that they would vote to exclude his business. Douglas then argued that the slaveholder should run an identical set of risks. But his southern enemies in effect responded to the fact that their slaves were not inanimate objects. Instead they were men and women. Liquor could not

---

[14] Richmond *Enquirer*, 28 September 1860; *De Bow's Review*, XXVIII (1860) 382; *Address to the Democracy and the People of the United States By the National Democracy Executive Committee* (Washington DC, 1860), p. 2.

flee of its own accord. Slaves could. Liquor could not rise up against its owner. Slaves could. Once again therefore the resistance, actual or potential, between master and slave had a decisive effect on the politics of the final antebellum years. The Democratic schism, the split that pitted Douglas Democrats against southern militants, saw both sides claiming that slavery was simply a form of property that should be placed on an equal footing with other forms of property. But in reality because of the conflict between master and slave, slavery was a profoundly different form of property and no equality was actually possible. Nor could the two positions be reconciled.

As a result, no compromise was possible at Charleston between the supporters of Douglas and his southern enemies either. After days of fierce and bitter debate, the Douglas men had their platform adopted, whereupon some fifty delegates from the Deep South walked out. Douglas, however, could not obtain the two-thirds majority needed to win the nomination and so the Convention adjourned, agreeing to meet again some six weeks later, this time in Baltimore. But time could not heal the breach. At Baltimore another bolt took place, and for the same reason. The bolters now nominated their own candidate, John C. Breckinridge, who of course endorsed a slave code for the territories. The remainder nominated Douglas for the presidency, on a platform that most assuredly did not endorse a slave code for the territories.

Between the dates of the two Democratic conventions, the Republicans met in Chicago to choose their presidential ticket. Since 1856 it had been assumed by many that the nomination would go to William Seward of New York, by far the best-known Republican in the nation. But Seward had major liabilities. His political manager, Thurlow Weed, had a reputation for dishonest or at least disreputable political dealings that many thought would be fatal for the party's prospects in 1860. Seward had also been a virulent critic of the Know Nothings, for whose principles the Republicans had shown little sympathy but whose supporters they did not wish to repel. Most of all Seward had a reputation for radicalism on the slavery question that many thought would damage the party in the crucial states of the Lower North.

Abraham Lincoln was only one of the alternative candidates. He was far less eminent than Seward. But his debates with Stephen A. Douglas in Illinois in 1858 when contending for Douglas's seat in the United States Senate had given him some national prominence. What did Lincoln stand for? In his debates with Douglas and elsewhere, he had argued that slavery was and had been recognised by the Founding Fathers as a wrong, a moral, political and economic evil. It should be allowed to spread no further. Moreover Lincoln had argued on more than one occasion that the nation could not exist half slave and half free; either slavery or freedom must triumph. Lincoln was not a radical on the slavery question in that he did not argue, for example, that the Fugitive Slave law should be cast aside; nor did he advocate the ending of the interstate slave trade. But still less was he one of the conservatives, who tended to ignore or at least downplay the moral evil of slavery and who merely wished to remove slavery from the political arena but otherwise leave it intact. Again and again he insisted that slavery was immoral as well as being politically unjust and economically injurious and must be placed on the path to ultimate extinction.[15]

Lincoln lacked Seward's disadvantages. He was not identified with radicalism to anything like the same degree and could therefore be expected to run well in the Lower North. Although he had made no secret of his opposition to nativism, his nomination would not be an affront or humiliation for former Know Nothings as Seward's would. Moreover, as he recognised himself, he might be the first choice of relatively few but, unlike Seward, was the second choice of many. Finally Lincoln seemed to embody the values of the new party: he seemed to stand for social mobility, hard work, honesty and integrity. On 18 May 1860 "Honest Abe" won the nomination of his party for president of the United States.

Lincoln would be faced not only by Douglas and Breckinridge, representing the rival wings of the Democratic party, but also by a fourth candidate. The more conservative elements of the old Whig party had never been reconciled either to the Republicans or to the Democracy. They continued to stand for the traditional values of the Whig party and accordingly reconvened in 1860 under the title of Constitutional Unionists. Believing that political parties and demagogic statesmen were themselves responsible for injecting essentially artificial sectional issues into politics, these erstwhile Whigs concluded that it would be possible to set aside the slavery question entirely. Disinterested statesmen would

---

[15] There is, of course, a vast literature on Lincoln. A good recent biography is Richard J. Carwardine, *Lincoln* (Harlow, England, 2003). See also Henry W. Jaffa, *A New Birth of Freedom: Abraham Lincoln and the Coming of the Civil War* (Lanham, MD, 2000) and Eric Foner, *The Fiery Trial: Abraham Lincoln and American Slavery* (New York, 2010).

then rule in the national interest and bring harmony where there had previously been strife. The Constitutional Union party nominated John Bell of Tennessee, a slaveholder but one of the few who had opposed the Kansas–Nebraska Act in 1854. For Vice-President the party nominated Edward Everett of Massachusetts, a former Whig of the Webster stripe. The new party, as befitted conservative Whigs, adopted no platform and went into battle merely avowing itself in favour of "The Union, The Constitution, and the Enforcement of the Laws".

In terms of new ideas and new policies, the campaign was devoid of interest; in terms of dramatic outcomes, none has ever matched it before or since. In the North the Democrats as usual played the race card, charging that a Republican victory and the freeing of the slaves, whenever it might come, would spell ruin for white labour – and for white female virtue. But the Republicans had too much ammunition of their own. The failure of the Buchanan administration to pass homestead legislation damaged the Democrats, especially in the West. Even more damaging were the reports, accurate enough, of the administration's corrupt activities. There had been malfeasance in the awarding of government contracts, judges had been bribed, congressmen illegally induced to support the Lecompton constitution and numerous other instances of abuse. These charges were not new in the summer and fall of 1860, but from a Republican standpoint they were very timely.

In the North Breckinridge's support, like that of the Buchanan administration itself, was extremely limited. The contest there was between Lincoln and Douglas. Douglas broke with precedent by campaigning vigorously on his own account. He presented himself as the one candidate whose policies could command support in all corners of the Union. His supporters attempted, especially in the North East, to create "fusion" tickets whereby they would unite with Breckinridge and Bell men in order to defeat Lincoln. But major obstacles stood in the path of this strategy. Divisions within the Democratic party were too deep, and Bell supporters were naturally hostile to the Democrats, whom they in any case blamed for the eruption of sectional hostilities in 1854. Similarly Democratic voters, especially immigrants, were hostile to the Bell campaign, in which many former Know Nothings featured strongly. The attempts at fusion generally failed. In the Upper North Republicans were bolder than in the Lower North, as they always had been; here the antislavery message tended to be delivered in unmistakable terms.

This cartoon depicts the 1860 presidential contest and parodies all four candidates. It suggests that each candidate is dancing with one of his supposed supporters, while Dred Scott calls the tune. Upper left is Southern Democrat John C. Breckinridge paired with President James Buchanan. Upper right Republican Abraham Lincoln dances with an African American woman. Lower right Constitutional Union candidate John Bell dances with an Indian brave. (He had been involved in Indian removal much earlier.) At lower left Stephen A. Douglas dances with a scruffy Irishman. (The Irish voted Democrat in disproportionate numbers.)

THE POLITICAL QUADRILLE
Music by Dred Scott

The Presidential Election of 1860 (Electoral College Votes)

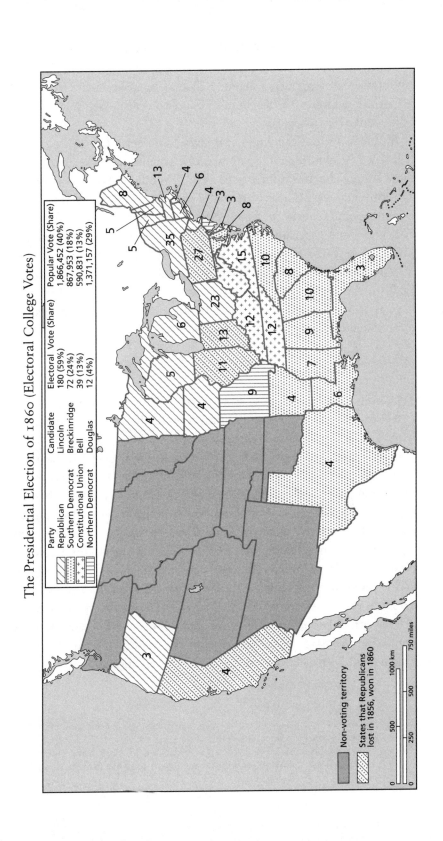

Party	Candidate	Electoral Vote (Share)	Popular Vote (Share)
Republican	Lincoln	180 (59%)	1,866,452 (40%)
Southern Democrat	Breckinridge	72 (24%)	867,953 (18%)
Constitutional Union	Bell	39 (13%)	590,831 (13%)
Northern Democrat	Douglas	12 (4%)	1,371,157 (29%)

Non-voting territory

States that Republicans lost in 1856, won in 1860

0 250 500 750 miles
0 500 1000 km

Although their opponents claimed that a Republican victory would jeopardise the future of the Union, Republicans dismissed such charges as fanciful or scaremongering.

In the South the campaign was quite different. Here Douglas and Bell faced Breckinridge; Lincoln was not even on the ticket in most of these states. The atmosphere especially in the Deep South was one of extraordinary fear. Alarms were sounded, not once but repeatedly. There were frequent reports of arson, poisonings, planned slave uprisings. Foreigners and especially northerners in the South were intimidated, forced to leave or subjected to violent attacks. Groups of vigilantes were formed. Once again southerners revealed their willingness to set aside the rule of law wherever slavery was threatened. Long before polling day it had become clear that a Republican victory would pose an unprecedented threat to national unity.

X

The result of the election was clear. Lincoln carried all eighteen free states except for New Jersey, whose electoral votes he shared with Douglas. He won each of his states apart from Oregon, California and New Jersey with an outright majority, not merely a plurality, which suggests he might have won the election even without the split in the Democratic vote.[16] Even though he won only thirty-nine per cent of the popular vote, his support was concentrated in states which he could carry. Douglas by contrast had support that was more scattered and he ended by carrying only Missouri (though he received a share of the electoral votes of New Jersey). In the South, Bell took Virginia, Kentucky and Tennessee, and Breckinridge the remaining eleven states. The election showed the extent of polarisation that had now taken place: Breckinridge obtained a derisory number of votes in the free states, Lincoln a still more derisory number in the slave states. Nevertheless the result was clear: Abraham Lincoln had been elected President of the United States.[17]

---

[16] This is of course a somewhat speculative claim, since the course of events and of the election itself would then have been different too.

[17] In his own right Breckinridge received fewer than 100,000 votes in the North compared to Lincoln's 1.8 million, though it is impossible to say what share he would have obtained of the 580,000 fusion votes.

8

SECESSION AND THE
OUTBREAK OF WAR,
1860–1861

The sixth of November 1860 saw extraordinary scenes in Springfield, Illinois. It was election day, the greatest election day in the history of the United States if by that we mean the one that produced the most important result in the nation's history. As the votes were counted across the nation and the news was telegraphed to Springfield, it became apparent that the Republican candidate, and the town's favourite son, Abraham Lincoln, was going to become the next president of the United States. Men and women alike displayed their elation visibly. Crowds cheered wildly, hats were thrown into the air and bands played. Cannon were fired and the celebrations went on into the night. Many understood that they were living through a decisive moment in the history of the Republic.

They were right, though in fact Lincoln's victory, as we have noted, was a modest one in that he polled only a minority of the votes cast and, as we have also noted, a particularly lopsided one in that he obtained not a single electoral vote from the fifteen slave states. Aware of the hatred with which so many southerners viewed Lincoln and his party, a minority of northerners refrained from celebrating and looked anxiously towards the South. How would her leaders react? In one very narrow sense the result was uncontroversial. Like the residents of Springfield all southerners now recognised that Lincoln would occupy the White House from March 1861.

Whether this should make him president of the nation in its present form was another matter. Here southerners were in no way agreed. There was a wide spectrum of opinion, ranging from outright secessionism, if necessary by a single state acting alone, to unconditional Unionism. These opinions, however, were not randomly distributed across the entire South; in general the Deep South was more militant on the slavery question than the Middle South, which in turn was less moderate than the Border South. This was the pattern that had existed for more than a generation.

What was it about Lincoln's election that most alarmed southerners? Those who wanted to leave the Union were not slow to spell out their reasons. Few of those reasons were new, though some were easier to state in public than others. But to understand the mind of the southern militant in 1860, it is necessary to reconstruct his view of the past, and in particular of the history of antislavery. In 1830 antislavery had been a feeble force in the North. But with each passing decade it had grown in strength, and southerners one after another recounted the events of the sectional controversy in order to demonstrate the truth of this claim. They were right. And now in 1860 the antislavery movement had elected a man who, though not an abolitionist in the generally accepted sense of the term, wanted to put slavery on the path to ultimate extinction. Where would this process end? Southerners looked ahead and projected the same line of development into the future. Within a short time yet more radically antislavery northerners would assume control of the North and of the nation. Was it not, therefore, supreme folly to wait and allow this to happen?[1]

These fears for the future were important. But Lincoln could begin the destructive process in his own term of office. What actions could he take? Southerners noted that possession of the executive power would

---

[1] On secession, see, for example, William L. Barney, *The Secessionist Impulse: Alabama and Mississippi in 1860* (Princeton, NJ, 1974); William Cooper Jr., *Liberty and Slavery: Southern Politics to 1860* (New York, 1983); Daniel Crofts, *Reluctant Confederates: Upper South Unionists in the Secession Crisis* (Chapel Hill, NC, 1993); Freehling, *The Road to Disunion: Secessionists Triumphant*; Michael P. Johnson, *Toward a Patriarchal Republic: The Secession of Georgia* (Baton Rouge, LA, 1977); Stephanie McCurry, *Masters of Small Worlds: Yeoman Households, Gender Relations, and the Political Culture of the Antebellum South Carolina Low Country* (New York, 1995); J. Mills Thornton III, *Politics and Power in a Slave Society: Alabama, 1800–1860* (Baton Rouge, LA, 1978); Christopher J. Olsen, *Political Culture and Secession in Mississippi: Masculinity, Honor, and the Antiparty Tradition, 1830–1860* (Oxford, 2000); George C. Rable, *The Confederate Republic: A Revolution Against Politics* (Chapel Hill, NC, 1994); Manisha Sinha, *The Counterrevolution of Slavery: Politics and Ideology in Antebellum South Carolina* (Chapel Hill, NC, 2000); Bertram Wyatt-Brown, "Shameful Submission and Honorable Secession", in *The Shaping of Southern Culture: Honor, Grace, and War, 1760s–1880s* (Chapel Hill, NC, 2001), pp. 177–202.

not only give antislavery a new prestige in the nation, it would allow the president to appoint officeholders throughout the South. These might be indifferent, or even hostile, to slavery. The president agreed not to appoint "strangers" to these offices but some of the enemies of slavery, especially in the Border States, men like Cassius Clay in Kentucky or Frank Blair in Missouri, were anything but strangers in their localities. A Republican president would be able to appoint such men to office; this would encourage others to support his party. Most of these officeholders would be postmasters, who might then allow the circulation of anti-slavery tracts within the South. Lincoln would also be able to confer government contracts upon favoured groups in the South. He would control the federal forts in the South too, which might become centres of antislavery agitation or sanctuaries for runaway slaves. Before long a Republican party would come into existence in the South. The party would first put pressure on the border states where slavery was weak-est. Slaveholders in these areas might then feel compelled to sell their slaves further south. With those states secured the Republicans could use their ever-increasing power to put pressure on the Middle South. The Deep South would then be the final domino to fall. How long would all this take? Southerners disagreed. Some conceded that it might take a long time. Robert Toombs of Georgia, however, one the South's leading statesmen, claimed that the result of a Republican victory would be to "abolitionize Maryland in a year, raise a powerful abolition party in Va., Kentucky and Missouri in two years, and foster and rear up a free labor party in [the] whole South in four years".[2]

These fears were extremely widespread and were voiced by dozens of leading southerners. They were probably even more important than their frequency of utterance suggests, however, because we should note that they betrayed a real lack of confidence in the non-slaveholding whites of the South: the implication was that a significant number of those whites were not entirely reliable. Some southerners proclaimed that the non-slaveholders were indeed entirely trustworthy; not all of them, however, said the same in private. Moreover the Republicans shared this view of the future in that they too expected their party

---

[2] Robert Toombs to Alexander H. Stephens, 10 February 1860, in Ulrich B. Phillips, ed. *The Correspondence of Robert Toombs, Alexander H. Stephens, and Howell Cobb*, American Historical Association *Annual Report 1911*, II (Washington DC, 1913), p. 462.

to acquire strength in the South. Little wonder that southerners who voiced these fears concluded that it was no longer safe for the South to remain in the Union.

This was not only because of the non-slaveholding whites, whose loyalty was, or might in the future become, suspect. It was also because of the slaves themselves who might be incited by Republicans to rise up in rebellion, precisely as John Brown had invited them to do in 1859. Although most Republicans had sincerely condemned the Brown raid, others had not, and southerners had not forgotten the reverence with which Brown the martyr was now viewed across much of the North.

As important as the fears over the executive's patronage were the policies that the new president would employ relating to slavery in the territories. Here the Republican party's refusal to countenance the creation of more slave states was vital. Secessionists focussed their attention, and that of their fellow southerners, on this. Their opposition sprang from many sources. Some revived the argument, heard since the time of the Wilmot Proviso, that without an "outlet" there would soon be too many slaves in the South, their value would plummet and emancipation would be forced upon their owners. Hence it might be necessary to spread slavery not only into Arizona, New Mexico and the South West, but also into Mexico, Cuba and other parts of Central America.

Other southerners, including many who favoured secession, however, did not believe that more territory was needed for slavery, at least not to secure its economic viability. Instead they stressed the political implications of the Republican policy of free soil. Again since at least the time of the Wilmot Proviso, southerners had fretted that the creation of more free states would result in the North possessing enough power to control the federal government absolutely and then ultimately amend the Constitution and secure the abolition of slavery even in the states where it already existed. Southerners did not always take care to distinguish northern free soilers from abolitionists. But this was in good part because they feared that free soil was itself abolition, though brought about more slowly and more insidiously.

Lincoln was strongly committed to the policy of free soil, and southerners attached great importance to the programme on which he had been elected. They also gave attention to the policies advocated by the more radical Republicans, in part because they feared that such policies would soon hold sway with the party as a whole. This would mean the abolition of slavery in the District of Columbia, in federal forts and dockyards, as well as the prohibition of the interstate slave trade. Such measures were explicitly intended by the radicals to ensure the abolition of slavery, not immediately but over a period of time, and without an unconstitutional direct assault on the institution within the states. Their cumulative effect, southerners feared, would be to promote insubordination among the slaves, who would be tempted by the prospect of escape into these antislavery enclaves within the South itself. Moreover the radicals, unlike Lincoln, refused to enforce the Fugitive Slave Act, in the absence of which the slaves would grasp at every opportunity for flight, and the masters suffer progressive demoralisation.

For all these reasons, then, southerners were convinced that slavery could not survive Lincoln's victory – if the South stayed in the Union. As one secessionist put it, in leaving the Union, his state had acted out of "a deep conviction" that "separation from the North" alone "could prevent the abolition of her slavery". And what did abolition mean? It was portrayed in apocalyptic terms by southerners in 1860 and 1861, as it had been for generations. To these southerners it meant that white men's livelihoods would be threatened, the "virtue" of their wives and daughters assaulted, the social system uprooted, all for the benefit of a hopelessly inferior, degraded race.[3]

Most secessionists were convinced that the North was gripped by fanaticism. Even if concessions could be obtained, could northerners be trusted to honour them? Some moderate southerners wanted to wait until Lincoln committed an "overt act" against the South. But others insisted that this was folly. In their view public opinion was what drove northern politicians on in their antislavery zeal. The North was hopelessly corrupt and beyond redemption.

Southerners who took this view wielded great influence in the Deep South, and it was logical for them to recommend immediate secession, as soon as Lincoln's victory was announced. Some of them did so. Others, however, avowed themselves willing to seek compromise with the Republicans. If the Republicans were to retreat from the platform on which they had been elected, secession might yet be averted and the Union preserved. Between November 1860 and March 1861 a series

---

[3] George H. Reese, ed. *Proceedings of the Virginia State Convention of 1861: February 13–May 1* 4 vols (Richmond, VA, 1965) I, pp. 62–66.

of attempts were made to broker a new agreement between North and South; on the success of these proposed compromises would hang the continued presence in the Union of the states of the Deep South.

II

"The South is of use to the North", said the Cleveland *National Daily Democrat* two weeks after Lincoln's election, "and the North is of use to the South". "Each State", the editor continued, was "as much a necessity to the others as a leg or an arm is to the body", and so "should be preserved at almost any and every sacrifice". Those who denied it were deluded because "as well might they argue, what use is a leg, or an arm, or an eye to man, he can get along without it". It was true that "man could hobble along with one leg gone – he could grope his way through life with his one eye – he could feed himself with his one arm". But "still he would be much better with the full compliment [sic]". If his analogy were accepted, the editor's logic was impeccable.[4]

These sentiments were those of an Ohio newspaper, but the attachment to the Union that they denoted was echoed throughout the nation. Many Americans wanted compromise as soon as, or even before, it became apparent that the states of the Deep South were preparing to leave the Union. A controlling body of opinion in the Upper South, though enormously disappointed and even alarmed by Lincoln's victory, did not consider it sufficient reason to break up the Union. Another swathe of southerners in the Deep South, as we have seen, at first thought that Lincoln might recede from his platform and thus save the day. In the North many Democrats and Constitutional Unionists, equally disappointed by Lincoln's triumph, were convinced of the need for compromise and accordingly sought a new resolution of the sectional controversy. Their supporters looked eagerly and hopefully to their Representatives and Senators in Washington DC.

There were various schemes of compromise put forward in the winter of 1860/1861, but the most important of them was advanced by John J. Crittenden of Kentucky. Crittenden had been a prominent Constitutional Unionist in 1860 and prior to that a still more prominent Whig. He was universally viewed as the heir of Henry Clay and

[4] Cleveland *National Daily Democrat*, 20 November 1860.

like Clay was a slaveholder but also a firm unionist. Clay had saved the Union repeatedly in the past, it was argued, most recently in 1850, and now his heir would do the same. The Kentuckian accordingly stepped forward with a package of measures that was designed to appeal to moderate sentiment throughout the nation and which, it was hoped, would consequently avert secession and, of course, civil war.

Crittenden proposed a new constitutional amendment to protect slavery in the states where it already existed. He also urged an extension of the Missouri Compromise line at 36° 30' which had formerly marked the boundary between slave and free territory in the land within the old Louisiana Purchase. North of that line slavery would be forbidden; south of it a slave code (whereby the federal government would if necessary protect slavery during the territorial phase) would be in operation. In addition to its clauses on slavery in the states and the territories, the Crittenden Compromise denied the power of the federal government to abolish slavery in federal forts and dockyards and in the District of Columbia, it guaranteed compensation to slaveholders who could not recover fugitive slaves and it explicitly prevented the federal government from obstructing the movement of slaves over state lines. Finally it stipulated that these clauses were to be incorporated as constitutional amendments and were themselves to be unamendable.

Crittenden's measures appear, at first glance, to have presented a real opportunity for the United States to avoid dismemberment. Appearances, however, are deceptive. If accepted, the measures would almost certainly have prevented the secession of every state in the Deep South, with the possible exception of South Carolina. But they were not accepted; they were not acceptable to the Republicans. The Republican party in general, and Lincoln in particular, would not tolerate them.

The key questions were those concerning the status of slavery in the territories, but we should note that even the guarantee offered to slavery in the states where it already existed proved highly controversial and was rejected by a majority of Republicans on the grounds that it meant for the first time the Constitution being polluted by direct reference to slavery. (To southerners, of course, their votes merely confirmed that it was sheer hypocrisy for Republicans to disavow any intention of interfering with slavery in the states.) But it was the territorial issue that was decisive. The great majority of Republicans refused to countenance an extension of the Missouri Compromise line, and this in effect doomed any hope of compromise.[5]

It is tempting to criticise the Republicans here for refusing to compromise and thus bringing on a civil war. This charge is particularly potent, since it is clear that, almost until the first shot had been fired, they hugely underestimated the gravity of the situation. They first grossly underestimated the likelihood of secession, then they grossly underestimated the danger of civil war. Nevertheless one should acquit the Republicans of blundering during the secession crisis, just as one should acquit southerners of irrationality in adopting their strategy. Once again it was not that the Republicans did not make these errors nor that they were unimportant. Rather it was that they flowed from the party's basic perceptions, its ideology or world view.

Prior to the election of 1860, as before the election of 1856, many southerners had threatened secession in the event of a Republican triumph. The Republicans had brushed such threats aside. In the immediate aftermath of Lincoln's election, they did the same. One Boston newspaper sounded a note struck by dozens of Republicans when its editor announced that "nobody in the free States need feel any anxiety about secession". "The slave States", the editor observed, "have neither the right, the power, nor the inclination to secede – therefore they will not". Why was this mistake made? It was essentially because the Republican view of the world necessitated it. The Republicans did not believe they were charting a new course for the Republic on the slavery question; on the contrary they believed they were bringing it back to the position it had held until diverted from it by the Slave Power. It followed, as Lincoln the presidential candidate put it in 1860, that "the people of the South have too much of good sense and good temper to attempt the ruin of the government rather than see it administered as it was administered by the men who made it".[6]

---

[5] Good accounts of these events may be found in Crofts, *Reluctant Confederates*; David Potter, *Lincoln and His Party in the Secession Crisis* (Baton Rouge, LA, 1995); Kenneth M. Stampp, *And The War Came: The North and the Secession Crisis, 1860–61* (Chicago, 1950).

[6] Boston, *Daily Atlas and Bee*, 12 November 1860, in Howard C. Perkins, ed. *Northern Editorials on Secession* 2 vols (Gloucester, MA, 1942), I, p. 88; Lincoln to John B. Fry, 15 August 1860, quoted in Potter, *Lincoln and His Party*, p. 18. See also *Congressional Globe*, 31st Congress, 1st Session, Appendix, p. 480.

This was one of the Republicans' controlling assumptions. Another was that slavery, because it was so clearly an unnatural system, with blatant moral, economic and political shortcomings, *needed* the Union; a labour system so contrary to human nature required support from a stronger one. A third, closely linked to the others, was that loyalty to the Union, despite current appearances to the contrary, was extremely widespread and intense throughout virtually the entire South. Hence it was only a matter of time before it resurfaced. These assumptions, which were all but universal within the party, explain the mistakes made in 1860 and 1861.

When Lincoln's victory was announced, and southerners began to issue threats, Republicans continued to scoff at them. Such threats had been made before. The South needed the Union. How else were fugitive slaves to be returned? How would slave insurrections be put down without federal forces? How could the slaveholders secure the loyalty of the non-slaveholding whites in their own localities? Had they not had to restrict their freedom of speech and opinion on the slavery question, using the most coercive of legislation? And how could the slaveholders cater to the economic ambitions of the non-slaveholding whites, who because of the inadequacies of the slave system were denied any real economic opportunity? The Republicans assumed that the free-labour society of the North was not simply the best available; it corresponded with the most fundamental aspirations, political, economic and moral, of humanity. Hence, once given their freedom, the non-slaveholding whites of the South would demonstrate their loyalty to the Union. And even if they did not, the slaveholders themselves would soon realise that secession was not in their interests and the secessionist bubble would burst.

All these perceptions played their part in the Republican response to southern threats. Beyond them, however, lay an equally vital tenet of the Republican faith. As we have seen, Republicans believed that the slaveholders constituted a Slave Power that had exercised a hugely disproportionate and entirely malign influence over the politics of the southern states and of the Union itself. How had this arisen? It had been not because of southern strength but instead because of northern weakness, the northern willingness to submit to dictation from the South. According to William Seward there had not been "one day from 1787 until now when slavery had any power in the government, except what it derived from buying up men of weak virtue, little principle and great cupidity, and terrifying men of weak nerves in the free states". Slavery was an inherently disorganising system which, as Lincoln himself insisted, posed the only threat to the survival and stability of the nation. Hence resistance to it was essential.[7]

Here of course the historian encounters the problems created by hindsight. All scholars know now that the consequence of the Republican refusal to compromise would be secession and then war. But this was not how it appeared to Republicans at the time. On the contrary they believed it indispensably necessary, and in the ultimate interests of peace, to face down the secessionist threat. Lincoln himself was adamant on this point: if he and his party backed down, then such was the inherent nature of slavery itself that the slaveholders would soon be knocking on the door again, demanding more territory, more concessions and more "compromises" from the North. Any compromise on the extension of slavery, he insisted, would mean that "all our labor is lost, and, ere long, must be done again". "The tug", he concluded, "has to come, & better now than at any time hereafter".[8]

To understand the Republican rejection of compromise (and especially of the only forms of compromise that would have satisfied the South), we must remind ourselves of their situation in 1860. They had just won an election. Now, at the very moment of victory, they were being asked to sacrifice the key principle for which they had been contending. A party which had come into existence in good part to battle the Slave Power was now being asked to make the ultimate and most humiliating concession to it. Compromise to many Republicans would make a mockery not only of the recent election but of American democracy itself. Most Republicans rejected compromise but, expecting a resurgence of southern Unionism, they failed until almost the final hour to recognise that this might mean the break-up of the nation.

III

On 20 December 1860 in Columbia, South Carolina, the convention that had been called to consider secession almost as soon as news of

---

[7] George E. Baker, ed. *The Works of William H. Seward* 5 vols (New York, 1853–1884), IV, pp. 344–345.
[8] Roy F. Basler, ed. *The Collected Works of Abraham Lincoln* 9 vols (New Brunswick, NJ, 1953–1955), IV, pp. 149, 152, 154, 172, 200.

Lincoln's election had reached the state took a unanimous decision. The state must leave the Union. The delegates then embarked on a train journey to Charleston and carried with them the state's Secession Ordinance, which explained to the world why South Carolina could no longer be one of the previously united states of America. There was then a formal ceremony in which each delegate added his name to the document, to the sound of rapturous applause from the thousands of delighted onlookers. The state had escaped "enslavement", the enslavement of the South to the North.

Events had moved quickly after the election results had been announced. South Carolina, with the heaviest concentration of slaves in its population, was the state in which secessionist sentiment had been for at least a generation strongest and the debate there had been over the process rather than the decision itself. As much as any southerners South Carolinians stressed the dangers of Lincoln using the patronage and stirring up both non-slaveholding whites and slaves against the slaveholders, ultimately in South Carolina herself, initially perhaps in the more lightly enslaved border areas. Nor had they wished to waste time inviting Lincoln to retreat from the Chicago platform, though some had been, for tactical reasons, prepared to attempt this, correctly predicting that it would fail.

Where South Carolina led, the other states of the Deep South followed. Mississippi and Alabama were next in rank in pro-secessionist sentiment. The arguments advanced differed in some respects from those heard in South Carolina. As they had been for a generation, these south-westerners were less elitist than the South Carolinians and less contemptuous of a mere "democracy of numbers". They also gave more attention to the need for additional territory (a need which many South Carolinians simply did not see). But these differences were differences of emphasis: most of the arguments made for secession could be found throughout the South. Georgia was a key battleground in that loyalty to the Union was deeper than in South Carolina, Mississippi or Alabama. But the same arguments carried the day – once it became apparent that the measures of compromise under consideration at Washington were doomed. It is extremely likely that major concessions from the Republicans, along the lines of those proposed in the Crittenden Compromise, would have kept all these states of the Deep South in the Union but, as we have seen, there was little prospect of this.

Accordingly, between 1 January and 1 February 1861, six more states of the Deep South – Mississippi, Alabama, Florida, Georgia, Texas and Louisiana – left the Union.

How popular was secession in the South? Some historians have suggested that it lacked popularity. It is certainly true that when elections were being held to the conventions considering secession intimidation was used against those who either dragged their feet or were openly hostile. But there is no evidence that these tactics were needed for a secessionist victory. In the Deep South the overwhelming majority of political figures argued either for immediate secession upon Lincoln's election, or secession if major concessions could not be obtained. As we have observed, the Republican world view meant that, in practice, there was little difference between these two positions. There was little true "Unionism" in the Deep South, and it is significant that those opposing immediate secession took the name Cooperationists rather than Unionists. The leaders of the South had been announcing since 1846 that a policy of no more slave states would drive them out of the Union. This after all had been the essence of the Georgia Platform, a platform drawn up not by the secessionists but by the unionists in that state. Now a president had been elected who was inflexibly committed to that policy with all that it entailed. In these circumstances any reaction other than secession would have been quite extraordinary.

Nor could the southern masses have been expected to rebel against their leaders in the way that some historians have suggested. Long before 1860 the slaveholders had succeeded in equating the rights of "the South" with the rights of slaveholders. There was no reason to expect in 1860 that the non-slaveholding majority in the South would be able suddenly to achieve a radically new understanding of their situation and reverse this process.

It is important to understand that southerners who advocated secession still did not, for the most part, expect, still less advocate, war. A minority speculated that war might happen but most thought it unlikely. A few did believe that many of its effects would be benign. How could they be so confident? In a sense their attitude was the mirror image of the Republicans'. Each side was deeply convinced of the merits of its own social system, and equally convinced of the frailty of the other's. In the South secessionists drew the sharpest possible contrast between the fate of the South within the Union and her future outside it. The southern economy had flourished in the 1850s as never before, and even the financial panic that had struck the rest of the nation in 1857 had had little impact. Secessionists could see no reason to believe this would not continue. Moreover the South had at its disposal the cotton crop. In 1858 James Henry Hammond had announced that "cotton is king", and southerners did not doubt that this would continue into the foreseeable future. And just as northerners believed in the superiority of their free-labour society, so southerners were convinced that slavery gave them a unique stability and an immunity to the evils – class warfare, periodic economic depression, poverty-ridden cities – that disfigured a free society.

Together, cotton and slavery would ensure that there would be no war. Since southerners did not want an armed conflict, it could only come as a result of northern aggression. But northerners would be insane to attempt to challenge the South militarily. Alexander Stephens, soon to become Vice-President of the Confederacy, was not an ardent secessionist. But he struck the same note as the most extreme secessionist when he declared that there was "not a flourishing village or hamlet in the North, to say nothing of their towns and cities, that does not owe its prosperity to Southern cotton". Moreover "England, with her millions of people and billions upon billions of pounds sterling, could not survive six months without it". So in the unlikely event that the North was so deluded as to provoke war, Britain, deprived of the cotton on which she depended, would be obliged to enter on the side of the Confederacy and thereby ensure its victory. The slaves meanwhile would be another source of strength in war. In what would prove another ill-fated prediction, Thomas Clingman of North Carolina announced that the horses of the South were about as likely to demonstrate disobedience as the slaves, who would in war be "a positive element of strength, because they add to the production of the country, while the white race can furnish soldiers enough". So, in the secessionist reading of the future, war was extremely unlikely but in any event guaranteed to result in triumph.[9]

As a result of these preconceptions, and in the context of the northern refusal to offer sufficient concessions, secessionists raced ahead

[9] Phillips, ed. *Correspondence of Toombs, Stephens, and Cobb*, p. 415; *Congressional Globe*, 36th Congress, 1st Session, p. 454.

with the formation of their new Confederacy. In the sense that they were now embarking on the creation of a new nation, they were of course exhibiting nationalist sentiment. But this was different from the nationalisms that characterised much of contemporary Europe when new nations were being founded. It was not that southerners felt themselves removed or separated from American nationality and the traditions of the nation; on the contrary they believed that they were the true Americans. Again and again they compared themselves with the patriots of the Revolution and claimed that they were being loyal to the spirit of '76, engaged in a similar act of resistance against external oppression. Accordingly the new Confederate Constitution was closely modelled upon the Federal Constitution of 1787, differing primarily in the explicit references made, and protections given, to slavery. On 4 February 1861 delegates met to draw up this constitution. Their task was complete within a week.

IV

Lincoln took office on 4 March 1861. The situation he inherited was, as he himself acknowledged, unprecedented. The months since his election had witnessed the launching, and the failure, of the various attempts at compromise. President Buchanan, meanwhile, had been almost a complete irrelevance. Though a Pennsylvanian, he had spent most of his career blaming the North for the sectional controversy. Now he declared that secession was illegal and unacceptable. He genuinely could not contemplate a break-up of the nation. But he believed equally strongly that the Constitution gave him no powers to combat it. In common with Stephen A. Douglas and virtually all other northern Democrats, he could not conceive how the nation could survive on the basis of coercion, even if coercion itself were successful. What would become of the cherished principles of state's rights and limited government in the event of war? Buchanan's cabinet was hopelessly divided; he himself, like virtually his entire party in the North, was paralysed. Even Stephen A. Douglas, normally the most dynamic of statesmen, had little to offer, though he supported attempts to find a compromise solution. In the end President Buchanan could recommend nothing other than a settlement on the basis of a slave code for all the territories, the very policy which every northern state and thus a majority of the nation had emphatically repudiated in the election of 1860.

In one single respect, however, the President was decisive, or perhaps it was a combination of events that merely allowed him to appear so. The Confederates, after secession, had taken possession of most of the federal forts that lay within the South. At first Buchanan would not have them strengthened, on the grounds that such action was too provocative. Gradually they began to acquire huge symbolic, though scarcely military, significance, especially with the northern public. This was particularly true of the forts at Charleston. Major Robert Anderson was in command of the Union forces in Charleston harbour, and he had been occupying Fort Moultrie. Under cover of darkness on 26 December 1860, he moved to Fort Sumter, on the grounds that it would be more easily defended. Southerners then put pressure on Buchanan to order Anderson out of Sumter. But uncharacteristically, perhaps, Buchanan announced that he would not comply with the southerners' request. As a result he bequeathed the problem of Sumter to the new president.

No sooner was Lincoln inaugurated than he received disturbing news from Anderson: supplies were running dangerously short. This placed the President in a quandary. To surrender Sumter would confer enormous prestige upon the Confederacy and would similarly demoralise his own supporters, many of whom were even now clamouring for action against the "traitors" of the South. On the other hand to send in military reinforcements would be seen as provocation, and Lincoln was acutely aware of the effect this might have on opinion in the still-loyal states of the Upper and Border South, to say nothing of opinion in the world at large. He therefore announced that he would do neither. Instead he would send provisions, but not military reinforcements, to Sumter.

It is almost certain that Lincoln finally realised that this would mean war. This is not to say, however, that he wanted war or that he set out to trick the Confederates into firing the first shot. On the contrary his position was that war should be avoided if possible, but that if it came it must be the Confederacy that was seen to be the aggressor. The strategy of sending in provisions (which was actually identical to one that Buchanan had employed in relation to a different fort) was partly successful in that the Confederates did indeed fire the first shot.

By the same token it was, of course, enormously unsuccessful in that it precipitated the war that the President had been so keen to avoid.

Thus there were two fateful decisions taken in regard to Fort Sumter. The first was Lincoln's decision not to surrender it. The President almost certainly still believed that secession was unpopular with a large majority of southerners (even from the Deep South), and he could not consent to give it further legitimacy and popularity by conceding the Confederacy's right to have the federal forts. Although not every Republican agreed with him, basic Republican principles were once again involved. To relinquish the fort would be to encourage the aggressions of the Slave Power, the very aggressions that Lincoln's party, and his presidency, had come into existence to combat. As he would also remind fellow northerners on many future occasions, to allow southerners to break up the nation simply because they had lost an election was an affront to the democratic principles to which the nation had been consecrated.

The second crucial decision was taken by the Confederates. Why did they decide to open fire on the federal troops seeking to re-provision Sumter? Although one or two voices urged caution, the predominant and entirely understandable view was that it was intolerable to allow the fort to remain in the hands of what was now after all a foreign power. Many Confederates hoped that armed conflict would induce some (or all) of the remaining slave states to secede from the Union and join them; in this they were not disappointed. Once again hubris, generated by confidence in the Confederate economy and social system, ruled the hour.

Even now few southerners understood what they had undertaken. With few exceptions they assumed the war would be short and glorious. There were predictions that it could all be wiped up by a pocket handkerchief or else contained in a lady's thimble. One or two read the future more clearly, including Confederate President Jefferson Davis. But none foresaw the carnage, the slaughter and the devastation that lay ahead.

V

"Let the Administration now know", the New York *Times* declared, "that twenty millions of loyal freemen approve its act, and imperiously demand the vindication of the integrity and majesty of the Republic". The firing at Sumter on 12 April 1861 launched the war; as the *Times* implied, it also produced an outpouring of patriotism in the North. There were Union meetings in every town, and the Stars and Stripes was paraded at every opportunity. Vengeance was threatened against the traitors of the South who finally, it now seemed, were to receive their just deserts. The nation could be cleansed. The North went into the war with as much self-belief as the Confederates: "the moral conscience of the world", declared the *Times*, "is on her side".[10]

The attack upon the Union forces at Sumter provoked widespread outrage and a new unity in the North. Most Republicans together with virtually all abolitionists, whether black or white, who had opposed concessions from the start, were now thirsting for action, and military action at that. The minority of Republicans together with the much larger numbers of Democrats and Constitutional Unionists in the North who had counselled moderation now with relatively few exceptions swung round in favour of decisive measures to combat the rebellion. Democrats, although strong believers in state's rights, had long been equally strong believers in the sanctity of the nation. Conservative Whigs, only recently ranged under the Constitutional Unionist banner, had tempered their antislavery sentiments and their resentment of the South with a deep regard for the Union. The nationalism of both groups now operated in a way antithetical to that in which it had previously functioned: it now produced, in the vast majority of cases, not a desire for compromise but rather a fierce determination to crush the Confederacy and thus reunite the nation. Even former President Buchanan fell into line.

For Lincoln and the administration, however, the immediate priorities were military. On 15 April the President issued a proclamation calling for 75,000 troops to be enlisted in a war whose purpose was to put down the southern Confederacy and thus maintain the Union.[11] The response in the North was overwhelming as men volunteered in their tens of thousands. Northerners too still believed that the war would

---

[10] New York *Times*, 15 April 1861.
[11] Not to be confused, of course, with the Emancipation Proclamation which did not come until much later. (It was announced in September 1862 and actually issued in January 1863.)

be over soon and many of them were even alarmed at the prospect of missing it.

If the reaction to the firing at Sumter united the North, the northern response now furthered southern unity. The states of the Upper and Border South had hitherto remained in the Union. After Lincoln's election, the balance of opinion there had been strongly against immediate secession. In Delaware, Maryland and Kentucky unionist sentiment was so strong that secession could not even be placed on the political agenda; in the other states of the Middle and Upper South (Virginia, North Carolina, Tennessee, Arkansas and Missouri), the voters rejected it outright. Where secession conventions did meet (Virginia, Arkansas, Missouri), unionist majorities quickly formed; in other states (North Carolina, Tennessee) popular referenda ruled even against their being called. Within these eight states, secessionist sentiment was probably strongest in Virginia and Arkansas, but an indication of its relative weakness even here is to be found in the composition of the Virginia convention in which only about one in five delegates favoured secession.

Moreover, prior to the firing at Sumter, the unionists had been gaining in strength in most of the region. After the seven states of the Deep South had seceded, a process completed by the first day of February 1861, the unionists of the Upper South saw a revival in their fortunes. They continued to hope that their fellow southerners might yet change their minds and rejoin the Union. But in some states unionist strength was more apparent than real. To be sure there were many unconditional unionists, mainly in the Border States (Kentucky, Missouri, Delaware and Maryland), where they were probably dominant though not (except in Delaware) unchallenged. But in the Middle South (Arkansas, Virginia, Tennessee and North Carolina), there was a much larger contingent of conditional unionists. The conditions upon which the loyalty of these groups to the Union depended differed somewhat and indeed were sometimes modified with the passage of time and the ebb and flow of events. But essentially the most important groups, who probably held the balance of power across the Middle South, would remain loyal provided the Lincoln administration committed no "overt act" against slavery and, equally important, took no coercive action against the seceding states. The problem was that for many of them the proclamation violated the second of these conditions. Arguing that

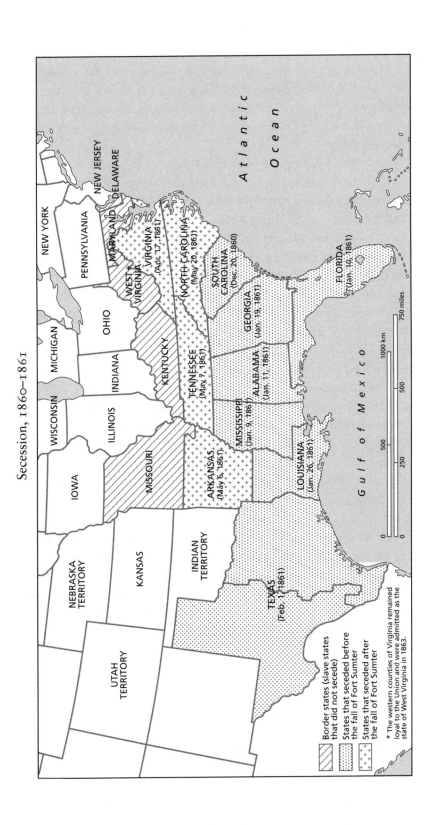

Secession, 1860–1861

NEW YORK

PENNSYLVANIA

NEW JERSEY

MARYLAND

DELAWARE

MICHIGAN

OHIO

WEST VIRGINIA

VIRGINIA
(Apr. 17, 1861)*

NORTH CAROLINA
(May 20, 1861)

SOUTH CAROLINA
(Dec. 20, 1860)

WISCONSIN

ILLINOIS

INDIANA

KENTUCKY

TENNESSEE
(May 7, 1861)

GEORGIA
(Jan. 19, 1861)

ALABAMA
(Jan. 11, 1861)

FLORIDA
(Jan. 10, 1861)

IOWA

MISSOURI

ARKANSAS
(May 6, 1861)

MISSISSIPPI
(Jan. 9, 1861)

LOUISIANA
(Jan. 26, 1861)

NEBRASKA TERRITORY

KANSAS

INDIAN TERRITORY

TEXAS
(Feb. 1, 1861)

UTAH TERRITORY

Atlantic Ocean

Gulf of Mexico

0   250   500   750 miles

0   500   1000 km

Border states (slave states that did not secede)

States that seceded before the fall of Fort Sumter

States that seceded after the fall of Fort Sumter

* The western counties of Virginia remained loyal to the Union and were admitted as the state of West Virginia in 1863.

the President should have relinquished the fort, they blamed him for the outbreak of hostilities. They blamed him even more for the proclamation itself which, they claimed, had turned what might have been a minor skirmish – there had been little bloodshed at Sumter – into a full-scale conflict.

Now these southerners were faced with an agonising dilemma, the dilemma they had sought to avoid for a generation. They had to choose between their nation and their fellow slaveholders farther south. Some of the residents of the Upper South, even some who eventually became Confederates, had deeply resented the secession of the Deep South. Some of them had scoffed at the military potential of the new "nation" and had predicted that war, whichever side won, would herald the end of slavery (which would prove too weak to withstand the pressures of a protracted armed conflict). Some of them felt that they had suffered the taunts and criticisms of secessionists in their home states for many years. They now felt betrayed by the Lincoln administration. Former Whig Vice-Presidential candidate William Graham of North Carolina was a distinguished representative of these groups. He complained bitterly that "it was not enough for the President that the conservative people of these [Upper South] states had been willing to acquiesce in his election". In addition Lincoln had demanded the impossible: southerners must "join with him in a war of conquest", using force against other southerners. But, he pointed out, "blood is thicker than water" and "however widely we have differed from, and freely criticised the course taken by those States [of the Deep South], they are much more closely united with us by the ties of kindred, affection, and a peculiar institution ... than to any of the Northern States". This was the logic that drove the four states of the Middle South out of the Union. On 17 April, two days after Lincoln's proclamation, Virginia seceded. Arkansas, North Carolina and Tennessee followed in May. There were now eleven states in the Confederacy. And the war was on.[12]

---

[12] William Graham, "Speech Upon the Political Situation April 27 1861", in J. G. De Roulhac Hamilton and Max R. Williams, eds. *The Papers of William Alexander Graham* 6 vols (Raleigh, NC, 1957–), IV, p. 245.

9

CONCLUSION

Slavery, Emancipation and the Civil War

I

Although the nation moved abruptly in April 1861 from peace to war, the critical processes and trends that had caused the conflict did not suddenly cease. As far as party politics were concerned, the Democrats even in the North retained a residual support for slavery. The party would for the duration of the military conflict contain the relatively small number of northerners who were adamantly opposed to the war. More important perhaps, it also contained that much larger number of northerners who, though quite willing to countenance, indeed eager to support, a war to maintain the Union, were not at all keen on a war to free the slaves. As we have seen, the Democratic party from the time of Jefferson had offered a disproportionate amount of support for slavery in the South. Northerners of this persuasion continued to display the racist hostility to African Americans that they had exhibited for more than a generation and to mistrust, again as they had for many decades, the motives of those who proclaimed a humanitarian concern for the slave. At the outset of the war this was not a problem; the goal of the Lincoln administration in prosecuting the war was the restoration of the Union, not the emancipation of the slaves.

Over time, however, the goal changed, despite the opposition of the Democrats. After the great Union victory at Antietam in September 1862, Lincoln issued his Emancipation Proclamation. Although its immediate impact was limited, it set in train a course of events that would culminate in the abolition of slavery in the United States. The war would become a war to free the slaves. How had this transformation occurred?

There were three factors, each of which we have encountered time after time. First the Republicans had been from the first genuinely opposed to slavery, which they saw as a disorganising element in the body politic. If this had been their core idea before the outbreak of hostilities, it had now been strongly reinforced. Indeed the disorganising force of slavery could scarcely have been more dramatically displayed. Slavery had now disorganised the nation to the extent of threatening its very continuance. It had even by the end of 1862 disorganised the nation to the extent of requiring the sacrifice of tens of thousands of lives, with the near certainty that tens of thousands more would go the same way in the coming months and years. Radical Republicans had always wanted to rid the nation of slavery as soon as constitutionally possible; accordingly many of them would have freed the slaves before Lincoln himself did so. Moderate Republicans, like the President himself, also wanted slavery to end in the United States. By late 1862 it struck almost all radicals and many moderates as absurd to be protecting slavery whilst making colossal sacrifices in a war that slavery had brought about. The Emancipation Proclamation thus put an end to this absurdity. At the same time it reflected the genuine antislavery, limited but real, that had characterised the Republican party from its very inception.

The second factor that brought about the shift in policy regarding emancipation was of almost equal importance. It was the attitude and the actions of the slaves themselves. During the war the opposition on the part of the slaves to their own enslavement became critical. It made itself felt in myriad ways. In their thousands, and without even being invited, slaves left their masters and entered the Union lines offering their labour and even risking their lives.[1] In the early stages of the conflict they were often sent back to their masters, but in time this policy was reversed. Their labour was too useful, and even the most confirmed northern racist came to see the logic of having blacks as well as whites run the risks that warfare entailed. More than 130,000 former slaves fought as soldiers. Others worked as teamsters, boatmen, butchers, bakers, cooks, nurses, laundresses, blacksmiths, carpenters. It soon

---

[1] On many occasions their masters reacted with genuine shock and disappointment, even accusing the slaves of disloyalty and ingratitude. There can be no more potent evidence of the slaveholders' lack of feelings of guilt. Until recently the role of the slaves in securing their freedom was almost entirely ignored. See Steven Hahn, *The Political Worlds of Slavery and Freedom* (Boston, 2009).

became apparent that each slave who came into the Union camps was a double gain: one slave fewer to aid the southern economy, one worker or soldier more to strengthen the Union. Many northerners had their opinions of blacks changed. One of them was President Lincoln himself, whose views underwent a series of revisions as the conflict intensified and the African-American contribution became ever more conspicuous. To reject this contribution would surely be folly; accepting it made the case for emancipation virtually unanswerable.[2]

Nevertheless there was another consideration that was still more important in bringing about not the goal of emancipation but its final realisation. Lincoln could announce that the slaves were free, but until the war was won the abolition of slavery could not be consummated. Abolition and Union victory became inextricably entwined.

II

Why did the Confederacy lose and the Union win? Historians have given many answers to this question, and it is beyond the scope of this volume to review them all extensively. But once again the processes that had been in train for many decades were crucial. A key factor was the North's economic superiority, long since visible. In 1861 the North enjoyed an enormous advantage in manpower and resources. For every two southerners there were five northerners. For every dollar of real and personal property in the Confederacy there were three in the North. For every dollar of bank capital in the Confederacy, four in the North. The North also had twice the railroad mileage and, most important, no less than ten times the value of manufactured products. This imbalance conferred an advantage that made a Confederate defeat almost (though not quite) inevitable. It meant that, other things being equal, the Union would win.[3]

---

[2] See Ira Berlin, "Who Freed the Slaves: Emancipation and Its Meaning", in David W. Blight and Brooks D. Simpson, eds. *Union and Emancipation: Essays on Politics and Race in the Civil War Era* (Kent, OH, 1997), pp. 105–122; James Oakes, *The Radical and the Republican: Frederick Douglass, Abraham Lincoln, and the Triumph of Antislavery Politics* (New York, 2007).

[3] Classic treatments of the reasons for northern victory or Confederate defeat can be found in David Donald, ed. *Why the North Won the Civil War* (New York, 1960); Gabor S. Boritt, ed. *Why the Confederacy Lost* (New York, 1992); Richard E. Beringer, Herman Hattaway, Archer Jones and William N. Still Jr., *Why the South Lost the Civil War*

Other factors were of course present, but most of them had relatively little impact. Historians have pointed to the allegedly superior military leadership of the Union, to its allegedly superior civilian leadership (and particularly that of Lincoln compared with Jefferson Davis) and even to the Confederacy's decentralised structure and attachment to state's rights (which allegedly prevented the development of a co-ordinated military or economic strategy). Some historians have argued that chance played a key part. But the truth is that the Union needed only to match the Confederacy in these respects. Then the massive superiority of the Union forces would bring triumph – eventually and as long as the Union was willing to accept the high casualty rates that war was bringing. Material advantage could not be brought to bear on the battlefield quickly; it could scarcely fail to have a decisive impact on the overall conflict in the longer term.

In effect the struggle was between heavyweight boxers, and it took four years for the Union advantage to make itself felt decisively. If the boxing metaphor can be pursued, the conflict was between not two but three heavyweights, two on the Union side, one on the Confederate. But the full strength of the North could not be brought to bear immediately: the second Union heavyweight could not take the ring until the first had exchanged blow after blow with his Confederate opponent. Thereafter he could enter the ring and win a victory against an exhausted enemy. When Robert E. Lee surrendered to Ulysses S. Grant at Appomattox, he observed that his Army of Northern Virginia had "been compelled to yield to overwhelming numbers and resources". Lee was right.

III

Nevertheless there is one factor that is even more fundamental than the one Lee cited. If lack of resources and manpower were critical, what explains the lack of resources and manpower? It is ironic but also profoundly appropriate that the most important factor of all in Confederate defeat was also the one for which the Confederacy came into existence. The ultimate cause of the Civil War was also the ultimate cause of Confederate defeat. This was slavery.

(Athens, GA, 1986). I have reviewed these works at some length in *Slavery, Capitalism and Politics in the Antebellum Republic* vol 2, *The Coming of the Civil War 1850–1861* (Cambridge, 2007), pp. 651–672.

The impact of slavery is apparent both before the war and during it. Before the war it had much to do with the minority status of the South, a fact which, as we have seen, haunted southerners and which made them view a future within the Union with so much trepidation. Long before 1861 slavery had shown itself unable to compete with northern free labour as far as states and territory are concerned. In 1776 when the nation was formed, slavery had been present throughout the former colonies. But it failed to sustain itself except in the South. Only where large-scale agriculture was possible, in highly favourable climatic conditions and where there was massive overseas demand for the staple crops produced, did the institution thrive and expand. In most of the West it was unable to compete. In the Border South it was weakening, most dramatically perhaps in the case of Missouri, where its defenders, as we have noted, sought to stem or reverse the process, and as far as events in Kansas were concerned, with strikingly counterproductive results. The Confederate war effort was greatly damaged by the failure to secure the primary loyalties of the four slaveholding states of Delaware, Maryland, Kentucky and Missouri. Whatever the role of the political and moral indictments of slavery, it was its economic shortcomings, in comparison with a free-labour system, that were decisive here.

This was one of two major factors accounting for the South's lack of manpower. Other things being equal, less territory implied fewer people. But the other factor was still more important: immigration. Natural reproduction meant that on each side of the Mason–Dixon line, population would increase at approximately the same rate. But this equilibrium was disrupted by immigration. Why did immigrants prefer the North? The reason had little or nothing to do with the region's natural endowment but everything to do with slavery. It was the far greater opportunities available in the free-labour North that proved decisive. Moreover, as we have seen, many southerners simply did not want immigrants, whose potential political power they feared. The result was that southerners were compelled to watch helplessly as the northern population outstripped their own.

Finally slavery retarded both industrialisation and urbanisation in the South. Slavery slowed the development of industry in the Old South, as almost all historians acknowledge. Data on urbanisation point strongly in the same direction. The result was that the more entrenched slavery was in a region, the less industry and the fewer cities were to be found there. For this the regime would pay the ultimate price between 1861 and 1865.[4]

Slavery had thus inflicted enormous damage upon the Confederate war-making potential before the first shot had even been fired. The smaller population of the South and the smaller absolute size of the slave economy were themselves the most dramatic illustrations of the weaknesses, ultimately to prove fatal, of slavery in the United States. But they were not the only illustrations. As we have seen, the actions of the slaves themselves during the war proved a huge liability for the Confederacy. Moreover their very existence precluded certain military options. Some military historians have suggested that the Confederates ought to have resorted to a guerrilla war and that such a strategy might have brought victory. But this was never a realistic option for a number of reasons, chief among them the dangers that such a strategy would have brought to slavery. A temporary surrender of territory was impossible if it allowed large numbers of slaves to flee or in other ways to subvert the authority of their masters.

Even this does not exhaust the list of weaknesses slavery brought to the Confederates. As we have seen again and again, the slaveholders of the South failed to understand the system they had created. They were confident that the northern social order faced ultimate or even imminent collapse as a result of the disaffection of its subordinate class of wage earners. Slavery, on the other hand, they believed, was almost perfectly attuned to the biological capabilities of blacks (or to the lack of them) and would therefore display a unique strength and stability. As a result the Confederates grossly overestimated their chances of victory in the war. "It may be safely estimated", a writer in *De Bow's Review* claimed, "that a population of twelve million, one third of whom are slaves, are equal in time of war to a population of twenty million without slaves". This was a catastrophically ill-fated prediction. Not least among the significant weaknesses induced by slavery was the conviction that slavery had produced a nation that was uniquely free from significant weaknesses.[5]

---

[4] Robert W. Fogel and Stanley L. Engerman, *Time on the Cross, The Economics of American Negro Slavery* 2 vols (London, 1974), I, p. 257.

[5] *De Bow's Review*, XXXI (1861), p. 36.

Nevertheless slavery as a cause of Confederate defeat does not discredit many of the other causes that historians have cited. Instead it underlies them. It produced a huge and decisive imbalance in resources and manpower. It ruled out some military options. It had an enormously disruptive effect on the southern war effort as its victims engaged in sabotage, or flight and even open warfare against their masters. It operated therefore at a deeper level than the factors upon which historians have too often concentrated.

IV

As we have seen time and again, the fact that the slaves did not wish to be slaves was a constant theme of the antebellum years; it underpinned the sectional conflict at almost every point. Contented slaves would not have taken so many opportunities to flee from their masters: there would then have been no need for a Fugitive Slave Act with all the controversy that that measure entailed. Contented slaves would not have made slavery so vulnerable in places like Missouri, where openly avowed fears of arson, rebellion and slave flight prompted the state's slaveholders to take such draconian actions in neighbouring Kansas, actions which did so much to antagonise northern opinion. Contented slaves, for whom abolition would have truly held no appeal, could have been more easily employed in industry, in cities and in closer proximity to free blacks and to immigrant whites. But the fact of discontented slaves and their potential resistance, together with the structural rigidities of slavery,[6] placed constraints upon southern economic development, constraints that generated a potent economic critique of slavery and for which a heavy price would be extracted when armed conflict broke out. In 1860 and 1861 the states of the soon-to-be Confederacy seceded out of the fear that slavery would be abolished. If the slaves had not resisted slavery and had indeed been as content under slavery as their masters believed, this fear would have been of little import. Slave resistance was an essential precondition of the sectional conflict and thus, however frequently overlooked by historians, a paramount cause of the Civil War.

---

[6] By this I mean the constraint placed upon the southern economy by the slaveholders' inability to adjust their supply of slave labour – see Chapter 1.

V

It was not, however, the only vital cause. The nature of slavery is such that its victims are likely to resent and resist their enslavement at almost all times and in almost all places. In order to be the explosive force it had become in the United States by 1860, this resentment and resistance needed other elements blended in with it.

In the United States there were several such elements. The most important, however, was the growth of wage labour in the North. Historians have been extremely reluctant to recognise this process or to accord it the importance it merits. Yet it was a vital force. As we have observed, the contrast in developmental capacity and potential between the northern and southern economies was a main theme of almost every critique of slavery that was mounted in the decades before the Civil War. But northern economic development, as was apparent above all (though by no means exclusively) in the growth of manufacturing, rested on the employment for wages of tens of thousands of Americans. The spread of wage labour, which underwrote the diversification of the northern economy, in this way underlay the economic critique of slavery.

The moral critique of slavery had a similar underpinning. In previous generations it had been assumed that the ownership of productive property, especially in land, was the indispensable qualification for republican citizenship. But across much of the North, men who worked for wages were now in a majority within the political community. What was it that maintained their loyalty to the nation? How were they to feel a stake in society? How should they be invited to view themselves? The predominant view within the Republican party, and also within the ranks of the abolitionists, was that these men enjoyed certain inestimable privileges. They had wives and families, which were indispensable sources of moral virtue and social cohesion. They had the right to respond to the prompting of the conscience, another vital source of moral rectitude and thus of social stability. But if conscience, family and home had now replaced the ownership of property as the foundation of republican freedom, where did this leave slavery, which obliterated the conscience of the slave and which trampled upon his right to home and family? The rights and privileges now associated with republican freedom thus made slavery increasingly unacceptable to increasing numbers of northerners.

VI

The Civil War was an armed conflict between a society based upon an old system of unfree labour and one based upon a system of free labour, a much newer one with the wage relationship at its heart. Slavery had been in existence for thousands of years. Wage labour on a large scale was in its infancy in the United States in the middle of the nineteenth century. On the battlefields of the Civil War the new system of wage labour defeated and destroyed the old system of slavery.

The destruction of slavery in the United States was achieved in a cataclysm of violence which had no parallel in other nations. Nevertheless it was part of a broader movement transcending national boundaries by which unfree-labour systems were dismantled across the long nineteenth century. Slavery had rarely been criticised before the final quarter of the eighteenth century, and serfdom too had a long history in nations like Russia. But in the first decades of the nineteenth century slavery was abolished in the northern states of the Union, in Haiti, in Argentina, Columbia, Chile and Central America (including Mexico). In the 1830s, 1840s and 1850s, Bolivia, Uruguay, Ecuador, Peru and Venezuela followed suit. By the time of the Civil War it had also been removed in all British, French and Danish colonies, while in the 1860s the Czar of Russia presided over the emancipation of the serfs. Over the nineteenth century as a whole, slavery was destroyed across the Americas, in most countries prior to the U.S. Civil War; in Cuba, Puerto Rico and in Brazil after it. So the freeing of the slaves, the most dramatic effect of the American Civil War, was part of a broader international movement that needs to be viewed in its wider chronological and geographical context.

Confederate defeat was itself a function of the weaknesses of slavery, weaknesses that transcended national boundaries. Throughout much of the developed and even semi-developed world, unfree-labour systems were being dismantled partly because they were thought to obstruct or impede economic growth and development.[7] So if we attribute the outcome of the Civil War to slavery and its weaknesses, we can then locate it within a broader international context. The suggestion is that

---

[7] This is not to say, of course, that a single formula can be offered which will explain the dismantling of unfree-labour systems throughout the world in these years. Rather the claim is that there were economic factors which transcended national boundaries.

the reasons for the dismantling of unfree-labour systems across many advanced or developing countries stemmed from a common root, the structural weaknesses of unfree-labour systems. It was this that generated not only opposition to slavery in the American South but also the superiority in resources and manpower and the strategic advantages visible in the war that brought ultimate ruin to the newly created southern Confederacy.

It remains true, of course, that in the United States the ending of unfree labour could be secured only by a blood-letting that had no equivalent in the rest of the world. This reminds us that slavery in the South, though unable to compete with the free-labour system of the North, either before the war or during it, was nevertheless immeasurably stronger than any other system of unfree labour observed in the modern world. This relative strength was in part political: it enabled the slaveholders to control a large slice of the United States and to shape to an extraordinary degree the destinies of at least eleven of the states of the antebellum Republic. It was also economic in that for all its weaknesses, the slave system of the South was nevertheless able to mount for four years an extraordinary struggle against an enemy that could boast one of the world's most dynamic economies. Indeed the Civil War reflects a perverse reality about slavery in the South: it was strong enough to make at least plausible the conviction that it could survive a protracted war with the North and it was strong enough to withstand four long years of destructive warfare and unparalleled slaughter. Yet it was not, as the history of the pre-war decades suggested and as the war years confirmed, strong enough to combat the free-labour system of the North. This too reflects a fundamental fact about unfree-labour systems. In terms of its productive power, slavery in the South was the strongest, most mature form of unfree labour the world has ever seen. But it was destroyed by the wage-labour system even though that system, as of 1860, was merely in its infancy. Here is the comparative perspective in which southern slavery should be seen.

VII

It fell to Abraham Lincoln to present the Civil War to northerners, to interpret it to them and to explain precisely what the Union represented and what they were fighting for. He did so in ways which served to make its meaning and its place in American history clear to subsequent generations.

In his message of 4 July 1861, the President proclaimed that the struggle upon which the Union had now embarked was one that concerned not merely the United States but all of humanity. It was not simply the American Constitution that was under threat or on trial. Instead it was democracy itself, in the United States and the world over. The conflict made Americans ask a vital question: "Must a government of necessity, be too strong for the liberties of its own people, or too weak to maintain its own existence?" The President in effect called upon the Union forces to supply an answer to this question and thus to confirm, before the eyes of the world, the viability of democratic government.[8]

For Lincoln American democracy was not simply a form of government. In addition it embodied a social system. Lincoln described the war as "a People's contest". By this he meant that it was "a struggle for maintaining in the world, that form, and substance of government, whose leading object is, to elevate the condition of men – to lift artificial weights from all shoulders – to clear the paths of laudable pursuit for all – to afford all, an unfettered start, and a fair chance, in the race of life". So the war was a test of democracy. And democracy meant social mobility.[9]

How was mobility to be secured? Those who heard his words in July 1861 would have known. In all Lincoln's descriptions of mobility, the need for wage labour was either explicit or implicit. Two years earlier he had actually defined free labour in terms of the individual's progress from the rank of wage labourer to that of employer. According to Lincoln, "the prudent, penniless beginner in the world, labors for wages awhile, saves a surplus with which to buy tools or land for himself, then labors on his own account another while, and at length hires another new beginner to help him". Lincoln even described this system as "free labor", thus ignoring the fact that wage labour is merely one variant of free labour. For most of human history free labour has not meant wages. But Lincoln's equation of the two underlines the importance of wage labour in his thinking, in the outlook of the Republican party and in the coming of the Civil War.[10]

[8] Roy F. Basler, ed. *The Collected Works of Abraham Lincoln* 9 vols (New Brunswick, NJ, 1953–1955), IV, p. 426.
[9] Basler, ed. *Collected Works of Lincoln*, IV, p. 438.
[10] Basler, ed. *Collected Works of Lincoln*, III, pp. 478–479.

According to Lincoln the glory of the wages system was that it "opens the way for all – gives hope to all, and energy, and progress, and improvement of condition to all". In that same year, 1859, he had announced that the very purpose of American democracy was to facilitate the progress of the wage labourer. "This progress", he had told a Cincinnati audience, "by which the poor, honest, industrious, and resolute man raises himself, that he may work on his own account, and hire somebody else", was "that progress that human nature is entitled to" and was "that improvement in condition that is intended to be secured by those institutions under which we live". This was nothing less than "the great principle for which this government was really formed". For Lincoln democracy, the Union, freedom, equality, even the Declaration of Independence could not be understood except in terms of social mobility. And social mobility rested upon wage labour.[11]

These were the ideals for which the Union would strive and suffer, and make appalling sacrifices for four years. We should remind ourselves that the President and his party had here assembled a new combination of ideas. Lincoln had formerly been a Whig, but he had now left far behind the old Whig suspicion of democracy, of majority rule and of popular power. In his eulogies of American democracy he sounded very much like a Democrat, or rather as the Democrats had sounded before the sectional conflict of the 1840s and 1850s had prompted a new conservatism within the party. But in his emphasis upon social mobility, his repeated insistence that wage labour was essential if the ambitions of millions of Americans were to be met, he sounded once more like a Whig. In effect Lincoln and the Republicans had achieved a synthesis of Democratic views of popular government with Whiggish views of capitalism. The antislavery implications of this world view did much to bring on the conflict of 1861–1865. And the northern triumph in 1865 would ensure that these values became then the values of the nation. So they remain.

---

[11] Basler, ed. *Collected Works of Lincoln*, III, p. 479; Basler, ed. *Collected Works of Lincoln: Supplement* (Westport, CT, 1974), pp. 43–44.

INDEX